From Lorca's Theatre

From Lorca's Theatre

Five Plays of
Federico García Lorca

In the authorized translation by

Richard L. O'Connell and James Graham L.

With a Foreword by

Stark Young

Charles Scribner's Sons, New York
1941

COPYRIGHT, 1941, BY
CHARLES SCRIBNER'S SONS

Printed in the United States of America

*All rights reserved. No part of this book
may be reproduced in any form without
the permission of Charles Scribner's Sons*

For dramatic production of these translations written
permission must be secured from the translators.

A

To the friends of Federico

Contents

FOREWORD NOTE	ix
NOTES ON THE PLAYWRIGHT	xi
THE DRAMATIC VALUES	xxiii
THE SHOEMAKER'S PRODIGIOUS WIFE	1
THE LOVE OF DON PERLIMPLÍN	47
IF FIVE YEARS PASS	73
YERMA	141
DOÑA ROSITA, THE SPINSTER	193

FOREWORD NOTE

It could be said, I think, that since the World War there has been no more beautiful mind in the theatre than Lorca's. It was a mind at the same time passionate, complex and natural and, as the theatre must be contagious and friendly. No modern dramatist has shown more instinct for using the theatre, working fully and freely in all the mediums that go to make up the theatre art. If there is a dramatist anywhere who suggests the stage's true vehemence in tone it is Lorca, and the stage's lyricism, shadow, light and spring.

We feel in these plays the effect of space and energy that belongs to the classical and Mediterranean. We are likely to feel even more a sense of irregularity, wilfulness and violence. That is partly true of Lorca's particular genius and practice; and is the defect of a great excellence in him. It may appear to us as a greater defect than it should because we are used to a drama that is lazy and plain and not very exacting in imagination and variety and that moves under cover of a mild realism. Lorca's theatre has only its own reality; it is never seen as anything but theatre, and it uses the theatre medium as frankly and directly as an artist uses paint.

Slowly, surely, as the great saints follow their destinies or a star follows its course, does art develop and unfold itself, every work of art. Whether or not these Spanish plays so notably translated in this volume fit into our conceptions of what drama is, they have the originality of what is true. Very few indeed of their most seemingly extravagant or complex images and motifs are not organic to the scene and its characters; they are a part of all that blaze of invention and fecundity and perception that Lorca exhibits.

This flowering in Lorca's plays is alive and can announce and convey its colors. To be violent or glowing and at the same time articulate does no harm in art, especially the art of the theatre. It implies here with him a necessity for expression, a pouring out, a love that fills up with abundance and knows all sweet device. Lorca's bold and poetic mind expects a movement toward the splendor and rigor and gravity of the heart. The key for our approach to his work is to accept it naturally, with all the natural eloquence of the blood, as it were, and so far as we are able, to take for granted all its choric passion, its glowing simplicity and its basis in a Latin tongue.

STARK YOUNG

FEDERICO GARCÍA LORCA

NOTES ON THE PLAYWRIGHT:

The friends of young Federico García Lorca, remembering him, recall most vividly of all his generous warmth. He was the greatest Spanish poet and playwright of our day, and there was about him a very personal magic. For that reason biographical preliminaries seem almost impersonal. His charm, his talents are the important things.

He was born in Fuentevaqueros, Granada, in 1899. Lorca himself liked merely to say that he was born at the close of the nineteenth century. That kind of statement would come only from a poet who realized that sometimes ambiguity of language produces dramatic mystery. In 1936, in the outskirts of his own beloved Granada at dawn, a Fascist firing squad composed of Civil Guardsmen took the young poet out and shot him. The authorities, when H. G. Wells questioned them, said they had no information on the subject. Writing now of his life, it may be best to let the subject of his death end on that same note of ambiguity.

When he was a boy, Lorca read much of Spanish and Greek classic drama, and of the Europeanized Spanish literature then in vogue: all of this was apprenticeship to an awareness of form he was later to use well. Meanwhile, his delights were always the music and legend of Spain, and later he was not only to use these, but to enrich them. In Spain each little town makes its own holiday sweetcakes, called *panes*. One summer in Mexico City we talked to a childhood friend of Lorca's, Eduardo Ugarte. Remembering his friend, he told us that Lorca could describe the *panes* characteristic to each little town. In the poet, such concerns with the diminutive in folklore indicate a lifelong love for his Spain and a child's tenderness he was, happily, always to keep.

Young Federico García lived for a time at the *Residencia de Estudiantes* in Madrid. There, in a company of talented young scholars from the university, he sang his songs. He seldom wrote these down; he had a prodigious memory, and he performed them very well. That is his personal magic again, and the prodigality of a talent given generously for the enjoyment of friends. Those who knew him say there has never been another like him for charm. In New York, when he lived for a year as a student at Columbia University, there was an echo of that Madrid situation. One of those who was his friend in New York remembers Federico at her piano, playing, as she says, in the most unpianistic and untheatrical of manners. He would stoop over the keys and bend his fingers in such a fashion that he seemed hardly to move them as he played. His harmonic patterns were very elementary, and his voice was a dark baritone, but he could bring to life before every one's eyes the most flashing of all *flamencos* whom he created, Antoñito el Camborio.

Now that we know these things about him, it is strange to hear that he received a degree in law and philosophy from the University of Granada in 1923. His interests were still music and poetry and drama. He had studied music with Manuel de Falla, a friend who thought he could have made of Lorca a great composer. Certainly their talents—Lorca's and de Falla's—are much alike. Another friend whose kindness guided the youngster lives now in New York. He is Don Fernando de los Rios, who has long been a friend of the poet's family. So, out of all these interests, and despite the law degree, came books of poetry remarkable for the crystallized purity of its language: *Impresiones y Paisajes* (1918), *Libro de Poemas* (1921), *Primeras Canciones* (1922), *Canciones* (1927). The dates when these poems were published do not at all coincide with their creation; for Federico García was lazy in the matter of getting a book together. It was also his habit, as a meticulous craftsman, to let his songs crystallize so that he could present them for reading when they had attained a shining clarity. The result was that these books commanded critical attention and brought him early success. With success came stature among other poets of undoubted brilliance who were also writing at the time.

In between these poems were two plays, almost poems both. One was called *El Maleficio de la Mariposa* ("The Evil-doing of the Butterfly"). It opened at the Teatro Eslava, Madrid, 1920, after the poet had lavished on it the intensity of his attention. Its failure was a defeat to him. No copy of the play is preserved, but we can tell this much about it: that the title is a beautiful one, and that it is a play about insects with no similarity to Maeterlinck's, and written before Ĉapek's satire. Young García had been much intrigued with the personal histories, the tragedies in miniature, of the little animals. He talked about *los animalitos:* the ants, the frogs, and the spiders. Years later he was to recite a long poem to a friend. This poem, whether it was ever written down or not, was in the classic *octavas reales,* and in it the *animalitos* played hero and villain. He speaks of them in the play "If Five Years Pass"—of

> "the he-lizard and she-lizard
> with little white aprons . . ."

or again he may look into the lives of this husband and wife and

> "their tiny children, which are many."

One of his early poems is about an adventuresome snail, "bourgeois of the footpaths." Federico fills it with a diminutive enchantment and with the light of a compassion that is Christ-like. So, to get back to "The Evil-doing of the Butterfly," we may guess that his unsuccessful play was written in his tight-knit early verse, that it was full of songs, and that it was probably more suitable for a salon reading (or for Federico to recite to his friends) than for the projection and broadness very often expected in the Spanish theatre.

Still, the dramatic poet was emerging toward theatrical clarity. He was on the way toward becoming a poet-dramatist: in his second attempt at the theatre it was evident that he had learned much. This second play was *Mariana Pineda*, subtitled "A Popular Ballad in Three Lithographs." In that beautiful subtitle lay two clues to the play's effectiveness. One was its conception in three romantic sets, like reproductions of old lithographs. The idea gave it beauty and theatricality, since, by placing the action before these lithographs, the mood was instantly established in the understanding and the affection of the audience. Moreover, its scenes of a heroic, semi-tragic melancholy brought to life in the playhouse the spirit of the popular ballad—a second clue. For here Federico's experiment with the ballad (the Spanish *romance*) was sure and successful. García Lorca was to become a greater balladeer than even the great Góngora of the sixteeenth century. So the audiences liked the play and its songs, since the play was stated in terms of setting and of language that they could understand. The dramatic verse was received with critical appreciation which made its opening an event of importance. Two of the ballads from the play—"The Death of Torrijos" and "The Ronda Bullfight" were everywhere repeated as popular songs. These ballads had the sentimental beauty, the vigor, and the color the Iberian popular song boasts. One other factor aided the young dramatist: that was the talent and intelligence of the actress who played the part of Mariana—Doña Margarita Xirgu. The plot of the play is a slender thing, like a sad little song, or the memory of a little musical theme. It tells of the life of a young heroine from the poet's Granada who was executed by the tyrant Pedroso under the absolutist reaction of Ferdinand VII. Mariana had embroidered a flag for the liberals. She would not reveal the names of her friends to Pedroso because one of the leaders was her lover, and so Pedroso ordered her execution. The audiences found grave pathos in Xirgu's playing of the young woman sitting in her room embroidering, in the sort of reflective mood that the Spanish call *asimismada*. This mood was heightened to tragedy when Mariana, sentenced to death, waits for it at the convent, bewildered by the refusal of her friends to come to her aid.

So the ballad of the *triste Marianita* gave the young poet a taste of the success other ballads were to bring him. Now he had put into actuality something he had always known: a formula of drama which stirs the Spanish and which is never absent from their popular art. But before the meaning of the *romance* in literature and in contemporary Spanish life can be understood, we must look at it a little more generally.

Sometimes in Spain even a cabaret song may have something of artistic worth. Certainly the regional songs, the songs of Andalucía and Málaga are pure and vital poetry. Very often into the making of a song have gone elements which give it a distinguished simplicity. The *cante jondo* is a case in point. This is a type of gypsy singing descended from archaic times. Its emotional and direct lines result in a verse *genre* too little known for its great strength. For a literary example of it, there is Lorca's own *Poema del Cante Jondo* of 1921. The *romance* is another illustration. It is a styled, deceptively simple ballad, written in octosyllabic lines that admit an infinity of effect. At best it has the clarity and economy toward which a sonneteer might labour without achieving the lyricism (albeit cheap sometimes) which the *romance* at its worst achieves.

The difference between this song and our love-haunted lyrics of the radio and cinema is as great as the difference between a baseball player and a bullfighter. That difference lies not in the danger of the bullfighter's profession, but in that he is considered an artist. No baseball player has yet laid claim to such title. In the same way, the Spanish songwriter (or those folk elements which may eventually produce a song) may have an artistic intelligence and discrimination which set the resulting song far above those of our American tunesmiths. And in this ballad, Federico García Lorca in 1928 with his *Romancero Gitano* (his gypsy balladeer) achieved as great a success as almost any poet ever has. He was then compared to Góngora, whose metaphorism he seemed to echo. No one, however, could deny the extremely individual artistry of the great new balladeer. The writings of both the young García and Góngora could be classified in the latter's phrase, *escandalo bizarro*. Both had learned how to mould obscurantism, strangeness, ambiguity, and ancestral echoes into a delicate instrument of song.

Because in Spain such a thing as a medieval-born ballad may still be vivid and alive, and because García Lorca knew and loved his Spain, his *romances* instantly flowed into the life of the towns. It is true of almost all Spanish art, as it was true of Lorca's, that the themes of death, religion, love, and betrayal are ever recurrent. These ideas had never been far from Lorca's own vision. As an artist, then, he was moving within his range. He was writing of that betrayal, death, love, and religion which are the sum total of the life of the *flamenco*.

The word *flamenco* means Flemish, and was first applied to those Spaniards who came back as the proud conquerors of Flanders. Today the *flamenco* is a gypsy of southern Spain. His speech is very special—a dark, emotional tongue, full of metaphor, itself almost poetry. His songs are barbaric, very Moorish of melody, conceived out of deep emotion. Their effect is very intense. The *zambra* is oriental, danced without castanets, the body held very low. The *bulerias* is a gay three-quarter rhythm to which the listeners or the dancers clap on the second and third beats of a measure. More often than not, dancers and singers improvise to the guitars and the explosive handclapping. The most amazing and hypnotic rhythms are produced, and hardly ever reproduced because variations surge instantly. Castanets or heels sound contrapuntally and can be modulated from a brisk staccato to a snakelike, sinister hiss. The effect is aphrodisiac. Improvisations are showpieces of virtuosity or spontaneous releases of emotion. All this is a part of the *flamencos* about whom García Lorca wrote. For the *flamenco* is a person of deep feeling, pride, and disdain, who, when he must think of earning a living, commits instead small robberies.

Knowing all these beautiful things, Lorca gave the gypsy to the literature of his country. He created scenes of splendid violence, so that his *flamencos* rose as half-illusory beings. They bore such vivid names as Amargo, Soledad Montoya, and Antoñito el Camborio. And such was the rightness of these ballads that they were everywhere sung, even by the

Notes on the Playwright

gypsies themselves, without, sometimes, any consciousness of their authorship—in that anonymity which the great acquires.

The *gitanos* were created in the romantic and desperate elements of idealized characters sprung to life in a drama. They were not the cigar-box creations of Prosper Merimée. They were exotic, resourceful beings, who rode head-high, glancing out of slow green eyes, while their curvetting Andalusian mares characteristically "sounded the drum of the fields!" These were the gypsies the poet had seen first as a boy. Their lives and their feelings, their violent attachments, were those of any repressed, socially desperate class. Their classic enemy was the insolent, tricorne-wearing Civil Guard. The outlines of these ballad-dramas are etched with an audacious economy to be essayed only by a masterful observer.

While the young poet wrote of this world of dramatic beings, there was

". . . nothing toward which his eyes looked which was not a reminder of death."

But from there he turned toward the bright sunshine of a farce. It was a play about a rebellious little cobbler's wife. Federico García called it *The Shoemaker's Prodigious Wife*. It is the first play in this collection—and the more appropriately so because in the prologue the playwright states his thesis as a dramatist. It is also rightly first because it is his masterpiece after serving a dramatist's apprenticeship.

In the prologue to the farce will be found the poet's concept of the theatre. There is in the play also what Lorca brings to the theatre: observation, compassion, love for Andalucía.

The chief charm of this play is in its interpretation of village life. When Federico turns away from his Spain, his talents falter a little. A year after the success of the *Romancero*, in 1929, Federico had gone to New York to live as a student in Columbia University. This is the period of his experiments with surrealistic verse. It is a paranoiac phase of his work that lacks the discipline without which his brilliant imagination produces almost chaos. It is necessarily an obscure period. His work is tortured, strangely moving. It is unfair to pass judgment on these poems, published posthumously. What was left to us would have been sure to change if the poet had lived longer and had had the desire to polish and edit.

If Five Years Pass is the third play in this collection. It also resulted from his preoccupation with the ironies and exquisite perversions of surrealism. Perhaps this play would be more truthfully labelled fantasy. (Federico did complete one surrealist play, now lost, called *El Público*.) *If Five Years Pass* was rehearsed, but the playwright was not satisfied with it and thought it needed changing. We are told this by Ernesto Pérez Da Cal, who took part in several of the Lorca productions. Finally, rehearsals were abandoned altogether. The mere production of the play was very difficult. Besides that, the playwright said this was a part of his writing which had only momentarily interested him.

We do not know how near the playwright's final conception the version we have translated is. We include it because it has theatrical effectiveness and great beauty. For in this play are found a richness of innovation and conception which other more finished plays do not boast. When we see the implications in the pun on the word *time* in the play's subtitle ("A Legend of Our Time") it is to realize how exultantly sure the dramatist's skill moves. The baroque fancies of the play have been developed with an eye to their truly fine plastic values. There are themes which are integrated with mastery and with distinction. There is the little thread of plot about the dead child. The little boy flees from the nightmare of preparations for his burial and meets a hurt kitten whom he seeks to comfort. The playwright shows this theme first as a mere foreshadowing, then in the anguished realization of the scenes of the dialogue of the dead cat and child; finally, as an echo, when the servant says he must remove a dead kitten from the roof. There clings to this diminutive incidental dramatic theme the air of a medieval *mystère*. Lorca's compassion toward little things, which had served for his poems, is here in dramatic use.

If Five Years Pass is a legend of our time—but also of the integrity of its author. Those who rehearsed it believed in the play, but the writer was not satisfied. Perhaps a reason for this dissatisfaction had been the felicity of the production of another of his plays: *The Love of Don Perlimplín*. It is the second play in this book, and its theme is somewhat like *The Shoemaker's Prodigious Wife*. In both we find an old bachelor urged into marriage by an interfering household. In both it is an old man who marries a young woman who is too beautiful. Both had been afraid of marriage; Perlimplín talks of a cobbler "who had been strangled by his wife." There all except incidental similarity ends. If *Shoemaker's Wife* is a *farsa violenta,* this is a styled satire whose wit derives as much from the balance of its form as from the story. The play is rich in plastic values. Too, that early admiration for classic Spanish drama finds concrete expression here. In the plays of Lope de Vega, the name *Belisa* often appears among the characters. Belisa's song in the third scene of *Don Perlimplín* was once headed *Homenaje a Lope de Vega*. There is a Lope madrigal on which this song of Belisa's is a variation. In Lope, as in Lorca, a song often serves to intensify a dramatic situation. The analogy goes beyond the immediate one: Lope, as an old man, was troubled with erotic visions, just as the aging Perlimplín must sublimate his sexual desires.

The better to understand Lorca's theatre, it is advantageous to know Lope's *Peribañez, Fuente Ovejuna,* and *El Caballero de Olmedo*. Particularly in this last play the little song,

> *Que de noche le mataron al caballero*

holds kinship in handling with Lorca's drama.

In *Don Perlimplín* the symbol of the youthful red cloak on the oldish man is not a facile theatricality—an accidentally effective device. García Lorca had become a producer-director whose practical insight aided his imagination. The Republic had been declared in Spain in 1931. Through the intervention of Don Fernando de los Rios, Lorca and Eduardo Ugarte directed a subsidized travelling universitarian theatre called *La Barraca*. For this organization, which carried classic and modern drama through Spain, Lorca set music, staged, directed, designed, and even took parts. There were other proofs of his theatrical maturity. In Buenos Aires he staged Lope's *La Dama Boba* for Margarita Xirgu. In the songs he found for the play, in the costumes and staging, there was complete theatrical excitement. Amazingly enough, Lorca had infused this old play with a contemporary social commentary that made it the success of the season, and later carried this success to Spain. The star of *La Dama Boba* in 1934 acted in another of Lorca's plays—*Yerma*.

Lorca had planned a trilogy on the theme of rural, woman-inspired tragedy. *Yerma* is the second play of the trilogy. The first, *Blood Wedding*, had been a fine success when produced. Later it was translated into French by Jean Prevost and Marcelle Auclair, and the translation published in the *Nouvelle Revue Française* is excellent for its truth, insight, and adaptive authenticity. In March, 1935, the play (inexplicably retitled "Bitter Oleander") was produced in English translation in New York at the Neighborhood Playhouse on the occasion of the twentieth anniversary of the Playhouse's founding.

With Margarita Xirgu in the title role, *Yerma* was mature, complete, successful drama. It carried the name of Lorca again to the stages of Spain, Mexico, and South America. The play seems curiously pagan. Its boldness and clarity are like Greek tragedy. As drama, it is a study in the mounting intensity of Yerma's anguish. The conflict turns on the double battle Yerma must wage against the sullen complacency of Juan and her own creed of a Spanish Catholic. This is pitted against the hypocrisy of the pilgrim women looking for new men under the pretext of praying to a shrine of fertility. That Yerma is a Catholic makes her the victim of a virtue that serves as noble maladjustment until it maddens her. One of the effects comes as Lope would have handled it. That is the scene of the laundresses at the stream. This scene and the songs of the pilgrimage provide the only relief from the relentless approach of Yerma's madness. The play is in bolder outline than any the poet had before attempted. But Lorca was travelling toward the intensity and even greater boldness of his last play of the trilogy, a play in which only women take part: *La Casa de Bernarda Alba*. This final work was thought lost for some time after Lorca's death, but it was brought to New York by the poet's family in the summer of 1940. It has not yet been published even in Spanish. Those who heard the poet's readings from it have for years talked of it as his greatest play. We hope to include it in a second volume of translations.

Sometimes Lorca, because he could not bear to say no, made changes in his plays. The mother in *Blood Wedding* has the final speech because a certain actress wanted the curtain line. For this reason there are variants in both plays and poems, but Lorca's own clear eye for rightness never permitted distortion. Lorca is capable of his best work when it is identified with his own experience, so that his personal charm shines through. The last of these translations is such a play—*Doña Rosita, the Spinster.*

The gentle sanity of the playwright's love for his Granada attends this play. To many of his friends, this was their favorite. Eduardo Ugarte likes it best of all, and always liked it so much that Lorca dedicated it to him. The poet's family home in Granada was model for the play's setting. The housekeeper is a portrait of the nurse of Paquito, his younger brother. When this play was produced in 1935, the author had lavished all his love and care on the staging. In the case of the costumes of the spinsters, he had produced such a heartbreaking attempt at elegance that it was said the audience didn't know whether to laugh or weep. That is the sort of effect toward which Chekhov strives, and which we call Chekhovian comedy. That sort of feeling is here in abundance and with exquisite rightness. To the translators, this seems "that kind of comedy," as Bernard Shaw writes, "which is so true to life that we have to call it tragi-comedy, and which is not only an entertainment, but a history and criticism of contemporary morals."

There are other plays from Lorca's theatre that are not included here and that we may undertake in another volume, perhaps. A puppet play, for example, remains—*Little Portrait of Don Cristobal*. There is another rather similar but more important hand puppet farce which Lorca left with Mildred Adams, *The Puppets of Cachiporra*. *Blood Wedding* and *The Home of Bernarda Alba* complete the trilogy to which *Yerma* belongs. Also, there is a piece of great charm, *The Dreams of My Cousin Aurelia*, which is yet to be translated. Finally, provided, that is, we can unearth it in some South American research we are undertaking, we shall bring back the surrealist study, *The Public*.

To this project of translation, Miss Janet Collett, of the Janet Collett School of Dancing in Austin, Texas, has been, as it were, the godmother. Professor Sawyer Falk, Director of Dramatic Activities at Syracuse University, lent us valuable aid in his own university theatre for a performance of *The Shoemaker's Prodigious Wife*. To Mr. Stark Young we must express a great indebtedness in that our approach to the theatre in general took form from his writings on principles of dramatic theory as did, also, our approach to the practice of translation from his translations of Chekhov, Molière and Goldoni. To Miss Mildred Adams we owe more than gratitude. Her knowledge of translation and her insight into Lorca's theatre were always at our command. By reason of her suggestions this book is better than it otherwise would have been.

Finally, in view of the fact that many unauthorized translations of Lorca's work have already appeared, we must mention the help of Francisco García Lorca, younger brother of the poet. Through his cooperation and endorsement we have been able both to use the most authentic version yet published of the plays, and to present this, the only authorized translation of them.

THE DRAMATIC VALUES IN LORCA'S PLAYS

Too often the poet in the theatre is treated with a benevolence that implies a lack of theatricality in his plays, however abundant they may be in poetic worth. Lorca feels this attitude with all its patronizing quality when he has The Author in the prologue to *The Shoemaker's Prodigious Wife* say that the poet "does not ask benevolence, but attention." Why there should be this attitude is difficult to say. The greatest dramatists in the history of theatre have been poets, which means nothing more than that theatre artists must have a keen sense of form, sound, light and color, and the body of emotion that may be conveyed by these things.

Lorca is a poet-playwright with this theatre sense. It is the quality or sense that leads an audience into the ecstasy of belief and participation which is the true miracle of theatre. To those who have acted in plays, or fought with all the elements of production to create a vitality of emotional excitement, this quality is evident. For example, an actor reading the lines is aware of the complete logic contained in them. They are conceived in acting terms which prompt the gesture, the inflection, the body position and movement that will make them effective in the theatre.

This "acting logic" may appear at times to the layman as a baffling lack of amplification on the part of the playwright. The thing to remember is that in the theatre words are not all, or even the greater part, of a production. The tone and color of voice, costume, setting and lighting; the rhythm of voice and movement, are the means of creating the body of theatric excitement. To the actor, designer, and director, these means of giving life to the playwright's score are stirred and excited by reading Lorca's plays. They speak of such plays as being "wide open" for acting and directing and designing. One artist senses in another a vision of form, light and color, respects it, and recreates it in its own terms. To the layman reader of plays these means of enlivening are not as habitual and do not as readily bring the play to life; and it need hardly be pointed out here again that the ability to read a play requires somewhat the same talent and concentration as that of the professional musician's in silently reading a score and creating in his mind its melodies and harmonies.

Lorca was amazingly sensitive to all the elements that make a theatric whole. His plays are not theatrical jig-saw puzzles neatly fitted together in the terms of the well-made play, or the pseudo-slickness of plays without a generic mood, theme, or idea to give them life. They are each one fully formed and generated. There is a completeness, a perfect arrangement in the visual, auditory, emotion-giving images that is like the arrangement of a completely satisfying symphony. His plays leave that image of completeness, of emotional follow-through, of a form met with and mastered, of a single mood. They are persuasive by an inner life which is met with seldom in any theatre.

"The poet does not ask benevolence, but attention." In the theatre (and this Lorca knew wisely and deeply) we are persuaded not by logic, but by surges of emotion. To these emotions he demanded attention with the full heart and "willing suspension of disbelief" of the religious zealot who relives in his ceremonials the miracle by which belief was first created. This is a very fundamental and right concept of theatre. It needs to be stressed here because it illuminates Lorca's theatre, and also because it is a concept that is almost lost in theatre today. We have forgotten how to give attention with the full heart and believing mind because the playwrights have forgotten that the theatre is in its basic concept a temple and a religion. By its miracle we perceive the comic or tragic forms of our destinies.

"If you can believe that a tree may be changed into a puff of smoke because I tell you it can, and for the purpose of enjoying my play you must believe it; if you will believe so far with me for the theatre moment, then we have created a miracle of belief, a theatre image that has charmed or deeply moved us both. That is all there is to it; we were both pretending. But the results of our pretense were thrilling, moving. I have shown you images and emotions you had never felt before. You have laughed or cried; but if I have created well you will always carry with you the magical and enticing forms and rhythms." This is Lorca's approach to theatre. It is not strange or new. It is only startling to those who have forgotten what the elements of theatre are. Lorca's peculiar power is to be the revivifier of anciently accepted truths—to present them once again with a vitality, with a joy of giving that makes them seem discovered now for the first time.

No amount of careful structuralizing will give even the semblance of theatric life that the true theatre poet can conjure out of the elements of belief and acceptance. In Lorca these elements are secured by dramatic values which are partially analyzable. At least it is important they be pointed out as convincing demonstrations of the great delight and skill with which Lorca controlled his vision of the light, sound, color and movement in his plays.

The stage directions, the subtitles, even the simple listing of the characters of the plays, are clues to the terms in which Lorca conceived a whole play, its degree of stylization let us say, or the way the accents should fall in a particular scene. The actual form of the language, its style, may show an actor how to play his part, or the director how to stage a scene. These are all spurs to what Robert Edmond Jones in his recent volume has called "the dramatic imagination."

The subtitles are one of the most revealing indications of the dominant mood. What could be more delicious—and immediately indicative of the spirit of a play—than the subtitle to *Don Perlimplín?* "An Erotic Allelujah in Four Scenes." In *The Shoemaker's Prodigious Wife* the subtitle—"A Violent Farce in Two Acts"—and the names of the characters—Red Neighbor, Purple Neighbor, Over-Pious Women, Don Blackbird—suggest at once not only the mood, but the degree of selection, of stylization, the play will require. They suggest a whole scheme of production and are very plain hints to the director, costumer, and designer. The subtitle for *Rosita,*

The Spinster is a similarly provocative and unmistakable indication of Lorca's feelings. It is: "The Language of the Flowers, A Poem of 1900 Granada, Divided into Various Gardens, with Scenes of Song and Dance." Again the names of the characters—Manolas, Spinsters—demonstrate the degree of contrast and the styling Lorca wished the play to have. "A Tragic Poem in Three Acts" sets at once the somber classic simple outlines of *Yerma*. The *dramatis personæ* in *If Five Years Pass*—The Young Man, The Old Man, The Cat, The Harlequin, The Masks, The Echo—in conjunction with the second title, "A Legend of Our Times," prepare for the elements of fantasy in the play. All of these subtitles in Lorca are as explicit as the instructions a musician affixes to his score—as Beethoven might say, *Sonata, quasi una fantasia*—or the more usual directions for tempo, mood or spirit—*allegro vivace, diminuendo, adagio sostenuto*.

In all of Lorca's plays music is of great dramatic importance. The songs in the plays serve always an organic effect. They create a mood, a body of emotion, on which the dramatic essence of a scene is conveyed. There are no songs, or music, simply for the sake of the song or music.

Don Perlimplín; Doña Rosita, The Spinster; and *The Shoemaker's Prodigious Wife* are the plays in which music and song are most satisfyingly used, though this is a difficult distinction to make, since in each play charming, dramatically right effects are created with music, song, or dance. The music was written or adapted by Lorca as an integral part of each play. This explains the complete unity of effect. This music is to be published in a volume of Lorca's songs edited by Señor Federico de Onis, Director of La Casa de Las Españas at Columbia University.

In *Don Perlimplín,* before we see Belisa we hear a piano playing her song—and then her voice singing from within the house. The song she sings is languorous with passionate desiring:

> Love, love
> Enclosed within my thighs,

Notes on the Playwright   xxvii

> *The sun swims like a fish.*
> *Like warm water among the rushes,*
> *Love.*
> *Morning cock, the night is going!*
> *Don't let it vanish, no!*

To end this scene, *The piano is heard. The theatre is in darkness, Belisa opens the curtains of her balcony, almost naked, singing languidly.* She repeats the song.

Belisa's serenade with the chorus of voices in the garden, the final scene of the play, is exquisitely right for the moment, for the mood; and by it the scene is suspended languorously.

A sweet serenade begins to sound.

> BELISA (*Within, singing*):
> Upon the river shores
> The passing night is moistened.

> VOICES:
> The passing night is moistened.

> BELISA:
> And in Belisa's breasts
> The flowers die of love.

And so on. This song has much the same feeling as De Falla's suite for piano and orchestra called *Noches en Los Jardines de España*. Certainly a director would do well to think of the scene in terms of that music.

The music in *Perlimplín* is baroque, justly ornamented; the music in *Doña Rosita* is sentimental, over-ornamented. *Rosita* is a delicate, charming picture of 1900 Granada. But, too, it is more than that by the tremulously longing sighs of its characters. The songs are sugared Victorianism. Lorca with his ability delicately to stylize, raises these songs to a plane of quaint charm and makes one of them the allegorical outline for his play. This is the *Rosa Mutabile* poem which is never sung, but which acts as a song by the beauty of its verse. It appears almost immediately in Act One:

> When it opens in the morning
> red as blood it is.
> The dew does not dare touch it
> for fear that it will burn.

And so on through the stages of this marvellous rose's life which exactly parallel the events that are to happen in Rosita's life.

To speak of the *songs* in these plays is to include the poetic passages that are not actually sung. These passages are purest song and create a heightening of emotional effect in the same way the songs with music do. The scene of Rosita and her fiancé at the end of Act One is an example of this song without music. For in it not only is a contrast with the scene before immediately secured by the introduction of verse, but the sense of forward-sweeping emotion is also created. The whole scene of the lovers' farewell is a finely wrought Victorian Valentine—except that it has more heart-moving emotion. The punctured paper lace is there to frame the scene ever so delicately with its heart-shaped outline, and Lorca has skillfully indicated the profile of the scene by most specific directions for the posturings of Rosita and The Nephew.

The stage is empty. Pause. The Nephew enters and on reaching the center of the room stops because Rosita enters. The two stand regarding each other face to face. The Nephew advances. He takes her by the waist. She leans her head on his shoulder.

ROSITA:
> Why were your treacherous eyes
> so to my own welded?
> And why did your hands weave,
> over my head, flowers?

And so on. Then the scene moves to its second profile—a

handsome Victorian one—for he *takes her to a "vis a vis" and they sit down."* The love scene that follows is moving, tenderly shaped. It is restrained, but abandoned; delicious, but salt-bitter. Then, *They embrace in the "vis a vis." The piano is heard distantly. The Nephew leaves. Rosita is left weeping.* The *Rosa Mutabile* theme is repeated. The curtain falls.

The device of changing from prose dialogue to poetic dialogue is used with great effect earlier in Act One, in the scene of Rosita and the Manolas (page 203). Here a different mood is created. It is the verse and its quality of tinkling, naughty gossip-gaiety that evokes the spirit of the scene.

The actual songs are precociously satiric. They are, too, strangely intense for all their quaintness. This is part of the strange quality of *Rosita, The Spinster.* You want to laugh at the sentimentality satirized, but so truly crystalline has it become in Lorca's hands that you are weeping too "for all lost joyous things."

In Act Two the song of the *Language of the Flowers* is precious. Good dramatic use is made of it. The Spinsters and Rosita sing it, each one taking a section. Rosita's verses are a restatement of the *Rosa Mutabile* theme. A satiric-comic effect is secured by having the most ardent verses sung by the Spinsters. Even the Mother of the Spinsters and Rosita's Aunt sing a verse apiece, so that the scene is lively in that parlor-decorous entertainment sense, that evening-well-spent-at-home sense of the 1900's. As this song ends the stage direction is exactly right—"The piano plays a last *arpeggio* and stops." The act itself ends with another song and a dance (page 232).

The songs in *The Shoemaker's Prodigious Wife* are lively folk tunes in the farce tempo of the play. They are Andalusian. In the latter part of this preface they are discussed and their dramatic value pointed out. There is another version of this play that was produced in Spain which has many, many more songs and dances in it than the version here translated. Señor Francisco García Lorca, the poet's brother, describes the effect of that version as being "almost that of a ballet." This is a clue to a treatment of the *Prodigious Wife*. It is a ballet. We recognize in it all the elements of such ballets as "The Three-Cornered Hat."

Yerma has two scenes in which songs and dances are used to produce an orgiastic effect. The song of the village women in Act Two, scene one, as they wash their clothes in the icy stream is a pæan to the god of fertility in praise of the joys of wedlock. It dramatizes for us what Yerma sees all around her every day. It helps us to understand her feeling of deep frustration in desiring the son her husband denies her. In the play, it presents the villagers' point of view—the outer forces acting on Yerma. In the final scene of the play (page 184 and ff.) the choruses of song and dance impel the play to its tragic climax.

There are tender songs in *Yerma*. Her lullaby to the imagined child in Act One, scene one, very gently establishes her great desire for a child. Victor's song, *Why, shepherd, sleep alone?* is dramatically effective because it suggests to Yerma the remedy for her childlessness, the means she cannot in honor bring herself to take. And again there is the song without words in Act Two, scene two, when Yerma reviews her longings and in a surge of emotion begins the beautiful *Oh what a field of sorrow,* verses.

If Five Years Pass is symphonic in the arrangement and relationship of its fantastic and realistic elements. Roughly, a distinction is tried for by casting the scenes of fantasy in verse—a wildly surrealistic verse. But at the same time the prose is imagistic and startling.

Songs and music are indicated all through the play. Snatches of old refrains interweave with the verse. There are poetic passages of a startling, frightening, clean kind of beauty. In Act One occurs the dialogue of the Dead Child and the Dead Cat (page 84 and ff.). Both are afraid to be buried and they talk of this fear while they wander in a naive terror, that is most pitiable in effect. They are one of the play's recurring motives. In Act Two (page 108 and ff.) there is another dialogue, that of The Manikin and The Young Man. All the sorrow of an unfulfilled betrothal is sung in a trembling freshness of pain, and with something of the warm enthusiasm of the gypsy for *esta pena negra de mi corazon*. Act Three, scene one, is sheer ballet,—harlequinade. With its combination of dance movement, brilliantly styled costumes, gleaming verse, and music, it has all the excitement of a terror-stricken dream; a nightmare tremendously dreamed (page 116).

If Five Years Pass is chaotic, unfinished. It is also a challenge. It strikes sparks in every direction. Its contribution to theatre lies in the depth and richness of conception. It demands much because it is boldly outlined, deeply exciting. The sheer imagination of even its stage directions starts the artist's fingers itching for a chance to try to bring them to theatric life. Read, for example, the one of Act Two's setting (page 97), or this one (page 116) from Act Three, scene one, beginning:

A Forest. Great tree trunks. In the center a theatre surrounded by baroque hangings with the curtains drawn. A small set of stairs unites the little scaffold with the stage.

And so on. Later in the same scene (page 127) there is a stimulating concept of décor and staging in the direction that begins:

The curtains of the little stage are drawn open. The library of the first act appears, reduced and in pale tones.

The plays in this volume were chosen from the ten or more plays Lorca wrote because they show the variety of his interests and the facility with which he vitalized old forms. There are: the farce, the fantasy, the satiric comedy, the poetic tragedy, and the realistic, gentle comedy. In each one of these types the dramatic values are beautifully outlined and maintained. Even in the fantasy—*If Five Years Pass*—with its surrealistic elements and the resultant confusion—there is the impression of tremendously stirring moods arranged and played off one against the other to give an excitement that makes the audience realize it has experienced, without completely understanding, something deep and true. *If Five Years Pass* is not clearly worked out. The basic idea is left too much suspended, but its quality is that it can still move us in precisely the same way that a piece of music can, emotionally, without our understanding completely the relationship of all its parts.

The Shoemaker's Prodigious Wife contains, especially in its prologue, dramatic values which are an exposition of Lorca's approach to theatre. The device of the prologue is a very right way of indicating to an audience the attitude it should maintain—the esthetic distance, the perspective—that is the essence of enjoyment of drama. The play is begun with an indication of the just relationship of playwright and play, playwright and actor, audience and actor. The conventions, the mechanics of theatre and its elements, are demonstrated. The dramatic value of such a prologue is that it lifts the play to the plane where it belongs: that of storybook once-upon-a-timeness, which is the plane on which Lorca conceived it.

The stage directions for the setting carry out this level of conception. *A completely white room. Large window and door.* The street seen through the large window is *also white with some small doors and windows in gray.* These are indications of the degree of selection, the lack of a cluttered quality, that Lorca desires in his setting. He then adds:

All this scene shall have an air of optimism and exalted happiness to the smallest details.

An appeal for an emotional effect to the designer, but no very specific instructions given. In the next line—*The soft orange light of afternoon pervades the scene*—we see his interest in color. He tells us, too, that *The Wife* is *dressed in angry green*. This, remembered in conjunction with the names of the neighbors which are also the colors of their costumes (red, green, yellow, purple, black) gives an idea of the crescendo in color and movement which will occur at the end of Act One when the following direction is carried out:

Neighbors dressed in various violent colors and carrying glasses of cooling drinks begin to enter through the door. They turn, run, go and come around The Wife, who is sitting on the floor shouting, with the quickness and rhythm of a dance.

Notes on the Playwright xxxiii

The great skirts open with their turns. All adopt a comic attitude of pain.

Here Lorca's power of visualizing a scene is evident. Again, in the stage directions at the opening of Act Two these sentences indicate his attention to acting:

At the right appears the Sashmaker's Apprentice. He is sad. His arms hang and he looks at The Wife in a tender fashion. If the actor exaggerates this character in the slightest he should be hit over the head by the director . . . Don Blackbird and the other apprentice turn their heads to look at him. This is almost a movie scene. The glances and expressions taken together create the effect.

There are many more of these directions that crystallize a theatre image of character or situation. Of Don Blackbird he says, *He is dressed in a black swallow-tail coat and short breeches. His voice trembles and he moves his head like a wire doll.*

Equally careful attention is given to the auditory dramatic values. Instrumental music, couplets, bells, shouts and shrieks, trumpet calls, all enliven the play with auditory rhythms. After a violent scene with the Shoemaker, The Wife relaxes and, *outside a flute is heard accompanied by a guitar playing an old polka with the rhythm comically stressed.* In another scene, as twilight falls, The Wife is alone on the stage, *she lights the lamp. From the street comes the sound of the bells of the flock returning to the village.* At the opening of the second act there is the comical pattern made by the three sighs of The Wife's would-be lovers. In this act, too, we have the couplets sung about The Wife by The Neighbors.

> *Mistress Cobbler, Mistress Cobbler,*
> *Since her husband went away,*
> *Turned her house into a tavern*
> *Where the men go night and day.*

They are at first *heard distantly* and then *distinguished near and clearly with their accompaniment of tambourines.* And when The Shoemaker returns disguised as a puppeteer he announces his arrival in the village by *a trumpet call—florid and most comical.*

The point about all of these is that they are beautifully placed, spaced so as to fall with the greatest dramatic effect. For example, in Act Two when The Shoemaker is reciting his ballad of the murder, The Neighbors are in a high pitch of expectancy and, *quickly, there is heard offstage a most loud and anguished shout; The Neighbors rise. Another shout nearer.* This coincides with and augments the climax of the ballad. At the same time it is a transition back to the play. At the end of the play with The Wife shouting and throwing chairs at The Shoemaker, *the rhymes are heard quite near. The Neighbors appear at the window. . . . The noise of the rhymes fills the stage. A bell begins to ring distantly and furiously.* And on this pandemonium, the curtain falls. No director could ask for more specific staging directions, or for more implications of emotional values.

Don Perlimplín is distinguished by its delicacy of styling in language. This bright balance of words, phrases, and scenes should make very clear the directorial treatment that is necessary: certainly a formal, balanced quality, a classic passivity that will contain decorously the emotions of the play. (Lorca suggested that the music of Scarlatti might be used.) The prologue with its staccato lines, its little theme of the first five lines (repeated later), sets this mood. *Don Perlimplín* is decorous and formal—but that is not to say that it has no verve or sweep of emotion. It has great, clean, incisive emotion. Always this emotion is focussed, clarified, by an emphasis on form which serves to hold attention on the idea—on Don Perlimplín's neatly worked out intellectualization of the loves and emotions he can no longer participate in. There is an impersonal quality in even the most ardent scenes, even in the language of love. A maintenance of this just balance between form and emotion secures the satiric effect.

In addition to the language, the effect of *Perlimplín* is carried out by careful attention to stage settings and costumes. For example, Belisa, in the prologue, is made the center of attraction by making the balcony where she first appears the focus of attention.

The house of Perlimplín is simply *green walls, chairs and furniture painted black*, so that when *the balcony opens and Belisa appears, resplendent in her loveliness*, she is fixed immediately as the image of erotic love. Nor did Lorca in this scene desert Don Perlimplín; for he is described as wearing *a green cassock and a white wig full of curls*. The two whitenesses (Belisa is *half naked*) create a visual relationship, focusing the two elements of importance in the play.

The wedding night scene is described in this way:

At the center there is a great bed piled high with pillows, spread with down comforters, and topped by a canopy with plume ornaments. IT IS ARRANGED SLANTING AS IF IN AN OLD PICTURE WITH BAD PERSPECTIVE. In the round back wall there are six doors.

And again in this scene attention is given to costuming. Perlimplín enters *magnificently dressed in the style of the eighteenth century, wearing a green coat trimmed with fur and a cravat of real lace*. Then, *Belisa appears, dressed in a great sleeping garment full of laces. Her hair is loose and her arms bare.* When the soft music of serenading guitars is heard, *Belisa throws a great CAPE OF RED VELVET over her shoulders and walks about the room*. In this same scene, when the Two Sprites open the curtains (which they drew to conceal Belisa and Perlimplín in the bed):

Don Perlimplín appears on the bed, completely dressed; on his forehead are two enormous horns, gilded and beflowered. Belisa is at his side. The five balconies of the stage are open and through them the white light of dawn enters.

Belisa falls asleep as the scene ends and *Perlimplín tiptoes over, covers her with the RED CAPE. An intense golden light enters through the balconies. Bands of paper birds cross amidst the sound of the morning bells.*

The two emphases—the primitive perspective of the painting and the red cape—recur consistently.

Scene Two. Perlimplín's dining room. The perspectives are deliciously wrong. All the objects on the table are painted as in a primitive Last Supper.

In the last scene when Perlimplín is dead Marcolfa says: *Now we shall have to bind him in the youthful red suit in which he used to walk under his own balconies.*

It should be clear that Lorca as an active playwright requires no benevolence. He stands successfully as a dramatic craftsman and brings besides to the theatre his gift of a poet's imagination. The beauty, force and compelling strength of his language, its fitness for the theatre, and its contribution of thrilling life, are manifest on every page of these plays. There is in them a direct truth. They are not sterile forms, for they grow and open inward with each repetition. By their delight they invite repetition; and they repay it in a hundred subtle ways. Themes and motifs that registered emotionally, suddenly appear in a clarity of intellectual ratiocination. This isolated singing phrase suddenly sparkles and bursts in the radiance of the unexpected perception of its relationship to a main motif. Best of all, these relationships grow in terms that live in the theatre and demand its images to give them life. They are theatre size. The skill that evolved these relationships is intuitive and practical. It is Lorca's contribution of genius. He, in *playing in the theatre* (as it has sometimes derogatorily been said), met it with freshness on its own terms, and by his faith perceived and performed its miracle.

The Shoemaker's Prodigious Wife

A Violent Farce in Two Acts

(1930)

CHARACTERS

Shoemaker's Wife
Red Neighbor
Purple Neighbor
Green Neighbor
Black Neighbor
Yellow Neighbor
First Over-Pious Woman
Second Over-Pious Woman
Sacristan's Wife
The Author
The Shoemaker
The Boy
The Mayor
Don Blackbird
The Sashmaker's Apprentice
The Hatmaker's Apprentice
Neighbors, Over-Pious People, Priests and Villagers.

PROLOGUE

(*Gray curtain.*)

(*The Author appears. He enters rapidly. He carries a letter in his hand.*)

THE AUTHOR: Worthy spectators . . . (*Pause.*) No, not "worthy spectators"; merely "spectators." And not because the author doesn't consider the public worthy—quite the contrary. It's only that behind that word "worthy" there seems to be a slight tremor of fear and a sort of plea that the audience should be generous with the mimicking of the actors and the workmanship of the playwright's genius. The poet does not ask benevolence, but attention, since long ago he leapt that barbed fence of fear that authors have of the theatre. Because of this absurd fear, and because the theatre on many occasions is run for financial reasons, poetry retires from the stage in search of other surroundings where people will not be shocked at the fact that a tree, for example, should become a puff of smoke, or that three fishes through their love for a hand and a word should be changed into three million fishes to feed the hunger of a multitude. The author has preferred to set the dramatic example in the live rhythm of an ordinary little shoemaker's wife. Everywhere walks and breathes the poetic creature that the author has dressed as a shoemaker's wife with the air of a refrain or a simple ballad, and the audience should not be surprised if she appears violent or takes bitter attitudes because she is ever fighting, fighting with the reality which encircles her and with fantasy when it becomes visible reality. (*Shouts of the Shoemaker's Wife are heard: "I want to come out!"*) I'm hurrying! Don't be so impatient to come out; you're not going to wear a dress with a long train and matchless plumes; but just a torn dress; do you hear? The dress of a shoemaker's wife. (*Voice of the Shoemaker's Wife is heard: "I want to come out!"*) Silence! (*The curtain is drawn and the darkened stage appears.*) Every day in the cities it dawns like this, and the audience forgets its half-world of dreams to go to market just as you do from your house on the stage, prodigious little shoemaker's wife. (*The light is increasing.*) To begin with, you reach the street. (*Voices arguing are heard. To the audience.*) Good evening. (*He takes off his tall silk hat and it becomes illuminated with a green light from within. The Author tips it over and a gush of water falls from it. The Author looks at the audience a bit embarrassedly, and retires backwards, with great irony.*) I beg your pardon. (*Exit.*)

ACT ONE

(*The Shoemaker's house. Shoemaker's bench and tools. A completely white room. Large window and door. The backdrop seen through the large window is a street, also white with some small doors and windows in gray. To the right and left, doors. All this scene shall have an air of optimism and exalted happiness to the smallest details. The soft orange light of afternoon pervades the scene.*)

When the curtain rises the Shoemaker's Wife enters furiously from the street and pauses at the door. She is dressed in angry green, and wears her hair drawn back tight and adorned with two big roses. She has an aggressive and a sweet air at the same time.)

WIFE: Be quiet, long tongue! Ugly Kate! Because if I've done it . . . if I've done it—it's because I wanted to. If you hadn't run into your house I would have dragged you along, you dusty little snake; and I say this so that all those who are behind the windows may hear me. For it's better to be married to an old man than to a one-eyed one as you are. I don't want any more conversation—not with you nor with you—nor with any one—nor with any one! (*Enters, slamming door.*) I knew that with that kind of people one couldn't talk even for a second . . . but I'm to blame—I and I . . . because I ought to stay in my house with . . . I almost don't want to believe it, with my husband. If anybody had told me, blonde and dark-eyed—and what a good combination that is, with this body and these colors so very very beautiful—that I was going to marry a . . . I would have pulled my hair out. (*She weeps. There is a knock at the door.*) Who is it?

(*Another knock at the door. No answer.*) Who is it? (*Furiously.*)

BOY (*Fearfully, outside*): A peaceful person.

WIFE (*Opening*): Is it you? (*Sweetly and touched.*)

BOY: Yes, Mrs. Shoemaker. Were you crying?

WIFE: No. It's just that one of those mosquitoes that go ping——ng bit me in the eye.

BOY: Do you want me to blow in it?

WIFE: No, my child, it's gone. (*She caresses him.*) And what is it you want?

BOY: I brought these patent leather shoes, which cost five dollars, for your husband to repair. They are my older sister's, the one who has the nice skin and wears two bow-knots because she's got two—one for one day and the other for the other—at her waist.

WIFE: Leave them here. They'll be repaired sometime.

BOY: My mother says you must be careful not to hammer them too much because patent leather is very delicate— so the patent leather won't be hurt.

WIFE: Tell your mother my husband knows what he's doing. And that she wishes she knew how to season a good dish with pepper and bay the way my husband knows how to repair shoes.

BOY (*His face puckering*): Don't be angry at me; it's not my fault. And I study my grammar very well every day.

WIFE (*Sweetly*): My child! My treasure! I'm not angry at you! (*Kisses him.*) Take this doll. Do you like it? Well, take it.

BOY: I'll take it because, well—since I know you're not going to have any children. . . .

WIFE: Who told you that?

BOY: My mother was talking about it the other day. She was saying: "The shoemaker's wife won't have any children," and her friend Rafaela and my sisters laughed.

WIFE (*Nervously*): Children? Maybe I'll have better looking ones than all of them—and with more courage and honor—because your mother—I think you ought to know this...

BOY: You take the doll. I don't want it!

WIFE (*Changing*: No, no—you keep it, son. This has nothing to do with you!

(*The Shoemaker appears at left. He wears a velvet suit with silver buttons, short trousers and a red tie. He goes toward his bench.*)

WIFE: May God help you!

CHILD (*Frightened*): Good health to you! Till I see you again! Congratulations! Deo Gratias! (*Goes running to the street.*)

WIFE: Good-bye, child. If I had burst before I was born I wouldn't be suffering these trials and tribulations. Oh, money, money! The one who invented you should have been left without hands or eyes.

SHOEMAKER (*At the bench*): Woman, what are you saying?

WIFE: Something that doesn't concern you!

SHOEMAKER: Nothing concerns me. I know I must control myself.

WIFE: I also have to control myself. . . . Just think of it: I'm only eighteen years old.

SHOEMAKER: And I—fifty-three. That's why I hush up and am not angry with you! I know too much! I work for you, and may God's will be done . . .

WIFE (*Her back is to her husband, but she turns and advances tenderly, moved*): Not that, my child. Don't say that!

SHOEMAKER: But, oh, if I were only forty years old, or forty-five even! (*Hammers the shoe furiously.*)

WIFE (*Aroused*): Then I would be your servant; isn't that so? One can't be good. What about me? Am I not worth anything?

SHOEMAKER: Woman, control yourself.

WIFE: Aren't my freshness and my face worth all the money in this world?

SHOEMAKER: Woman—the neighbors will hear you!

WIFE: Cursed be the hour, cursed be the hour, when I listened to my friend Manuel.

SHOEMAKER: Would you like me to make you some lemonade?

WIFE: Oh, fool, fool, fool! (*Strikes her forehead.*) With as good suitors as I've had.

SHOEMAKER (*Trying to soften her*): That's what people say.

WIFE: People? It's known everywhere. The best in these parts. But the one I liked best of all of them was Emiliano. You knew him, Emiliano—the one who used to ride a black mare full of tassels and little mirrors, carrying a willow wand in his hand, with his copper spurs shining. And what a cape he had for winter! What sweeps of blue broadcloth and what trimmings of silk!

SHOEMAKER: I had one like that too; they're lovely capes.

WIFE: You? What could you have had? Now why do you fool yourself? A shoemaker has never in his life had a prize like that.

SHOEMAKER: But, woman, can't you see? . . .

WIFE (*Interrupting him*): And then I had another suitor.

(*The Shoemaker hammers the shoe furiously.*)

He was rather young. . . . He was maybe eighteen years old. That can be said very quickly! Eighteen years!

(*The Shoemaker twists uncomfortably.*)

SHOEMAKER: I was eighteen once, too.

WIFE: You never in your life were eighteen years old! But he was. And such things as he used to say to me. Look . . .

SHOEMAKER (*Hammering furiously*): Will you be quiet? You're my wife whether you like it or not—and I'm your husband. You were perishing without a dress or a home. Why did you love me? Deceiver! Deceiver! Deceiver!

The Shoemaker's Prodigious Wife

WIFE (*Rising*): Shut up! Don't make me speak more than is wise—and get to your duty. I can hardly believe it!

(*Two neighbors wearing "mantillas" cross the window smiling.*)

Who could have told me, old bag-o'bones, that you would repay me like this? Hit me if you want. Go on, throw the hammer at me!

SHOEMAKER: Oh, woman, don't raise such a row. Look, the people are coming—oh, my God!

(*The two neighbors cross again.*)

WIFE: I've gone below my station. Fool, fool, fool! Cursed be my friend Manuel. Cursed be the neighbors. Fool, fool, fool. (*Leaves, striking her forehead.*)

SHOEMAKER (*Looking in a mirror, counting his wrinkles*): One, two, three, four . . . and a thousand. (*Puts up the mirror.*) But it serves me right, yes sir. Because, let's see: why did I marry? I should have known after reading so many novels that men like all women—but women don't like all men. And I was so well off! My sister, my sister is to blame. My sister who kept saying: "You're going to be left alone." You're going to be this and that. And that was my undoing. May lightning strike my sister, may she rest in peace!

(*Outside, voices are heard.*)

What could that be?

RED NEIGHBOR (*At the window, with great spirit. She is accompanied by her two daughters dressed in the same color*): Good afternoon!

SHOEMAKER (*Scratching his head*): Good afternoon.

RED NEIGHBOR: Tell your wife to come out here. Girls, will you please stop crying! Tell her to come out here and we'll see if she gossips as much to my face as behind my back!

SHOEMAKER: Oh, neighbor of my soul, don't raise a row, by the little nails of Our Lord! What do you want me to do? Understand my situation; all my life fearing marriage . . .

because marriage is a very serious thing, and then, finally, what you can see.

RED NEIGHBOR: You poor man! How much better off you would have been if you had married with people of your own kind, these girls, for example, or others of the village.

SHOEMAKER: And my house is not my own. It's a tower of Babel!

RED NEIGHBOR: You tear my soul! As good a name as you've had all your life.

SHOEMAKER (*Looking to see if his wife is coming*): Day before yesterday, she cut to bits the ham that we had saved for Christmas—and we ate it all. Yesterday we ate nothing but egg soup and parsley; well then, because I didn't protest over that, she made me drink three glasses of unboiled milk one right after the other.

RED NEIGHBOR: How brutal!

SHOEMAKER: And so, little neighbor of my heart, I would be grateful to you with my whole soul, if you would leave.

RED NEIGHBOR: Oh, if your sister still lived! Now there was a . . .

SHOEMAKER: You see . . . and on your way you can take these shoes that are ready.

(*The Shoemaker's Wife looks in at the door on the left where she watches the scene unnoticed from behind the curtain.*)

RED NEIGHBOR (*Ingratiatingly*): How much are you going to charge me for these? Times are always getting harder.

SHOEMAKER: Whatever you want. Whatever isn't too hard on either of us . . .

RED NEIGHBOR (*Nudging her daughters with her elbow*): Are two *pesetas* all right?

SHOEMAKER: I leave that to you!

RED NEIGHBOR: Oh, well, I'll give you one then . . .

WIFE (*Entering furiously*): Thief! (*The women squeal and are frightened.*) Do you have the face to rob a man this

The Shoemaker's Prodigious Wife

way? (*To her husband.*) And you to let yourself be robbed? Give me those shoes. Until you give me ten *pesetas* for them, I'll keep them here.

RED NEIGHBOR: Lizard! Lizard!

WIFE: Be very careful what you're saying!

GIRLS: Oh, let's go, let's go! For heaven's sake!

RED NEIGHBOR: It serves you right, having such a wife! Make the most of it!

(*They go out quickly. The Shoemaker shuts the door and the window.*)

SHOEMAKER: Listen to me a moment . . .

WIFE (*Mulling*): Lizard . . . Lizard. What? What? What? . . . What are you going to tell me?

SHOEMAKER: Look, my child: all my life it has been my constant lookout to avoid rows. (*The Shoemaker is constantly swallowing.*)

WIFE: Have you got the courage to tell me I cause a row when I come out to defend your interests?

SHOEMAKER: I don't say any more, except that I have fled from rows just as salamanders do from cold water.

WIFE (*Quickly*): Salamanders! Oh, how nasty!

SHOEMAKER (*Armed with patience*): They have provoked me; they have, at times, even insulted me, and I not being even a little bit of a coward, would give up my soul for fear of seeing myself surrounded by people and carried here and there by gossips and idlers. Therefore, you're warned. Have I spoken clearly? This is my last word.

WIFE: Well, now, let's see. What does all that matter to me? I married you. Isn't your house clean? Aren't you fed? Don't you wear collars and cuffs such as you had never in your life worn before? Don't you carry your watch—so beautiful with its silver chains and charms—which I wind every night? What more do you want? Because I will be everything except a slave. I'll always do just as I want to.

SHOEMAKER: No need to tell me. We've been married three months. I loving you and you turning me green. Can't you see that I can't stand jokes like that?

WIFE (*Seriously, as if dreaming*): Loving me, loving me . . . but (*roughly*) what is that about loving me? What do you mean, "loving me"?

SHOEMAKER: You may think I'm blind, but I'm not. I know what you do and what you don't do; and now I'm fed up with it—to here!

WIFE (*Furious*): Well, it's all the same to me whether you're fed up or not. Because you don't matter three whistles. Now you know! (*Weeps.*)

SHOEMAKER: Couldn't you speak a little lower?

WIFE: What you deserve—you're such a fool—is for me to fill the street full of shouting.

SHOEMAKER: Fortunately, I think this will end soon; because I don't know how I have the patience.

WIFE: Today we don't eat here—so you can go somewhere else to look for your food. (*The Wife leaves quickly in a fury.*)

SHOEMAKER (*Smiling*): Tomorrow, maybe you will have to look too. (*Goes to bench.*)

(*Through the central door the Mayor appears. He is dressed in dark blue, wears a large cape, and carries the long wand of his office with silver decorations. He speaks slowly and with great sluggishness.*)

MAYOR: Working?

SHOEMAKER: Working, Mr. Mayor.

MAYOR: Much money?

SHOEMAKER: Enough. (*Shoemaker continues working. The Mayor looks everywhere curiously.*)

MAYOR: Everything's not all right with you.

SHOEMAKER (*Without raising his head*): No.

MAYOR: Your wife?

SHOEMAKER (*Assenting*): My wife.

MAYOR (*Sitting*): That comes of marrying at your age. At your age, one should be a widower from at least one wife as a minimum. I'm a widower of four: Rosa, Manuela, Visitación and Enriqueta Gómez, who was the last one—nice looking girls all of them—fond of dancing and clean water. All, without exception, have felt this stick time and again. In my house—in my house they must sew and sing.

SHOEMAKER: Well, you can see for yourself what my life is. My wife . . . does not love me. She talks through the window with every one. Even with Don Blackbird, and it's setting my blood on fire.

MAYOR (*Laughingly*): It's just that she's a happy little girl. It's only natural.

SHOEMAKER: Bah! I'm convinced . . . I believe she does this to torment me, because I'm sure . . . she hates me. First I thought I would tame her with my sweet character and my little presents: coral necklaces, little belts, tortoise shell combs—even a pair of garters! But she—she's always herself!

MAYOR: And you, always yourself, devil take it! Come now, I see it, and it seems unbelievable how a man who calls himself a man can't dominate not one, but eighty females. If your wife talks through the window with every one, if she becomes bitter with you, it's because you want her to, because you have no comeback. Women should be squeezed at the waist, stepped upon strongly, and always shouted at. And if with all this they dare to say cock-a-doodle-doo, the stick; there's no other remedy. Rosa, Manuela, Visitación, and Enriqueta Gómez, who was the last one, can tell you that from the other world, if by any chance they happen to be there.

SHOEMAKER: But it so happens that there's one thing I don't dare to say to her. (*Looks about cautiously.*)

MAYOR (*Commandingly*): Say it to me!

SHOEMAKER: I understand it's a beastly thing, but—I'm not in love with my wife.

MAYOR: The devil!

SHOEMAKER: Yes, sir. The devil!

MAYOR: Then, you great rascal, why did you marry?

SHOEMAKER: There you have it. I can't explain it myself. My sister, my sister was to blame. "You're going to be left alone! You're going to this—you're going to I don't know what else!" I had a little money and my health so I said: "Well, here goes!" But Lord help us . . . Lightning strike my sister—may she rest in peace!

MAYOR: Well, you've certainly outshone yourself!

SHOEMAKER: Yes, sir—I have outshone myself. Now, when I can't stand it any longer. I didn't know what a woman was. I say—and you four! I'm not of an age to stand this jigging.

> WIFE (*Singing within—lustily*):
> Ay, my joyful heart,
> when the shouting's over,
> let the shooting start!

SHOEMAKER: There you are!

MAYOR: And what do you intend to do?

SHOEMAKER: Fly the coop! (*Makes a gesture.*)

MAYOR: Have you lost your senses?

SHOEMAKER (*Excited*): This business of "shoemaker stick to your shoes" is over for me. I'm a peaceful man. I'm not used to all this shouting—and being talked about by everyone.

MAYOR (*Laughing*): Consider what you have said you are going to do; for you're able to do it—so don't be foolish. It's a shame that a man like you should not have the strength of character he ought.

(*Through the door at the left the Shoemaker's Wife appears, powdering herself with a pink powder puff and accentuating her eyebrows with a finger wet in her mouth.*)

WIFE: Good afternoon!

The Shoemaker's Prodigious Wife

MAYOR: A very good afternoon. (*To the Shoemaker*) How handsome! She's very handsome!

SHOEMAKER: You think so?

MAYOR: What well-placed roses you wear in your hair—and how delightfully they smell!

WIFE: It's many that you have in the balconies of your house.

MAYOR: Quite so. Do you like flowers?

WIFE: Me? Oh, I love them! I'd have flower pots on the roof even—at the door—on the walls. But he—that one—doesn't like them. Naturally, making his boots all day, what would you expect? (*She sits at the window.*) And good afternoon! (*She looks toward the street and flirts.*)

SHOEMAKER: You see that?

MAYOR: A little bit brusque—but she's a very handsome woman. What an ideal waist!

SHOEMAKER: You just don't know her.

MAYOR: Tssch! (*Leaving majestically.*) Until tomorrow! And let's see if that head of yours clears. To rest, child! Too bad about that figure! (*Leaves, looking at the Shoemaker's Wife.*) Because, well,—and you ought to see those waves in her hair! (*Leaves.*)

SHOEMAKER (*Singing*):
If your mother has a king,
Any deck of cards has more;
King of hearts and diamonds,
King of spades and clubs—that's four!

(*The Wife takes a chair and seated at the window begins to spin it.*)

SHOEMAKER (*Taking another chair—and making it spin in the opposite direction*): You know that's a superstition of mine. You might just as well shoot me. Why do you do it?

WIFE (*Letting go the chair*): What have I done? Didn't I tell you you don't even let me move.

SHOEMAKER: I'm tired of explaining to you—it's useless. (*Starts to leave, but the Wife begins once more to spin her chair and the Shoemaker runs back from the door to spin his chair.*) Woman, why don't you let me go?

WIFE: Heavens! Why it's just what I'm hoping—that you'd go.

SHOEMAKER: Then let me!

WIFE (*Infuriated*): Well, go on!

(*Outside a flute is heard accompanied by a guitar playing an old polka with the rhythm comically accented. The Wife begins to nod her head in rhythm and the Shoemaker leaves through the left door.*)

WIFE (*Singing*): La-ran, la-ran . . . Well, maybe I've just always liked the flute a lot. I've always been crazy about it. It almost makes me cry. What a delight! La-ran, la-ran. Listen. I wish he could hear it. (*She rises and begins to dance as if she were doing it with imaginary suitors.*) Oh, Emiliano! What beautiful little ribbons you have! No, no! It would embarrass poor little me. But, José María, don't you see that they're looking at us? Take a handkerchief then, for I don't want to stain my dress. It's you I love, you. Ah, yes! Tomorrow when you bring the white mare, the one I like. (*Laughs. The music stops.*) Oh, too bad. That's just like leaving one with honey at her lips. How . . .

(*At the window Don Blackbird appears. He is dressed in a black swallow-tail coat and short breeches. His voice trembles and he moves his head like a wire doll.*)

DON BLACKBIRD: Ssst!

WIFE (*Without looking, her back turned to the window, imitates a bird*): Caw, caw—cheep, cheep!

DON BLACKBIRD (*Coming nearer*): Ssst! Little white Mistress Shoemaker, like the heart of an almond—but a little bit bitter, too. Little Mistress Shoemaker—burning golden reed—little Mistress Shoemaker, beautiful temptress of my heart.

WIFE: What a lot of things, Don Blackbird. I didn't know that big buzzards could talk. If there's a black blackbird flut-

The Shoemaker's Prodigious Wife

tering around here—black and old—he'd better realize that I can't listen to him sing until later. Tweet, tweet—chirp, chirp.

DON BLACKBIRD: When the crepuscular shadows invade the world with their tenuous veils, and the public walk finds itself free of pedestrians, I shall return. (*Takes snuff and sneezes on the Wife's back.*)

WIFE (*Turning wilfully, and hitting at Don Blackbird, who trembles*): A-h-h-h!! (*Her face full of loathing*) And even if you don't return it'll be all right, indecent thing! Wire blackbird! Stove lamp smudge! Run, now run! Did you ever see such a thing? Look what's sneezing! God go with you! How loathsome!

(*At the window the Sashmaker's Apprentice stops. His straight-brim hat is down over his face and he shows signs of great sadness.*)

APPRENTICE: Taking the air, Mistress Shoemaker?

WIFE: Exactly as you are.

APPRENTICE: And always alone. What a pity!

WIFE (*Sourly*): And why a pity?

APPRENTICE: A woman like you—with that hair and that bosom so very beautiful . . .

WIFE (*More sourly*): But, why a pity?

APPRENTICE: Because you're worthy of being painted on a picture postcard—and not to be just here—at this little window sill.

WIFE: Yes? I like postcards very much, especially those of sweethearts about to go on a trip.

APPRENTICE: Oh, little Shoemaker's Wife, what a fever I have!

(*They continue talking.*)

SHOEMAKER (*Entering, then retreating*): With the whole world, and at this hour! What will the people coming from rosary at the church say? What will they say at the club? How

they must talk about me! In each house they must discuss me—suit, underclothes and all.
(*Shoemaker's Wife laughs.*)
Oh, my lord! I have cause to leave! I'd like to listen to the wife of the sacristan. But the priests; what will the priests say? They are the one I ought to hear. (*He is desperate.*)
APPRENTICE: How do you want me to say it? I love you, I love *thee* like . . .
WIFE: Really, that about "I love you, I love thee," has a style about it that makes me think some one is tickling me behind the ear with a feather. "I love thee, I love you."
APPRENTICE: How many seeds has a sunflower?
WIFE: How should I know?
APPRENTICE: Every minute I sigh that many times for you, for *thee*. (*Very near.*)
WIFE (*Brusquely*): Stop that. I can listen to you talk because I like it and it's pretty—but that's all, do you hear? A fine thing that would be!
APPRENTICE: But that cannot be. Is it that you've given your word elsewhere?
WIFE: Now look here; go away.
APPRENTICE: I won't move from this spot until you say yes. Oh, my little Shoemaker's Wife, give me your word! (*Starts to embrace her.*)
WIFE (*Closing the window violently*): What an impertinent man! What a fool! If I have turned your head you'll just have to bear it! As if I were here just to . . . just to . . . well, can't one talk to anybody in this town? From what I can see there are but two extremes in this town: either a nun or a dishrag. That's all I needed to know! (*Pretending she smells something, running.*) Oh, my dinner's on the stove! Evil woman!
(*It is growing dark. The Shoemaker enters wearing a great cape and with a bundle of clothes in his hand.*)

The Shoemaker's Prodigious Wife 19

SHOEMAKER: I'm either another man or I don't know myself! Oh, my little house! Oh, my little bench! Wax, nails, calf-skins . . . well. (*He goes toward the door and retreats because he runs into the two Over-Pious Women.*)

FIRST OVER-PIOUS WOMAN: Resting, aren't you?

SECOND OVER-PIOUS WOMAN: You do well to rest!

SHOEMAKER (*In a bad humor*): Good night!

FIRST OVER-PIOUS WOMAN: To rest, master.

SECOND OVER-PIOUS WOMAN: To rest, to rest! (*They leave.*)

SHOEMAKER: Yes, resting—but they weren't looking through the keyhole! Witches! Ugly things! Be careful of that insinuating tone in which you speak to me. Naturally, since in the whole village they talk of nothing else—he this, she that, the servants something else! Ay! May lightning strike my sister, may she rest in peace! But better alone than pointed at by everybody!

(*He goes out rapidly, leaving the door open. Through the left door the Wife appears.*)

WIFE: Supper's ready. Do you hear me? (*Goes toward the door on the right.*) Do you hear me? Well, has he had the courage to go to the café, leaving the door open? And without finishing the boots? Well, when he returns he'll listen to me! He'll have to listen! How like men, men are! How abusive and how . . . how . . . well! (*Changing*) Oh, what a nice little breeze. (*She lights the lamp and from the street comes the sound of the bells of the flock returning to the village. The Wife looks out the window.*) What lovely flocks! I'm just crazy about little sheep. Look, look at that little white one that can just barely walk! Ay! But look at that big ugly one that keeps trampling on her and nothing . . . (*Shouts*) Shepherd, day dreamer! Don't you see that they're stepping on the new-born lamb? (*Pause.*) Certainly it's my business. Why shouldn't it be my business? Big brute! You . . . (*She moves away from the window.*) Well, sir, where could that wandering man have gone? Well, if he delays two minutes more, I'll eat by myself, for I'm self-sufficient and more than that. With such a good supper as I've prepared! My sweetmeat with the fresh wild potatoes, two green peppers, white bread, a bit of lean bacon, and squash conserve with lemon peel for the top. Because I have to take care of him! I have to take care of him! I take care of him by hand! (*During all this monolog, she gives evidence of great activity, moving from one side to the other, arranging the chairs, taking lint off the curtains, and removing threads from her dress.*)

BOY (*At the door*): Are you still angry?

WIFE: My little darling of a neighbor, where are you going?

BOY (*At the door*): You won't scold me, will you? Because my mother, who sometimes beats me, I love twenty bushelsful but I love you thirty-two and a half.

WIFE: Why are you so lovely? (*Seats him on her lap.*)

BOY: I came to tell you something that nobody else wants to tell you. "You go, you go, you go"—and no one wanted to go. And then, "Well, let the child go," they said—because it's some bad news that no one wants to carry.

WIFE: Then, tell me quickly. What has happened?

BOY: Well, don't be frightened—because it's not about dead people.

WIFE: Go on . . .

BOY: Look, little Shoemaker's Wife! (*Through the window a butterfly enters and the boy, getting down from her lap, begins to run after it.*) A butterfly! A butterfly! Don't you have a hat? It's yellow with blue and red marks—and I don't know what all!

WIFE: But child, weren't you going to . . . ?

BOY (*Sternly*): Be quiet and speak in a low voice. Don't you see it will get frightened if you don't? Oh, give me your handkerchief!

The Shoemaker's Prodigious Wife

WIFE (*Already intrigued by the hunt*): Take it.

BOY: Shh! Don't stamp your feet.

WIFE: You're going to let it get away.

BOY (*In a low voice, as though charming the butterfly, sings*):
>Wind butterfly,
>so lovely there,
>in gold and green,
>candlelight,
>stay there, there, there!
>You will not light,
>light you will not.
>Wind butterfly,
>in gold and green
>candlelight
>stay there, there, there!
>Oh please stay there,
>Butterfly, are you there?

WIFE: (*Jokingly*): Ye-e-e-s.

BOY: No, now that's not fair. (*The butterfly flies.*)

WIFE: Now! Now!

BOY (*Running happily with the handkerchief*): Won't you light? Won't you quit flying?

WIFE: (*Also running on the other side*): It'll get away! It'll get away!

(*The Boy runs out the door pursuing the butterfly.*)

WIFE: (*Sternly*): Where are you going?

BOY (*Suspended*): It's true. (*Quickly.*) But it's not my fault!

WIFE: Come now! Are you going to tell me what's happened? Quickly!

BOY: Oh! Well, look—your husband, the Shoemaker, has left never to return.

WIFE (*Terrified*): What?

BOY: Yes, yes. He said that at my house before he got on the stagecoach. I saw him myself—and he told us to tell you that—and the whole town knows it.

WIFE: (*Sitting deflated*): But it isn't possible. It isn't possible! I don't believe it!

BOY: Yes, it's true; don't scold me!

WIFE (*Rising in a fury, stamping on the floor*): And this is how he pays me? And this is how he pays me?

(*The Boy finds refuge behind the table.*)

BOY: Your hairpins are falling out!

WIFE: What's going to happen to me all alone in life? Oh! Oh! Oh!

(*The Boy runs out. The windows and the doors are full of Neighbors.*)

Yes, yes—come look at me! Rattlers, gossips! It's your fault . . .

MAYOR: Look, now, be quiet. If your husband has left you—it was because you didn't love him—because it couldn't be.

WIFE: But, do you think you know more than I do? Yes, I did love him. I should say I loved him. How many good and rich suitors I had—and I never said yes to them. Oh, my poor thing—what things they must have told you!

SACRISTAN'S WIFE (*Entering*): Woman, control yourself!

WIFE: I can't resign myself! I can't resign myself! Oh, Oh!

(*Neighbors dressed in various violent colors and carrying large glasses of cooling drinks begin to enter through the door. They turn, run, go and come around the Wife, who is sitting on the floor shouting, with the quickness and rhythm of a dance. The great skirts open with their turns. All adopt a comic attitude of pain.*)

YELLOW NEIGHBOR: A cooling drink?

RED NEIGHBOR: A little refreshment?

GREEN NEIGHBOR: For the blood?

BLACK NEIGHBOR: Lemon flavor?

PURPLE NEIGHBOR: Sarsaparilla?
RED NEIGHBOR: Mint is better.
PURPLE NEIGHBOR: Neighbor.
GREEN NEIGHBOR: Little neighbor.
BLACK NEIGHBOR: Shoemaker's Wife.
RED NEIGHBOR: Little Shoemaker's Wife.
(*The neighbors create a great excitement. The Wife is crying at the top of her lungs.*)

CURTAIN

ACT TWO

(*The same set. To the left the abandoned cobbler's bench. To the right a counter with bottles and a pan where the Wife washes the cups. The Wife is behind the counter. She wears a burning red dress with wide skirts. Her arms are bare. On the stage three tables. At one of them Don Blackbird is seated having a drink, and at the other the servant of the pulled-down hat.*)

The Wife washes glasses and cups with great ardour and places them on the counter. At the right appears the Sashmaker's Apprentice with the straight hat who was in the first act. He is sad. His arms hang at his sides and he looks at the Wife tenderly. If an actor exaggerates this character in the slightest he should be hit over the head by the director. No one should exaggerate. The farce always demands naturalness. The author has drawn the character and the tailor has dressed him. Simplicity. The Apprentice stops at the door. Don Blackbird and the other Apprentice turn their heads to look at him. This is almost a movie scene. The glances and expressions taken together create the effect. The Wife stops washing and looks fixedly at the Apprentice in the door. Silence.)

WIFE: Come in.

SASH APPRENTICE: If you wish it.

WIFE (*Amazed*): I? It absolutely does not matter to me one way or the other, but since I see you at the door . . .

SASH APPRENTICE: As you wish. (*He leans on the counter. Between his teeth*) This is that other one that I'm going to have to . . .

WIFE: What will you take?

The Shoemaker's Prodigious Wife

SASH APPRENTICE: I'll follow your suggestions.

WIFE: Then—take the gate.

SASH APPRENTICE: Oh, Lord, how times change!

WIFE: Don't think I'm going to start crying. Come now. Are you going to have a drink? Coffee? A cold drink? What?

SASH APPRENTICE: A cold drink.

WIFE: Don't look at me so hard—you'll make me spill the syrup.

SASH APPRENTICE: It's only—I'm dying. Ay!

(*Past the window go two girls with immense fans. They look, cross themselves, scandalized, cover their eyes with their fans, and cross on with tiny steps.*)

WIFE: The drink.

SASH APPRENTICE (*Looking at her*): Ay!

HAT APPRENTICE (*Looking at the floor*): Ay!

DON BLACKBIRD (*Looking at the ceiling*): Ay!

WIFE (*Turns her head toward each of the three "ays"*): "Ay" some more! But what is this—a tavern or a hospital? Abusers! If I didn't have to earn my living with these little wines and sweets—because I'm alone since the poor little husband of my soul left me, through the fault of all of you—how would it be possible for me to bear this? What do you say to that? I'm going to have to throw you out into the nice, wide street.

DON BLACKBIRD: Well said; very well said.

HAT APPRENTICE: You have opened a tavern and we can stay inside here as long as we want.

WIFE (*Fiercely*): What? What?

(*The Sash Apprentice starts to leave and Don Blackbird rises smiling and acting as if he were in on the secret, and would return.*)

HAT APPRENTICE: Just what I said!

WIFE: Well whatever you say—I can say more. And you might as well know, and the whole village, that my husband has been gone four months, but that I'll never give in to anybody—never! Because a married woman should keep her place as God commands, and I'm not afraid of anybody; do you hear? For I have the blood of my grandfather, may he be in heaven, who was a horse tamer and what is called a man. Decent I was and decent I will be. I gave my word to my husband. Well, until death.

(*Don Blackbird goes rapidly to the door making motions that indicate a relation between him and the Wife.*)

HAT APPRENTICE (*Rising*): I'm so angry I could take a bull by the horns, bend his head to the ground, eat his brains raw with my teeth, and surely not tire myself with biting.

(*He strides out and Don Blackbird flees toward the left.*)

WIFE: (*With her hands to her head*): Lord, Lord, Lord and Lord! (*She sits.*)

(*Through the door the Boy enters. He goes toward the Wife and covers her eyes.*)

BOY: Who am I?

WIFE: My child, little shepherd of Bethlehem.

BOY: I'm here. (*They kiss.*)

WIFE: Did you come for your little lunch?

BOY: If you want to give me some.

WIFE: I have a piece of chocolate today.

BOY: Yes? I like to be in your house very much.

WIFE (*Giving him the chocolate*): Why do you just look out for yourself?

BOY: For myself? Do you see this red spot on my knee?

WIFE: Let me see. (*She sits on a low chair and takes the Boy in her arms.*)

BOY: Well, Cunillo did it because he was singing the rhymes they made up about you and I hit him in the face, and then he threw a rock at me that—bang! Look.

WIFE: Does it hurt very much?

BOY: Not now, but I cried.

WIFE: Don't pay any attention to what they say.

The Shoemaker's Prodigious Wife

BOY: Well, they were saying very indecent things. Indecent things that I know how to say, you understand. But that I don't want to say.

WIFE (*Laughing*): Because if you say them I'll take a hot pimiento and make your tongue like a red-hot coal. (*They laugh.*)

BOY: But—why should they blame you because your husband left?

WIFE: They, they are the ones to blame, and the ones who make me unhappy.

BOY (*Sadly*): Don't say that, little cobbler's wife.

WIFE: I used to see myself in his eyes. When I'd see him coming mounted on his white mare . . .

BOY (*Interrupting her*): Ha-ha-ha! You're fooling me. Mr. Shoemaker didn't have a mare.

WIFE: Boy, be more respectful. He had a mare; certainly he had one—but you . . . you weren't born yet.

BOY (*Stroking his face*): Oh!—That was it!

WIFE: You see, when I met him I was washing clothes in the little brook. Through half a yard of water the pebbles on the bottom could be seen laughing—laughing with little tremblings. He wore a tight black suit, a red tie of the finest silk, and four gold rings that shone like four suns.

BOY: How pretty!

WIFE: He looked at me and I looked at him. I lay back on the grass. I think I can still feel on my face that little fresh breeze that came through the trees. He stopped his horse and the horse's tail was white and so long that it reached down to the water in the brook. (*The Wife is almost weeping. A distant song begins to be heard.*) I was so flustered that I let two lovely handkerchiefs, just this tiny, flow down with the current.

BOY: How funny!

WIFE: He then said to me . . . (*The song is heard nearer. Pause.*) Shh!

BOY (*Rises*): The couplets.

WIFE: The couplets. (*Pause. The two listen.*) Do you know what they say?

BOY (*Gesturing with his hand*): Well, sort of.

WIFE: Well, sing them, then, because I want to know.

BOY: What for?

WIFE: So that I can find out once and for all what they're saying.

BOY (*Singing and marking time*): You'll see:

> Mistress Cobbler, Mistress Cobbler,
> since her husband ran away
> turned her house into a tavern
> where the men go night and day.

WIFE: They'll pay for this!

BOY (*He beats time on the table with his hand*):

> Who has bought you, Mistress Cobbler,
> all those dresses; may we guess?
> cambrics, batistes, bobbin laces,
> fit for a proprietress.
>
> Now she's courted by the Mayor,
> now it is Don Blackbird's turn,
> Mistress Cobbler, Mistress Cobbler,
> Mistress, you have men to burn!

(*The voices are distinguished near and clearly with their accompaniment of tambourines. The Wife takes up a Manila scarf and throws it over her shoulders.*)

Where are you going? (*Frightened.*)

WIFE: They're going to drive me to buying a revolver! (*The song grows faint. The Wife runs to the door. But she bumps into the Mayor who comes majestically, beating on the floor with his wand.*)

MAYOR: Who waits on one here?

WIFE: The devil!

The Shoemaker's Prodigious Wife 29

MAYOR: But what's happened?

WIFE: Something you must have known for several days. Something that you as Mayor ought not to allow. The people sing couplets to me, the neighbors laugh at their doors, and since I have no husband to watch out for me I'm going to defend myself—since in this town the authorities are pumpkin-heads, good-for-nothings, figureheads!

BOY: Very well said.

MAYOR (*Severely*): Child, child! Enough of this shouting. Do you know what I've just done? Well, I put in jail two or three of those who came along singing.

WIFE: I'd like to see that!

VOICE (*Outside*): So-n-n-y-y!

BOY: My mother's calling me! (*Runs to the window.*) Wha-a-a-t? Good-bye. If you want, I can bring you my grandfather's big sword—the one who went to war. I can't lift it, you see, but you can.

WIFE (*Smiling*): Whatever you want!

VOICE (*Outside*): So-n-n-y-y!

BOY (*Already in the street*): Wha-a-at?

MAYOR: From what I can see that precocious and unnatural child is the only person in the village you treat well.

WIFE: You people can't say a single word that isn't an insult. And what is your most illustrious self laughing about?

MAYOR: To see you so beautiful but going to waste!

WIFE: A dog first! (*Serves him a glass of wine.*)

MAYOR: What a disillusioning world! I've known many women just like poppies—like fragrant roses—dark women with eyes like inky fire, women whose hair smells of sweet oils and whose hands are always very warm, women whose waists you can encircle with these two fingers; but like you —there's no one like you. Day before yesterday I was sick all morning because I saw laid out on the grass two of your chemises with sky blue ribbons—and it was like seeing you, Cobbler's Wife of my soul.

WIFE (*Exploding furiously*): Be quiet, old man. Hush up! With grown daughters and a large family you shouldn't come courting in a manner so indecent and so bold-faced.

MAYOR: I'm a widower.

WIFE: And I'm a married woman!

MAYOR: But your husband has left you and will not return I'm sure.

WIFE: I'll live as if I still had him.

MAYOR: Well then, I can testify, because he told me, that he didn't love you even as much as this.

WIFE: Well, I can testify that your four wives—may lightning strike them—hated you to death.

MAYOR (*Striking the floor with his wand*): Now that's enough!

WIFE (*Throwing a glass*): Now that's enough!

(*Pause.*)

MAYOR (*Under his breath*): If I could have you for my own I'd show you if I could tame you.

WIFE (*Coyly*): What's that you're saying?

MAYOR: Nothing. I was just thinking that if you were as good as you ought to be, I would have let you know that I have the will and the generosity to make out a deed before a notary for a very beautiful house.

WIFE: And what of that?

MAYOR: With a drawing room that cost five thousand *reales*, with table cloths, brocade curtains, full-length mirrors ...

WIFE: And what else?

MAYOR (*Don Juan*): The house has a bed with a canopy upheld by copper birds and daisies, a garden with six palms and a leaping fountain, but waits—in order to be happy —for a person I know to want to take possession of those rooms where she would be ... (*Addressing the Wife directly*) Look, you'd be like a Queen!

The Shoemaker's Prodigious Wife

WIFE (*Coyly*): I'm not used to such luxury. You sit down in the drawing room, crawl into the bed, look in the mirror, and lie with your mouth open underneath the palm trees waiting for the dates to fall—because I'm not budging from being a shoemaker's wife.

MAYOR: Nor I from being Mayor. But it's time you knew that daylight won't break any earlier just for our disdaining it. (*In an affected tone of voice.*)

WIFE: And it's time you knew that I don't like you or any one in the village. An old man like you!

MAYOR (*Indignant*): I'll end by putting you in jail.

WIFE: Just you dare!

(*Outside there is heard a trumpet call—florid and most comical.*)

MAYOR: What could that be?

WIFE (*Happy and wide-eyed*): Puppets! (*She beats her knees. Two women cross the window.*)

RED NEIGHBOR: Puppets!

PURPLE NEIGHBOR: Puppets!

BOY (*At the window*): Do you think they have any monkeys? Let's go!

WIFE (*To the Mayor*): I'm going to close up.

BOY: They're coming to your house.

WIFE: Yes? (*Goes toward the door.*)

BOY: Look at them!

(*At the door the Shoemaker, disguised, appears. He carries a trumpet and a scroll at his back. The people surround him. The Wife waits with great expectancy and the Boy leaps in through the window and holds on to her skirts.*)

SHOEMAKER: Good afternoon!

WIFE: Good afternoon to you, Mr. Puppeteer.

SHOEMAKER: May a person rest here?

WIFE: And drink if you like.

MAYOR: Enter, my good man. And drink what you like, for I'll pay. (*To the Neighbors*) And you others, what are you doing here?

RED NEIGHBOR: Since we are out in the broad street, I don't believe we're in your way.

(*The Shoemaker, looking at all with calmness, leaves the scroll on the table.*)

SHOEMAKER: Let them be, Mr. Mayor—for I imagine you are he—I must make my living with these people.

BOY: Where have I heard this man talk before? (*Throughout all this scene the Boy looks at the Shoemaker with a puzzled air.*) Work your puppets! (*The Neighbors laugh.*)

SHOEMAKER: As soon as I drink a glass of wine.

WIFE (*Happily*): But are you going to work them in my house?

SHOEMAKER: If you will permit me.

RED NEIGHBOR: Then, may we come in?

WIFE (*Serious*): You can come in. (*Gives a glass to the Shoemaker.*)

RED NEIGHBOR (*Seating herself*): Now we shall enjoy ourselves a little.

(*The Mayor sits.*)

MAYOR: Do you come from very far?

SHOEMAKER: From very far.

MAYOR: From Seville?

SHOEMAKER: Leagues farther.

MAYOR: From France?

SHOEMAKER: Leagues farther.

MAYOR: From England?

SHOEMAKER: From the Philippine Islands.

(*The Neighbors give signs of admiration. The Wife is ecstatic.*)

MAYOR: You must have seen the Insurrectionists, then?

SHOEMAKER: Just the same as I am looking at you now.

BOY: And what are they like?

The Shoemaker's Prodigious Wife

SHOEMAKER: Unbearable. Just imagine, almost all of them are shoemakers.

(*The Neighbors look at the Wife.*)

WIFE (*Blushing*): And aren't they in any other profession?

SHOEMAKER: Absolutely not. In the Philippines—shoemakers!

WIFE: Well, perhaps in the Philippines shoemakers are stupid, but in this country there are some who are smart—and very smart at that.

RED NEIGHBOR (*Flatteringly*): Very well spoken.

WIFE (*Brusquely*): No one asked your opinion.

RED NEIGHBOR: But, child!

SHOEMAKER (*Sternly, interrupting*): What rich wine! (*Louder*) What rich wine indeed! (*Silence.*) Wine from grapes black as the souls of some women I have known.

WIFE: If any of them had souls!

MAYOR: Shh! And of what does your work consist?

SHOEMAKER (*Drinks wine, rolls his tongue, looks at his wife*): Ah! It is a work of small show but much science. I present life from within. There are the couplets of the "Henpecked Shoemaker," and the "Roaring Girl of Alexandria," "Life of Don Diego Corrientes," "Adventures of the Handsome Francisco Esteban," and above all, "The Art of Closing the Mouths of Gossipy and Impudent Women."

WIFE: My poor husband knew all those things!

SHOEMAKER: May God forgive him!

WIFE: Now you listen . . . (*The Neighbors laugh.*)

BOY: Hush!

MAYOR (*Imperiously*): Quiet! These are teachings like any Scripture. (*To the Shoemaker*) Whenever you wish.

(*The Shoemaker unrolls the scroll on which the story is painted, divided into tiny squares, drawn in red ochre and violent colors. The Neighbors start moving closer, and the Wife takes the Boy upon her knees.*)

SHOEMAKER: Attention.

BOY: Oh, how pretty! (*Embraces the Wife, whispering.*)

WIFE: Now pay good attention in case I don't understand everything.

BOY: It's surely not harder than sacred history.

SHOEMAKER: Worthy spectators. Listen to the true and moving ballad of the rubicund wife and the poor, patient little husband, that it may serve as warning and example to all the people of this world. (*In a lugubrious tone.*) Prick up your ears and understanding. (*The Neighbors crane their necks, and a few of the women take hands.*)

BOY: Doesn't the puppeteer remind you of your husband when he talks?

WIFE: He had a sweeter voice.

SHOEMAKER: Are we ready?

WIFE: I feel so excited.

BOY: Me too!

    SHOEMAKER (*Pointing with a wand*):
    In Córdoba within a cottage
    set about with trees and rosebays,
    once upon a time a tanner
    lived there with the tanner's wife.
                     (*Expectancy*)
    She a very stubborn woman—
    he a man of gentle patience;
    though the wife had not turned twenty,
    he was then well over fifty.
    Holy Lord, how they would argue!
    Look now at that beastly woman,
    laughing at the poor weak husband
    with her glances and her speaking.
(*On the scroll is drawn a woman who looks infantile and slightly wall-eyed.*)

WIFE (*Whispering*): What an evil woman!
SHOEMAKER:
Dark hair worthy of an empress
had this little tanner's wife.
and her flesh was like the water
from Lucena's crystal sources.
When she moved her skirts and flounces,
as she walked about in springtime,
all her clothes gave off the fragrance
lemon groves and mint exhale.
Oh what lemons, lemons
of the lemon grove!
Oh what a delicious
little tanner's wife!

(*The Neighbors laugh.*)

And now look how she was courted
by young men of striking presence
riding sleek and shining stallions
harnessed in fine silken tassels.
Elegant and charming persons
would come riding past the doorway,
making shine a happy luster
from their coin-hung golden watch-chains.
And the tanner's wife was willing
to converse with all these worthies,
while the mares they rode went prancing
on the cobbles of the roadway.
Mark her how with one she's flirting,
dressed and combed with fullest grooming,
while the poor long-suffering tanner
sticks his awl into the leather.

(*Very dramatically, crossing his hands.*)

Old and decent acting husband,
married to a wife too youthful,
who could be that scoundrel horseman
come to steal love from your doorway?

(*The Wife who has been sighing, bursts into tears.*)

SHOEMAKER (*Turning*): What's happened to you?

MAYOR: But, child! (*Beats with his wand on the floor.*)

RED NEIGHBOR: A person who has something to shut up about always bawls.

PURPLE NEIGHBOR: Please go on!

(*The Neighbors murmur and shush.*)

WIFE: It's just that I'm filled with pity and can't contain myself. You see? I can't contain myself. (*Weeps, trying to control herself, hiccuping most comically.*)

MAYOR: Quiet!

BOY: You see?

SHOEMAKER: Do me the favor of not interrupting. How well one can tell you're not trying to repeat something from memory!

BOY (*Sighing*): How true!

        SHOEMAKER (*Ill-humored*):
So, upon a Monday morning,
just about eleven thirty,
when the sun left without shadow
honeysuckle vines and rushes,
when most happy danced together
winds and thyme plants in the forest,
and the leaves of green were falling
from the wild strawberry bushes,
there the spoiled wife was watering
gilliflowers in her garden.
Just then came her suitor trotting
mare of Cordovan extraction,
and he told her through his sighing:
"Sweetheart, if you only wished it,
we'd have supper this next evening,
we alone, but at your table."
"Yes, but what about my husband?"
"Husband? He won't know about it."

The Shoemaker's Prodigious Wife

"Then what will you do?" "I'll kill him."
"He's a quick one, you might fail.
Have you a revolver?" "Better!
I can use a barber's razor."
"Does it cut much?" "More than cold wind.

(*The Wife covers her eyes and squeezes the Boy. All the Neighbors are in a high pitch of expectancy which is shown by their expressions.*)

And the blade's without a nick yet."
"You're not lying?" "No, I'll give him
ten quite well-directed blade thrusts
in the following distribution,
which I really think stupendous:
four upon the lumbar region,
one just at his left side nipple,
one more at a place just like it,
two on each side of his buttocks."
"Will you kill him right away?"
"This same night when he's returning
with his leather and his horsehair,
where the water ditch starts curving."

(*During this last verse, quickly, there is heard offstage a most loud and anguished shout; the Neighbors rise. Another shout nearer. The scroll and the wand fall from the hands of the Shoemaker. All tremble comically.*)

BLACK NEIGHBOR (*At the window*): They've drawn their knives!

WIFE: Oh, my Lord!

RED NEIGHBOR: Holiest Virgin!

SHOEMAKER: What a row!

BLACK NEIGHBOR: They're killing themselves! They're ripping each other to pieces—all through the fault of that woman! (*Points to the Wife.*)

MAYOR (*Nervous*): Let's go see.

BOY: I'm very scared!

GREEN NEIGHBOR: Come on! Come on! (*They start leaving.*)

VOICE (*Outside*): Because of that evil woman!

SHOEMAKER: I can't stand this! I can't stand it! (*Runs around the stage with his hands at his head.*)

(*All are leaving rapidly, exclaiming and casting looks of hate towards the Wife. She quickly closes the window and door.*)

WIFE: Have you ever seen such hatefulness? I swear by the holiest blood of our Father Jesus that I'm innocent. Ay! What could have happened? Look, look how I'm trembling. (*Shows him her hands.*) It seems as if my hands want to fly off by themselves.

SHOEMAKER: Be calm, girl. Is it your husband in the street?

WIFE (*Bursting into sobs*): My husband? Oh, Mr. Puppeteer!

SHOEMAKER: What's the matter?

WIFE: My husband left me because of these people and now I'm alone—with nobody's warmth.

SHOEMAKER: Poor little thing.

WIFE: And I loved him so much! I adored him!

SHOEMAKER (*Starting*): That isn't true!

WIFE (*Quickly ceasing her sobs*): What did you say?

SHOEMAKER: I said it's such an incomprehensible thing that . . . it doesn't seem to be true. (*Disturbed.*)

WIFE: You're very right, but since then I haven't been able to eat nor sleep, nor live; because he was my happiness, my defense.

SHOEMAKER: And, loving him as much as you did, did he abandon you? I can see from that your husband was not very understanding.

WIFE: Please keep your tongue in your pocket. No one has given you permission to voice your opinion.

SHOEMAKER: You must excuse me; I didn't mean to . . .

WIFE: The idea! Why, he was so smart!

SHOEMAKER (*Jokingly*): Ye-e-e-s?

WIFE (*Sternly*): Yes. You know those ballads and little songs you sing and tell through the villages? Well, that isn't anything to what he knew. He knew—three times as much!

SHOEMAKER (*Serious*): That can't be.

WIFE (*Sternly*): Four times as much! He used to tell them all to me when we went to bed. Old stories that you probably haven't even heard mentioned, (*Coyly*) and I would get so frightened. But he would say to me: "Darling of my soul, these are just tiny little white lies!"

SHOEMAKER (*Indignant*): That's not true.

WIFE (*Surprised*): Eh? Have you lost your mind?

SHOEMAKER: It's a lie!

WIFE (*Angry*): What are you saying, you puppeteer of the devil?

SHOEMAKER (*Strongly, standing*): That your husband was quite right. Those stories are just lies—fantasy, that's all.

WIFE (*Sourly*): Naturally, my good sir. You seem to take me for a complete fool—but you won't deny that these stories make an impression.

SHOEMAKER: Ah, that is flour from another sack, then! They make an impression on impressionable souls.

WIFE: Every one has feelings.

SHOEMAKER: According to how one looks at it. I've known many people without feelings. And in my town there lived a woman at one time who had a heart so unfeeling that she would talk to her friends through the window while her husband made boots and shoes from morning to night.

WIFE (*Rising and taking up a chair*): Are you saying that because of me?

SHOEMAKER: What?

WIFE: If you were going to add anything else, go ahead! Be brave!

SHOEMAKER (*Humbly*): Miss, what are you saying? How do I know who you are? I haven't insulted you in any way.

Why do you treat me so? But that's my fate! (*Almost weeping.*)

WIFE (*Stern, but moved*): Look here, my good man; I spoke like that because I'm on pins and needles. Everybody besieges me—everybody criticizes me. How can I help but be looking out for the slightest opportunity to defend myself? Because I'm alone, because I'm young, and yet already live only for my memories.... (*Weeps.*)

SHOEMAKER (*Weepily*): I understand, you lovely young creature. I understand much better than you can imagine, because—you must know, most confidentially, that your situation is—yes, there's no doubt of it—identical with mine.

WIFE (*Intrigued*): Could that be possible?

SHOEMAKER (*Falls on the table*): I—was abandoned by my wife!

WIFE: Death would be too good for her!

SHOEMAKER: She dreamt of a world that was not mine. She was flighty and domineering; she loved conversation, and the sweets I could not buy for her, too much, and on a day that was stormy with a wind like a hurricane, she left me forever.

WIFE: And why do you wander over the world now?

SHOEMAKER: I search for her to forgive her and to live out with her the short time I have left in this world. At my age one is rather insecurely in this world of God's.

WIFE (*Quickly*): Take a little black coffee; it'll be good for you after all this hullabaloo. (*Goes to the counter to pour the coffee and turns her back on the Shoemaker.*)

SHOEMAKER (*Crossing himself exaggeratedly and opening his eyes*): May God repay you, my little red carnation.

WIFE (*Offers him the cup. She keeps the saucer in her hand. He drinks in gulps*): Is it good?

SHOEMAKER (*Flatteringly*): Since it was made by your hands!

WIFE (*Smiling*): Thank you!

The Shoemaker's Prodigious Wife

SHOEMAKER (*With a final swallow*): Oh, how I envy your husband!

WIFE: Why?

SHOEMAKER (*Gallantly*): Because he married the most beautiful woman in the world!

WIFE (*Softened*): What things you say!

SHOEMAKER: And now I'm almost glad I have to go, because here you are alone, and I'm alone, and you so beautiful and I, having a tongue,—it seems to me that I couldn't help making a certain suggestion . . .

WIFE (*Recovering*): My heavens, stop that! What do you think? I keep my whole heart for that wanderer, for the one whom I must, for my husband!

SHOEMAKER (*Very pleased—throwing his hat on the ground*): That's fine! Spoken like a real woman—fine!

WIFE (*Joking a little, surprised*): It seems to me that you're a little . . . (*Points to her temple.*)

SHOEMAKER: Whatever you say. But understand that I'm not in love with any one except my wife, my lawfully wedded wife!

WIFE: And I with my husband; and nobody but my husband. How many times I've said it for even the deaf to hear . . . (*With her hands crossed.*) Oh, Shoemaker of my soul!

SHOEMAKER (*Aside*): Oh wife of my soul!

(*Knocking at the door.*)

WIFE: Heavens! One is in a constant state of excitement. Who is it?

BOY: Open!

WIFE: How's this? How did you get here?

BOY: Oh, I've come running to tell you!

WIFE: What's happened?

BOY: Two or three young men have wounded each other with knives and they're blaming you for it. Wounds that bleed a lot. All the women have gone to see the judge to make you leave town. Oh! And the men wanted the sacristan to play the bells so they could sing you the rhymes . . . (*The Boy is panting and perspiring.*)

WIFE (*To the Shoemaker*): Do you see that?

BOY: All the plaza is full of people talking—it's like the fair—and all of them are against you!

SHOEMAKER: Villains! I'm of a mind to go out and defend you.

WIFE: What for? They'd just put you in jail. I'm the one who's going to have to do something desperate.

BOY: From the window in your room you can see the excitement in the plaza.

WIFE (*In a hurry*): Come on, I want to see for myself the hatefulness of those people. (*Runs out quickly.*)

SHOEMAKER: Yes, yes, villains! But I'll soon settle accounts with all of them and they'll have to answer to me. Oh, my little house! What a pleasant warmth comes from your doors and windows! Oh what terrible holes, what bad meals, what dirty cloth sheets out in the world's highways. And how stupid not to realize that my wife was pure gold, the best in the world! It makes me almost want to weep!

RED NEIGHBOR (*Entering rapidly*): Good man.

YELLOW NEIGHBOR (*Rapidly*): Good man.

RED NEIGHBOR: Leave this house immediately. You are a decent person and ought not to be here.

YELLOW NEIGHBOR: This is the house of a she-lion, of a she-hyena.

RED NEIGHBOR: Of an evil-born woman, betrayer of men.

YELLOW NEIGHBOR: But she'll either leave town or we'll put her out. She's running us crazy.

RED NEIGHBOR: I'd like to see her dead.

YELLOW NEIGHBOR: In her shroud, with her flowers.

SHOEMAKER: (*Anguished*): That's enough!

RED NEIGHBOR: Blood has been shed.

YELLOW NEIGHBOR: There are no white handkerchiefs left.

RED NEIGHBOR: Two men like two suns.

YELLOW NEIGHBOR: Pierced by knives.

SHOEMAKER (*Loudly*): Enough now!

RED NEIGHBOR: All because of her.

YELLOW NEIGHBOR: That one and no one else.

RED NEIGHBOR: We are really looking out for your good.

YELLOW NEIGHBOR: We're letting you know in time.

SHOEMAKER: You big liars! Evil-born women! Cats! I'm going to drag you by the hair . . .

RED NEIGHBOR (*To the other*): She's captured him too.

YELLOW NEIGHBOR: Her kisses must have done it.

SHOEMAKER: May the devil take you! Basilisks, perjurers!

BLACK NEIGHBOR (*At the window*): Neighbor, run! (*Leaves running. The two Neighbors do likewise.*)

RED NEIGHBOR: Another one ensnared.

YELLOW NEIGHBOR: Another one!

SHOEMAKER: Harpies! Jewesses! I'll put barber's razors in your shoes. You'll have bad dreams about me.

BOY (*Entering rapidly*): A group of men was just going into the Mayor's house. I'm going to hear what they're saying. (*Exits running.*)

WIFE (*Entering, courageously*): Well, here I am, if they dare to come. And with the composure of one descended from a family of horsemen who many times crossed the wilds without saddles—bareback on their horses.

SHOEMAKER: And will not your fortitude sometime weaken?

WIFE: Never. A person like me, who is sustained by love and honor, never surrenders. I am able to hold out here until all my hair turns white.

SHOEMAKER (*Moved, advancing toward her*): Oh . . .

WIFE: What's the matter with you?

SHOEMAKER: I am overcome . . .

WIFE: Look, the whole town is on me; they want to come

kill me, yet I'm not the least afraid. A knife is answered with a knife, and a club with a club, but at night, when I close this door and go to my bed—I feel such sadness— what sadness! And I suffer such smotherings! The bureau creaks—a fright! The windows sound with the rain against them—another fright! Without meaning to, I shake the bed hangings myself—double fright! And all this is nothing more than fear of loneliness—full of phantoms, which I have not seen because I have not wanted to—but which my mother and grandmother and all the women of my family who have had eyes have seen.

SHOEMAKER: And why don't you change your way of living?

WIFE: Are you crazy? What can I do? Where can I go? Here I am and God will say what is to happen.

(*Outside, distantly, shouts and applause are heard.*)

SHOEMAKER: Well, I'm sorry, but I must be on my way before night falls. How much do I owe you? (*Takes up the scroll.*)

WIFE: Nothing.

SHOEMAKER: I couldn't.

WIFE: What you ate for what you served.

SHOEMAKER: Many thanks. (*Puts the scroll to his back sadly.*) Then, good-bye—forever; because at my age . . . (*He is moved.*)

WIFE (*Recovering*): I wouldn't want to say good-bye like this. I am usually very gay. (*In a clear voice*) Good man, may God will that you find your wife so that you may once more live with the care and decency that you were used to. (*She is moved.*)

SHOEMAKER: I say the same about your husband. But, you know, the world is small: what do you want me to say to him if I meet him by chance in my wanderings?

WIFE: Tell him I adore him.

SHOEMAKER (*Coming near*): And what else?

The Shoemaker's Prodigious Wife

WIFE: That in spite of his fifty and some odd years, his most blessed fifty years, I find him more slender and graceful than all the men in the world.

SHOEMAKER: Child, how wonderful you are! You love him as much as I love my wife!

WIFE: Much more!

SHOEMAKER: That's not possible. I'm like a little puppy, and my wife commands in the castle. But let her command! She has more sense than I have. (*He is near and as though praying to her.*)

WIFE: And don't forget to tell him I'm waiting for him, for the nights are long in winter.

SHOEMAKER: Then, you would receive him well?

WIFE: As if he were the king and queen together.

SHOEMAKER (*Trembling*): And if he should by chance come right now?

WIFE: I would go mad with happiness!

SHOEMAKER: Would you forgive him his madness?

WIFE: How long ago I forgave him!

SHOEMAKER: Do you want him to come back now?

WIFE: Oh, if he would only come!

SHOEMAKER (*Shouting*): Well, he's here.

WIFE: What are you saying?

SHOEMAKER (*Removing his glasses and the disguise*): I can't bear it any longer! Wife of my heart!

(*The Wife is as though insane, with her arms held out from her body. The Shoemaker embraces her, and she looks at him intently in this critical moment. Outside, the murmuring of the rhymes is clearly heard.*)

VOICE (*Without*):
Mistress Cobbler, Mistress Cobbler,
since her husband went away,
turned her house into a tavern
where the men go night and day.

WIFE (*Recovering*): Loafer, scoundrel, rascal, villain! Do you hear that? All because of you! (*Begins throwing chairs.*)

SHOEMAKER (*Full of emotion, going toward the bench*): Wife of my heart!

WIFE: Vagabond! Oh, how happy I am you've returned! What a life I'm going to lead you! Not even the Inquisition could have been worse. Not even the templars at Rome!

SHOEMAKER (*At the bench*): House of my happiness!

(*The rhymes are heard quite near. The Neighbors appear at the window.*)

VOICES (*Outside*):
Who has bought you, Mistress Cobbler,
All those dresses, may we guess?
Cambrics, batistes, bobbin laces,
Fit for a proprietress.

Now she's courted by the Mayor,
Now it is Don Mirlo's turn;
Mistress Cobbler, Mistress Cobbler,
Mistress, you have men to burn!

WIFE: How unfortunate I am! With this man God has given me! (*Going to the door.*) Quiet, long tongues, red Jews! And now, come ahead, come ahead if you want to. There are two of us now to defend my house. Two! Two! My husband and I. (*To her husband*) With this scoundrel, with this villain!

(*The noise of the couplets fills the stage. A bell begins to ring distantly and furiously.*)

CURTAIN

The Love of Don Perlimplin and Belisa in the Garden

An Erotic Allelujah* in Four Scenes

Chamber Version—1931

---

*The Spanish of the subtitle means "An Erotic Lace Paper Valentine in Four Scenes." *Aleluya* is the name of a particular kind of decorated papers with flowery couplets printed on them that are distributed among the people on certain festive days. In *The Shoemaker's Prodigious Wife* these *aleluyas* are mentioned by the Shoemaker as part of his stock in trade when he returns disguised as a puppeteer. We have kept the title as it appears above for its purely evocative qualities.

CHARACTERS

Don Perlimplín
Belisa
Marcolfa
Mother of Belisa
First Sprite
Second Sprite

PROLOGUE

(*House of Don Perlimplín. Green walls; chairs and furniture painted black. At the rear, a deep window through which Belisa's balcony may be seen.*

(*Perlimplín wears a green cassock and a white wig full of curls. Marcolfa, the servant, wears the classic striped dress.*)

PERLIMPLÍN: Yes?

MARCOLFA: Yes.

PERLIMPLÍN: But why, 'yes'?

MARCOLFA: Just because yes.

PERLIMPLÍN: And if I should say no?

MARCOLFA (*Acidly*): No?

PERLIMPLÍN: No.

MARCOLFA: Tell me, Master, the reason for that 'no.'

PERLIMPLÍN: You tell me, you persevering domestic, the reasons for that 'yes.'

(*Pause.*)

MARCOLFA: Twenty and twenty are forty . . .

PERLIMPLÍN (*Listening*): Proceed.

MARCOLFA: And ten, fifty.

PERLIMPLÍN: Go ahead.

MARCOLFA: At fifty years one is no longer a child.

PERLIMPLÍN: Of course!

MARCOLFA: I may die any minute.

PERLIMPLÍN: Of course!

MARCOLFA (*Weeping*): And what will happen to you all alone in the world?

PERLIMPLÍN: What will happen?

MARCOLFA: That's why you have to marry.

PERLIMPLÍN (*Distracted*): Yes?

MARCOLFA (*Sternly*): Yes.

PERLIMPLÍN (*Miserably*): But Marcolfa . . . why 'yes'? When I was a child a woman strangled her husband. He was a shoemaker. I can't forget it. I've always said I wouldn't marry. My books are enough for me. What good will marriage do me?

MARCOLFA: Marriage holds great charms, Master. It isn't what it appears on the outside. It's full of hidden things . . . things which it would not be becoming for a servant to mention. You see that . . .

PERLIMPLÍN: That what?

MARCOLFA: That I have blushed.

(*Pause. A piano is heard.*)

VOICE OF BELISA (*Within, singing*):
Love, love.
Enclosed within my thighs,
the sun swims like a fish.
Warm water in the rushes,
love.
Morning cock, the night is going!
Don't let it vanish, no!

MARCOLFA: My master will see the reason I have.

PERLIMPLÍN (*Scratching his head*): She sings prettily.

MARCOLFA: She is the woman for my master. The fair Belisa.

PERLIMPLÍN: Belisa . . . but wouldn't it be better . . . ?

MARCOLFA: No. Now come. (*She takes him by the hand and goes toward the window.*) Say, 'Belisa.'

PERLIMPLÍN: Belisa . . .

MARCOLFA: Louder.

PERLIMPLÍN: Belisa!

(*The balcony of the house opposite opens and Belisa appears, resplendent in her loveliness. She is half naked.*)

Don Perlimplín and Belisa

BELISA: Who calls?

(*Marcolfa hides behind the window curtains.*)

MARCOLFA: Answer!

PERLIMPLÍN (*Trembling*): I was calling.

BELISA: Yes?

PERLIMPLÍN: Yes.

BELISA: But why, 'yes'?

PERLIMPLÍN: Just because yes.

BELISA: And if I should say no?

PERLIMPLÍN: I would be sorry, because . . . we have decided that I want to marry.

BELISA (*Laughs*): Marry whom?

PERLIMPLÍN: You.

BELISA (*Serious*): But . . . (*Calling.*) Mamá! Mama-á-á!

MARCOLFA: This is going well.

(*Enter the Mother wearing a great eighteenth-century wig full of birds, ribbons, and glass beads.*)

BELISA: Don Perlimplín wants to marry me. What must I do?

MOTHER: The very best of afternoons to you, my charming little neighbor. I always said to my poor little girl that you have the grace and elegance of that great lady who was your mother whom I did not have the pleasure of knowing.

PERLIMPLÍN: Thank you.

MARCOLFA (*Furiously, from behind the curtain*): I have decided that we are going . . .

PERLIMPLÍN: We have decided that we are going . . .

MOTHER: To contract matrimony. Is that not so?

PERLIMPLÍN: That is so.

BELISA: But, Mamá, what about me?

MOTHER: You are agreeable, naturally. Don Perlimplín is a fascinating husband.

PERLIMPLÍN: I hope to be one, madam.

MARCOLFA (*Calling to Don Perlimplín*): This is almost settled.

PERLIMPLÍN: Do you think so? (*They whisper together.*)

MOTHER (*To Belisa*): Don Perlimplín has many lands. On these are many geese and sheep. The sheep are taken to market. At the market they get money for them. Money produces beauty . . . and beauty is sought after by all men.

PERLIMPLÍN: Then . . .

MOTHER: She is ever so thrilled. Belisa, go inside. It isn't well for a maiden to hear certain conversations.

BELISA: Until later. (*She leaves.*)

MOTHER: She is a lily. You've seen her face? (*Lowering her voice.*) But if you should see further! Just like sugar. But, pardon. I need not call these things to the attention of a person as modern and competent as you . . .

PERLIMPLÍN: Yes?

MOTHER: Why, yes. I said it without irony.

PERLIMPLÍN: I don't know how to express our gratitude.

MOTHER: Oh, 'our gratitude.' What extraordinary delicacy! The gratitude of your heart and yourself . . . I have sensed it. I have sensed it . . . in spite of the fact that it is twenty years since I have had relations with a man.

MARCOLFA (*Aside*): The wedding.

PERLIMPLÍN: The wedding . . .

MOTHER: Whenever you wish. Though . . . (*She brings out a handkerchief and weeps.*) . . . to every mother . . . until later! (*Leaves.*)

MARCOLFA: At last!

PERPLIMPLÍN: Oh, Marcolfa, Marcolfa! Into what world are you going to thrust me?

MARCOLFA: Into the world of matrimony.

Don Perlimplín and Belisa

PERLIMPLÍN: And if I should be frank, I would say that I feel thirsty. Why don't you bring me some water?

MARCOLFA (*Approaching and whispering in his ear*): Who could believe it?

(*The piano is heard. The stage is in darkness. Belisa opens the curtains of her balcony, almost naked, singing languidly.*)

BELISA:
Love, love.
Enclosed within my thighs,
The sun swims like a fish.

MARCOLFA: Beautiful maiden.

PERLIMPLÍN: Like sugar . . . white inside. Will she be capable of strangling me?

MARCOLA: Woman is weak if frightened in time.

BELISA:
Love.
Morning cock, the night is going!
Don't let it vanish, no!

PERLIMPLÍN: What does she mean, Marcolfa? What does she mean?

MARCOLFA: What is this I feel? What is it?

(*The piano goes on playing. Past the balcony flies a band of black paper birds.*)

CURTAIN

THE ONLY ACT

SCENE ONE

(Don Perlimplín's room. At the center there is a great bed piled high with pillows, spread with down comforters, and topped by a canopy with plume ornaments. It is arranged slanting, as if in an old picture with bad perspective. In the round back wall there are six doors. The first one on the right serves as entrance and exit for Don Perlimplín. It is the wedding night.)

(Marcolfa, with a candelabrum in her hand, speaks at the first door on the left side.)

MARCOLFA: Good night.

BELISA *(Offstage)*: Good night, Marcolfa.

(Don Perlimplín enters, magnificently dressed in the style of the eighteenth century, wearing a green coat trimmed with fur and a cravat of real lace.)

MARCOLFA: May my master have a good wedding night.

PERLIMPLÍN: Good night, Marcolfa.

(Marcolfa leaves. Perlimplín tiptoes toward the room in front and looks from the door.)

Belisa, in all that froth of lace you look like a wave, and you give me the same fear of the sea that I had as a child. Since you came from the church my house is full of secret whispers, and the water grows warm of its own accord in the glasses. Oh! Perlimplín. . . . Where are you, Perlimplín?

(Tiptoes back. Belisa appears, dressed in a great sleeping garment full of laces. Her hair is loose and her arms bare.)

BELISA: The maid perfumed this room with lavender and not

Don Perlimplín and Belisa

with musk as I ordered . . . (*Goes toward the bed.*) Nor did she put on the fine linen and the bedcover she has. Marcolfa . . . (*At this moment there is a soft music of guitars. Belisa crosses her hands over her breast.*) Ah! Whoever seeks me ardently will find me. My thirst is never quenched, just as the thirst of the gargoyles who spurt water in the fountains is never quenched. (*The music continues.*) Oh, what music! What music! Like the soft warm downy feathers of a swan! Oh! Is it I? Or is it the music?

(*She throws a great cape of red velvet over her shoulders and walks about the room. The music is silent and five whistles are heard.*)

BELISA: Five of them!

(*Perlimplín appears.*)

PERLIMPLÍN: Do I disturb you?

BELISA: How could that be possible?

PERLIMPLÍN: Are you sleepy?

BELISA (*Ironically*): Sleepy?

PERLIMPLÍN: The night has become a little chilly. (*Rubs his hands. Pause.*)

BELISA (*With decision*): Perlimplín.

PERLIMPLÍN (*Trembling*): What do you want?

BELISA (*Vaguely*): It's a pretty name, 'Perlimplín.'

PERLIMPLÍN: Yours is prettier, Belisa.

BELISA (*Laughing*): Oh! Thank you! (*Short pause.*)

PERLIMPLÍN: I wanted to tell you something.

BELISA: And that is?

PERLIMPLÍN: I have been late in deciding . . . but . . .

BELISA: Say it.

PERLIMPLÍN: Belisa, I love you.

BELISA: Oh, you little gentleman! That's your duty.

PERLIMPLÍN: Yes?

BELISA: Yes.

PERLIMPLÍN: But why 'yes'?

BELISA (*Coyly*): Because.

PERLIMPLÍN: No.

BELISA: Perlimplín!

PERLIMPLÍN: No, Belisa, before I married you, I didn't love you.

BELISA (*Jokingly*): What are you saying?

PERLIMPLÍN: I married . . . for whatever reason, but I didn't love you. I couldn't have imagined your body until I saw it through the keyhole when you were putting on your wedding dress. And then it was that I felt love come to me. Then! Like the deep thrust of a lancet in my throat.

BELISA (*Intrigued*): But, the other women?

PERLIMPLÍN: What women?

BELISA: Those you knew before.

PERLIMPLÍN: But, the other women?

BELISA: You astonish me!

PERLIMPLÍN: The first to be astonished was I. (*Pause. Five whistles are heard.*) What's that?

BELISA: The clock.

PERLIMPLÍN: Is it five?

BELISA: Bedtime.

PERLIMPLÍN: Do I have your permission to remove my coat?

BELISA: Of course (*Yawning*), little husband. And put out the light, if that is your wish.

(*Perlimplín puts out the light.*)

PERLIMPLÍN (*In a low voice*): Belisa.

BELISA (*Loudly*): What, child?

PERLIMPLÍN (*Whispering*): I've put the light out.

BELISA (*Jokingly*): I see that.

PERLIMPLÍN (*In a much lower voice*): Belisa . . .

BELISA (*In a loud voice*): What, my enchanter?

PERLIMPLÍN: I adore you!

Don Perlimplín and Belisa

(*Two Sprites, entering from opposite sides of the stage, run a curtain of misty gray. The theatre is left in darkness. Flutes sound with a sweet, sleepy tone. The Sprites should be two children. They sit on the prompt box facing the audience.*)

FIRST SPRITE: And how goes it with you in this tiny darkness?

SECOND SPRITE: Neither well nor badly, little friend.

FIRST SPRITE: Here we are.

SECOND SPRITE: And how do you like it? It's always nice to cover other people's failings . . .

FIRST SPRITE: And then to let the audience take care of uncovering them.

SECOND SPRITE: And without this covering and uncovering . . .

FIRST SPRITE: What would the poor people do?

SECOND SPRITE (*Looking at the curtain*): Don't leave even a crack.

FIRST SPRITE: For the cracks today are darkness tomorrow.

(*They laugh.*)

SECOND SPRITE: When things are quite evident . . .

FIRST SPRITE: Man figures that he has no need to investigate them . . .

SECOND SPRITE: And he goes to dark things to discover in them secrets he already knew.

FIRST SPRITE: But that's what we're here for. We Sprites!

SECOND SPRITE: Did you know Perlimplín?

FIRST SPRITE: Since he was a child.

SECOND SPRITE: And Belisa?

FIRST SPRITE: Well. Her room exhaled such intense perfume that I once fell asleep and awoke between her cat's paws.

(*They laugh.*)

SECOND SPRITE: This affair was . . .

FIRST SPRITE: Ever so clear!

SECOND SPRITE: All the world imagined it.

FIRST SPRITE: And the gossip must have turned then to more mysterious things.

SECOND SPRITE: That's why our efficient and most sociable screen should not be opened yet.

FIRST SPRITE: No, don't let them find out.

SECOND SPRITE: The soul of Perlimplín, tiny and frightened like a newborn duckling, becomes enriched and sublime at these moments.

(*They laugh.*)

FIRST SPRITE: The audience is impatient.

SECOND SPRITE: And with reason. Shall we go?

FIRST SPRITE: Let's go. I feel a fresh breeze on my back already.

SECOND SPRITE: Five cool camellias of the dawn have opened in the walls of the bedroom.

FIRST SPRITE: Five balconies upon the city.

(*They rise and throw on some great blue hoods.*)

SECOND SPRITE: Don Perlimplín, do we help or hinder you?

FIRST SPRITE: Help: because it is not fair to place before the eyes of the audience the misfortune of a good man.

SECOND SPRITE: That's true, little friend, for it's not the same to say: "I have seen," as "It is said."

FIRST SPRITE: Tomorrow the whole world will know about it.

SECOND SPRITE: And that's what we wish.

FIRST SPRITE: One word of gossip and the whole world knows.

SECOND SPRITE: Sh . . .

(*Flutes begin to sound.*)

FIRST SPRITE: Shall we go through this tiny darkness?

SECOND SPRITE: Let us go now, little friend.

FIRST SPRITE: Now?

SECOND SPRITE: Now.

(*They open the curtain. Don Perlimplín appears on the bed, completely dressed; on his forehead are two enormous horns, gilded and beflowered. Belisa is at his side. The five balconies of the stage are wide open, and through them the white light of dawn enters.*)

PERLIMPLÍN (*Awakening*): Belisa! Belisa! Answer me!

BELISA (*Pretending to awaken*): Perlimplinpinito . . . what do you want?

PERLIMPLÍN: Tell me quickly.

BELISA: What do you want me to tell you? I didn't fall asleep much before you did.

PERLIMPLÍN (*Leaps from the bed. He has on his cassock*): Why are the balconies open?

BELISA: Because this night the wind has blown as never before.

PERLIMPLÍN: Why do the balconies have five ladders that reach to the ground?

BELISA: Because that is the custom in my mother's country.

PERLIMPLÍN: And whose are those five hats which I see under the balconies?

BELISA (*Leaping from the bed*): The little drunkards who come and go. Perlimplinillo! Love!

(*Perlimplín looks at her, staring stupefied.*)

PERLIMPLÍN: Belisa! Belisa! And why not? You explain everything so well. I am satisfied. Why couldn't it have been like that?

BELISA (*Coyly*): I'm not a little fibber.

PERLIMPLÍN: And I love you more every minute!

BELISA: That's the way I like it.

PERLIMPLÍN: For the first time in my life I am happy! (*He approaches and embraces her, but, in that instant, turns brusquely from her.*) Belisa, who has kissed you? Don't lie, for I know!

BELISA (*Gathering her hair*): Of course you know! What a playful little husband I have! (*In a low voice*). You! You have kissed me!

PERLIMPLÍN: Yes. I have kissed you . . . but . . . if some one else had kissed you . . . if some one else had kissed you . . . do you love me?

BELISA (*Lifting a naked arm to embrace him*): Yes, little Perlimplín.

PERLIMPLÍN: Then, what do I care? (*Embraces her.*) Are you Belisa?

BELISA (*Coyly, and in a low voice*): Yes! Yes! Yes!

PERLIMPLÍN: It almost seems like a dream!

BELISA (*Recovering*): Look, Perlimplín, close the balconies because, before you know it, people will be getting up.

PERLIMPLÍN: What for? Since we have both slept enough, we shall see the dawn. Don't you like that?

BELISA: Yes, but . . . (*She sits on the bed.*)

PERLIMPLÍN: I had never seen the sunrise.

(*Belisa, exhausted, falls on the pillows of the bed.*)

It is a spectacle which . . . this may seem an untruth . . . thrills me! Don't you like it? (*Goes toward the bed.*) Belisa, are you asleep?

BELISA (*In her dreams*): Yes.

(*Perlimplín tiptoes over and covers her with the red cape. An intense golden light enters through the balconies. Bands of paper birds cross them amidst the ringing of the morning bells. Perlimplín has seated himself on the edge of the bed.*)

PERLIMPLÍN:

Love, love
that here lies wounded.
So wounded by love's going;
so wounded,
dying of love.
Tell every one that it was just
the nightingale.
A surgeon's knife with four sharp edges;
the bleeding throat—forgetfulness.

Don Perlimplín and Belisa

Take me by the hands, my love,
for I come quite badly wounded,
so wounded by love's going.
So wounded!
Dying of love!

CURTAIN

SCENE TWO

(*Perlimplín's dining room. The perspectives are deliciously wrong. All the objects on the table are painted as in a primitive Last Supper.*)

PERLIMPLÍN: Then you will do as I say?

MARCOLFA (*Crying*): Don't worry, master.

PERLIMPLÍN: Marcolfa, why do you keep on crying?

MARCOLFA: Your grace knows. On your wedding night five men entered your bedroom—one through each balcony—and left forgotten behind them their hats and you quite tranquil! Five. My lord, five! Representatives of the five races of the earth. The European, with his beard—the Indian—the Negro—the Yellow Man—and the American. And you unaware of it all.

PERLIMPLÍN: That is of no importance.

MARCOLFA: Just imagine: yesterday I saw her with another one.

PERLIMPLÍN (*Intrigued*): Really?

MARCOLFA: And she didn't even hide from me.

PERLIMPLÍN: But I am happy, Marcolfa.

MARCOLFA: The master astonishes me.

PERLIMPLÍN: You have no idea how happy I am. I have learned many things and above all I can imagine many others.

MARCOLFA: My master loves her too much.

PERLIMPLÍN: Not as much as she deserves.

MARCOLFA: Here she comes.

PERLIMPLÍN: Please leave.

(*Marcolfa leaves and Perlimplín hides in a corner. Enter Belisa dressed in a red dress of eighteenth-century style. The skirt, at the back, is slit allowing silk stockings to be seen. She wears huge earrings and a red hat trimmed with big ostrich plumes.*)

BELISA: Again I have failed to see him. In my walk through the park they were all behind me except him. His skin must be dark, and his kisses must perfume and burn at the same time—like saffron and cloves. Sometimes he passes underneath my balconies and moves his hand slowly in a greeting that makes my breasts tremble.

PERLIMPLÍN: Ahem!

BELISA (*Turning*): Oh! What a fright you gave me.

PERLIMPLÍN (*Approaching her affectionately*): I observe you were speaking to yourself.

BELISA (*Distastefully*): Go away!

PERLIMPLÍN: Shall we take a walk?

BELISA: No.

PERLIMPLÍN: Shall we go to the confectioner's?

BELISA: I said no!

PERLIMPLÍN: Pardon.

(*A letter rolled about a stone falls through the balcony. Perlimplín picks it up.*)

BELISA: Give that to me.

PERLIMPLÍN: Why?

BELISA: Because it's for me.

PERLIMPLÍN (*Jokingly*): And who told you that?

BELISA: Perlimplín! Don't read it!

Don Perlimplín and Belisa

PERLIMPLÍN (*Jokingly severe*): What are you trying to say?

BELISA (*Weeping*): Give me that letter!

PERLIMPLÍN (*Approaching her*): Poor Belisa! Because I understand your feelings I give you this paper which means so much to you.

(*Belisa takes the note and hides it in her bosom.*)
 I can see things. And even though it wounds me deeply, I understand you live in a drama.

BELISA (*Tenderly*): Perlimplín!

PERLIMPLÍN: I know that you are unfaithful to me, and that you will continue to be so.

BELISA (*Fondly*): I've never known any man other than my Perlimplinillo.

PERLIMPLÍN: That's why I want to help you as any good husband should when his wife is a model of virtue . . . look. (*He closes the door and adopts a mysterious air.*) I know everything! I realized immediately. You are young and I am old . . . what are we going to do! But I understand perfectly. (*Pause. In a low voice.*) Has he come by here?

BELISA: Twice.

PERLIMPLÍN: And has he signalled to you?

BELISA: Yes . . . but in a manner that's a little disdainful . . . and that hurts me!

PERLIMPLÍN: Don't be afraid. Two weeks ago I saw that young man for the first time. I can tell you with all sincerity that his beauty dazzled me. I have never seen another man in whom manliness and delicacy meet in a more harmonious fashion. Without knowing why I thought of you.

BELISA: I haven't seen his face . . . but . . .

PERLIMPLÍN: Don't be afraid to speak to me. I know you love him . . . and I love you now as if I were your father. I am far from that foolishness; therefore . . .

BELISA: He writes me letters.

PERLIMPLÍN: I know that.

BELISA: But he doesn't let me see him.

PERLIMPLÍN: That's strange.

BELISA: And it even seems . . . as though he scorns me.

PERLIMPLÍN: How innocent you are!

BELISA: But there's no doubt he loves me as I wish . . .

PERLIMPLÍN (*Intrigued*): How is that?

BELISA: The letters I have received from other men . . . and which I didn't answer because I had my little husband, spoke to me of ideal lands—of dreams and wounded hearts. But these letters from him . . . they . . .

PERLIMPLÍN: Speak without fear.

BELISA: They speak about me . . . about my body . . .

PERLIMPLÍN (*Caressing her arms*): About your body!

BELISA: "What do I want your soul for?" he tells me. "The soul is the patrimony of the weak. Of frozen heroes and sickly people. Beautiful souls are at death's door, leaning upon whitest hairs and lean hands. Belisa, it is not your soul that I desire, but your white and soft trembling body."

PERLIMPLÍN: Who could that beautiful youth be?

BELISA: No one knows.

PERLIMPLÍN (*Inquisitive*): No one?

BELISA: I have asked all my friends.

PERLIMPLÍN (*Inscrutably and decisively*): And if I should tell you I know him?

BELISA: Is that possible?

PERLIMPLÍN: Wait. (*Goes to the balcony.*) Here he is.

BELISA (*Running*): Yes?

PERLIMPLÍN: He has just turned the corner.

BELISA (*Choked*): Oh!

PERLIMPLÍN: Since I am an old man, I want to sacrifice myself for you. This that I do no one ever did before. But I am

Don Perlimplín and Belisa

already beyond the world and the ridiculous morals of its people. Good-bye.

BELISA: Where are you going?

PERLIMPLÍN (*At the door, grandiosely*): Later you will know everything. Later.

CURTAIN

SCENE THREE

(*A grove of cypresses and orange trees. When the curtain rises, Marcolfa and Perlimplín appear in the garden.*)

MARCOLFA: Is it time yet?

PERLIMPLÍN: No, it isn't time yet.

MARCOLFA: But what has my master thought?

PERLIMPLÍN: Everything he hadn't thought before.

MARCOLFA (*Weeping*): It's my fault!

PERLIMPLÍN: Oh, if you only knew what gratitude there is in my heart for you!

MARCOLFA: Before this, everything went smoothly. In the morning, I would take him his milk and coffee and his grapes . . .

PERLIMPLÍN: Yes . . . the grapes! The grapes! But . . . I? It seems to me that a hundred years have passed. Before, I could not think of the extraordinary things the world holds. I was merely on the threshold. On the other hand . . . today! Belisa's love has given me a precious wealth that I ignored before . . . don't you see? Now I can close my eyes and . . . I can see what I want. For example, my mother, when she was visited by the elves. Oh, you know how elves are . . . tiny. It's marvellous! They can dance upon my little finger.

MARCOLFA: Yes, yes, the elves, the elves, but . . . how about this other?

PERLIMPLÍN: The other? Ah! (*With satisfaction.*) What did you tell my wife?

MARCOLFA: Even though I'm not very good at these things, I told her that the master had instructed me to say . . . that that young man . . . would come tonight at ten o'clock sharp to the garden, wrapped, as usual, in his red cape.

PERLIMPLÍN: And she?

MARCOLFA: She became as red as a geranium, put her hands to her heart, and kissed her lovely braids passionately.

PERLIMPLÍN (*Enthusiastic*): So she got red as a geranium, eh? And, what did she say?

MARCOLFA: She just sighed; that's all. But, oh! such a sigh!

PERLIMPLÍN: Oh, yes! As no woman ever sighed before! Isn't that so?

MARCOLFA: Her love must border on madness.

PERLIMPLÍN (*Vibrantly*): That's it! What I need is for her to love that youth more than her own body. And there is no doubt that she loves him.

MARCOLFA (*Weeping*): It frightens me to hear you . . . but how is it possible? Don Perlimplín, how is it possible that you yourself should encourage your wife in the worst of sins?

PERLIMPLÍN: Because Perlimplín has no honor and wants to amuse himself! Now do you see? Tonight the new and unknown lover of my lady Belisa will come. What should I do but sing? (*Singing.*) Don Perlimplín has no honor! Has no honor!

MARCOLFA: Let my master know that from this moment on I consider myself dismissed from his service. We servants also have a sense of shame.

Don Perlimplín and Belisa

PERLIMPLÍN: Oh, innocent Marcolfa! Tomorrow you will be as free as a bird. Wait until tomorrow. Now go and perform your duty. You will do what I have told you?

MARCOLFA (*Leaving, drying her tears*): What else is there for me to do? What else?

(*A sweet serenade begins to sound. Don Perlimplín hides behind some rosebushes.*)

BELISA (*Within, singing*):
Upon the river shores
the passing night is moistened.

VOICES:
The passing night is moistened.

BELISA:
And in Belisa's breasts
the flowers die of love.

VOICES:
The flowers die of love.

PERLIMPLÍN:
The flowers die of love!

BELISA:
The night is naked singing
upon the bridge of March.

VOICES:
Upon the bridge of March.

BELISA:
Belisa bathes her body
with briny water and oils.

PERLIMPLÍN:
The flowers die of love!

BELISA:
The night of anis and silver
is shining on the rooftops.

VOICES:
Is shining on the rooftops.

BELISA:
Silver of streams and mirrors
and anis of white thighs.

VOICES:
The flowers die of love!

(*Belisa appears in the garden splendidly dressed. The moon lights the stage.*)

BELISA: What voices fill the air with the sweet harmony of one nocturne alone? I have felt your warmth and your weight, delicious youth of my soul. Oh! The branches are moving . . .

(*A young man dressed in a red cape appears and crosses the garden cautiously.*)

BELISA: Sh! Here! Here!

(*The young man signals with his hand that he will return immediately.*)

Oh! Yes . . . come back my love! Like a jasmine floating and without roots, the sky will fall over my moistening shoulders. Night! My night of mint and lapislazuli . . .

(*Perlimplín appears.*)

PERLIMPLÍN (*Surprised*): What are you doing here?

BELISA: I was walking?

PERLIMPLÍN: Only that?

BELISA: In the clear night.

PERLIMPLÍN (*Severely*): What were you doing here?

BELISA (*Surprised*): Don't you know?

PERLIMPLÍN: I don't know anything.

BELISA: You sent me the message.

PERLIMPLÍN: Belisa . . . are you still waiting for him?

BELISA: With more ardour than ever.

PERLIMPLÍN (*Loudly*): Why?

BELISA: Because I love him.

Don Perlimplín and Belisa

PERLIMPLÍN: Well, he will come.

BELISA: The perfume of his flesh passes beyond his clothes. I love him! Perlimplín, I love him! It seems to me that I am another woman!

PERLIMPLÍN: That is my triumph.

BELISA: What triumph?

PERLIMPLÍN: The triumph of my imagination.

BELISA: It's true that you helped me love him.

PERLIMPLÍN: As now I will help you mourn him.

BELISA (*Puzzled*): Perlimplín! What are you saying?

(*The clock sounds ten. A nightingale sings.*)

PERLIMPLÍN: It is the hour.

BELISA: He should be here this instant.

PERLIMPLÍN: He's leaping the walls of my garden.

BELISA: Wrapped in his red cape.

PERLIMPLÍN (*Drawing a dagger*): Red as his blood.

BELISA (*Holding him*): What are you going to do?

PERLIMPLÍN (*Embracing her*): Belisa, do you love him?

BELISA: Yes!

PERLIMPLÍN: Well, since you love him so much, I don't want him ever to leave you. And in order that he should be completely yours, it has come to me that the best thing would be to stick this dagger in his gallant heart. Would you like that?

BELISA: For God's sake, Perlimplín!

PERLIMPLÍN: Then, dead, you will be able to caress him in your bed—so handsome and well groomed—without the fear that he should cease to love you. He will love you with the infinite love of the dead, and I will be free of this dark little nightmare of your magnificent body. (*Embracing her.*) Your body . . . that I will never possess! (*Looking into the garden.*) Look where he comes. Let go, Belisa. Let go! (*He exits running.*)

BELISA (*Desperately*): Marcolfa! Bring me the sword from the dining room; I am going to run my husband's throat through. (*Calling* . . .)
>Don Perlimplín
>Evil husband!
>If you kill him,
>I'll kill you!

(*A man wrapped in a large red cape appears among the branches. He is wounded and stumbling.*)

BELISA (*Embracing him*): Who opened your veins so that you fill my garden with blood? Love, let me look at your face for an instant. Oh! Who has killed you . . . who?

PERLIMPLÍN (*Uncovering himself*): Your husband has just killed me with this emerald dagger. (*He shows the dagger stuck in his chest.*)

BELISA (*Frightened*): Perlimplín!

PERLIMPLÍN: He ran away through the fields and you will never see him again. He killed me because he knew I loved you as no one else. . . . While he wounded me he shouted: "Belisa has a soul now!" Come near. (*He has stretched out on the bench.*)

BELISA: Why is this? And you are truly wounded.

PERLIMPLÍN: Perlimplín killed me. . . . Ah, Don Perlimplín! Youngish old man, manikin without strength, you couldn't enjoy the body of Belisa . . . the body of Belisa was for younger muscles and warm lips. . . . I, on the other hand, loved your body only . . . your body! But he has killed me . . . with this glowing branch of precious stones.

BELISA: What have you done?

PERLIMPLÍN (*Near death*): Don't you understand? I am my soul and you are your body. Allow me this last moment, since you have loved me so much, to die embracing it.

(*Belisa draws near and embraces him.*)

BELISA: Yes . . . but the young man? Why have you deceived me?

PERLIMPLÍN: The young man!

(*Closes his eyes. The stage is left in its natural light. Marcolfa enters.*)

MARCOLFA: Madame . . .

BELISA (*Weeping*): Don Perlimplín is dead!

MARCOLFA: I knew it! Now we shall bind him in the youthful red suit in which he used to walk under his own balconies.

BELISA (*Weeping*): I never thought he was so devious.

MARCOLFA: You have found out too late. I shall make him a crown of flowers like the noon-day sun.

BELISA (*Confused, as if in another world*): Perlimplín, what have you done, Perlimplín?

MARCOLFA: Belisa, now you are another woman. You are dressed in the most glorious blood of my master.

BELISA: But who was this man? Who was he?

MARCOLFA: The beautiful adolescent whose face you never will see.

BELISA: Yes, yes, Marcolfa—I love him—I love him with all the strength of my flesh and my soul—but where is the young man in the red cape? Where is he?

MARCOLFA: Don Perlimplín, sleep peacefully. . . . Do you hear? Don Perlimplín. . . . Do you hear her?

(*The bells sound.*)

CURTAIN

If Five Years Pass
(Así Que Pasen Cinco Años)

A Legend of Our Times in
Three Acts and Five Scenes

(1931)

CHARACTERS

The Young Man
The Old Man
The Stenographer
The First Friend
The Second Friend
The Child
The Cat
Juan, the servant
The Betrothed
The Football Player
The Maid
The Father
The Manikin
The Harlequin
The Girl
The Clown
The Masks
The Maidservant
First Cardplayer
Second Cardplayer
Third Cardplayer
The Echo

ACT ONE

(A library. The Young Man is seated. He wears blue pyjamas. The Old Man, who wears a gray Prince Albert, has a white beard and enormous gold-rimmed spectacles.)

YOUNG MAN: It doesn't surprise me.

OLD MAN: Pardon . . .

YOUNG MAN: It always happens to me this way.

OLD MAN (*Inquisitive and sympathetic*): Really?

YOUNG MAN: Yes.

OLD MAN: Is it . . .

YOUNG MAN: I remember . . .

OLD MAN (*Laughs*): I always remember.

YOUNG MAN: I . . .

OLD MAN (*Sighing*): Go on.

YOUNG MAN: I used to save the sweets and eat them last.

OLD MAN: Last? Really? They taste better. I also . . .

YOUNG MAN: And I remember that one day . . .

OLD MAN (*Interrupting with vehemence*): I like the word "remember" so much. It's a green word—juicy. Little threads of cold water spring from it endlessly. And it's strange: you can see it standing sharp against a clear dawn sky.

YOUNG MAN (*Happy and trying to convince himself*): Yes, yes! Of course. You're right. It's necessary to fight against the whole idea of decay, against those terrible scalings-off of walls. Many times I've got up at midnight to pull weeds in the garden. I don't want weeds in my house, nor broken furniture.

OLD MAN: That's it. Nor broken furniture because one must remember, only . . .

YOUNG MAN: Only live things, burning in their blood, with all their outlines intact.

OLD MAN: Very well. That is to say; (*Lowering his voice*) one must remember, but remember beforehand.

YOUNG MAN: Beforehand?

OLD MAN (*As though imparting a secret*): Yes, one must remember toward tomorrow.

YOUNG MAN (*Absorbed*): Toward tomorrow——

(*A clock sounds six. The Stenographer, crying silently, crosses the stage.*)

OLD MAN: Six o'clock.

YOUNG MAN: Yes, six, and it's awfully warm. (*He rises.*) There is a beautiful storm sky. Full of gray clouds . . .

OLD MAN: And so you . . . ? I was a great friend of that family. Of the father above all. He busies himself with astronomy. He's well, eh? And she?

YOUNG MAN: I've seen her very little. But that doesn't matter. I believe that she loves me.

OLD MAN: Of course.

YOUNG MAN: They went on a long trip. I was glad of that . . . these things take time.

OLD MAN (*Happy*): Certainly.

YOUNG MAN: Yes, but . . .

OLD MAN: But what . . .

YOUNG MAN: Nothing. (*Fanning himself.*) I wait.

OLD MAN: Did her father ever come?

YOUNG MAN: Never. It can't be, just now . . . not until five years pass.

OLD MAN: Very well. (*With happiness.*)

YOUNG MAN (*Serious*): Why do you say "Very well"?

OLD MAN: Because . . . (*Indicating the room.*) This is pleasant, isn't it?

YOUNG MAN: No.

If Five Years Pass

OLD MAN: Doesn't it cause you anguish, the hour of parting, the happenings, what must come right now?

YOUNG MAN: Yes, yes. Don't talk to me about that.

OLD MAN: It is so beautiful to wait.

YOUNG MAN: Yes, to wait—but to have! (*Passionately.*)

OLD MAN: What's happening in the street?

YOUNG MAN: Noise, noise always, dust, heat, bad smells. It annoys me to have the street winds enter my house. (*A long wail is heard. Pause.*) Juan, shut the window.

(*A thin servant walking on tiptoe closes the shutters.*)

OLD MAN: She . . . is she young?

YOUNG MAN: Very young. Fifteen years.

OLD MAN: Fifteen years that she has lived, that are she herself. But why not say that she is fifteen snows old, fifteen winds, fifteen dawns? Don't you dare to elope? To fly? To spread your love through all the sky?

YOUNG MAN (*He covers his face with his hands*): I love her too much.

OLD MAN (*Standing, with energy*): Or, better said, fifteen roses old, fifteen wings, fifteen little grains of sand. Do you not dare to concentrate your love, to make it tiny, wounding and sharp within your breast?

YOUNG MAN: You want to separate me from her. But I know your plan. It's enough merely to observe a live insect on the palm of the hand, or to look at the sea some afternoon, concentrating on the form of each wave, in order to make the face or the wound that we carry in our breast vanish in bubbles. But I am in love, and I want to be in love, as much in love as she is with me, and that is why I can wait five years, in the hope of being able at night—the whole world forgotten—to bind her gleaming braids about my throat.

OLD MAN: I take the liberty of reminding you that your fiancée . . . has no braids.

YOUNG MAN (*Irritated*): I know that. She cut them off, without my permission, naturally, and this (*With anguish*) changes her image for me. (*Angrily.*) I know she has no braids. (*Almost furious.*) Why did you remind me of that? (*With sadness.*) But in these five years she will have them again.

OLD MAN (*With enthusiasm*): And more beautiful than ever. They will be such braids . . .

YOUNG MAN: They are, they are. (*With joy.*)

OLD MAN: They are such braids that with their perfume one can live without bread or water.

YOUNG MAN: She thinks so much.

OLD MAN: She dreams so much.

YOUNG MAN: What?

OLD MAN: She thinks so much that . . .

YOUNG MAN: That my flesh is raw. All inwards. All burning.

OLD MAN (*Handing him a glass*): Drink.

YOUNG MAN: Thanks. If I begin thinking of the child, my little girl . . .

OLD MAN: Say "sweetheart." Dare.

YOUNG MAN: No.

OLD MAN: But why?

YOUNG MAN: Sweetheart . . . you know why, if I say "sweetheart" I see her, without wanting to, shrouded in a sky, held down by enormous braids of snow. It is very easy for her nose to grow sharp and for the hand she places on her breast to become like five green stems down which the snails go. No, she is not my sweetheart—(*He makes a gesture as of pushing away the image that was about to capture him.*)—she is my little girl, my child.

OLD MAN: Go on, go on.

YOUNG MAN: Well, if I begin thinking about her, I draw her, I make her move white and living, but suddenly—who changes her nose, breaks her teeth, or makes her some one else all in rags, running through my head looking the way she would in one of those distorting mirrors at a circus?

OLD MAN: Who? It seems a lie for you to say "who." Yet, they change more, those things which are before our eyes than those which live without resistance within the mind. The water coming down the river is completely different from that which goes on down. And who remembers exactly a map of the sands of the desert . . . or the face of any friend?

YOUNG MAN: Yes, yes. That which is inside is more alive even if it should also change. The last time I saw her I couldn't look at her closely because she had two tiny furrows in her brow, that, if I shouldn't watch out, you understand, would fill her whole face and leave her faded, old, as if she had suffered much. I had to leave her in order to crystallize her—that is the word—in my heart.

OLD MAN: Isn't it true that in the moment you saw her old she was completely yours?

YOUNG MAN: Yes.

OLD MAN (*Exalted*): Isn't it true if she had in that very instant admitted she had deceived you and did not love you, the tiny furrows would have changed to the most delicate roses in the world?

YOUNG MAN (*Exalted*): Yes.

OLD MAN: And you would have loved her more, exactly because of that.

YOUNG MAN: Yes, yes.

OLD MAN: Then? Aha!

YOUNG MAN: Then . . . it is very difficult to live.

OLD MAN: That is why one must fly from one thing to another until he is lost. If she is fifteen years old she can be fifteen dawns, or fifteen skies. Things inside are more alive than those outside exposed to air or death. Because of that let us . . . not go—or wait. Because the other is to die right now and it is more beautiful to think that tomorrow we shall see the five golden horns with which the sun raises the clouds.

YOUNG MAN (*Stretching out his hand*): Thank you, thank you for everything.

OLD MAN: I'll come back this way.

(*The Stenographer appears.*)

YOUNG MAN: Did you finish writing the letters?

STENOGRAPHER (*Tearfully*): Yes, sir.

OLD MAN (*To the Young Man*): What has happened to her?

STENOGRAPHER: I want to leave this house.

OLD MAN: Well, that's very easy, isn't it?

YOUNG MAN (*Troubled*): You'll see.

STENOGRAPHER: I want to go and I cannot.

YOUNG MAN (*Sweetly*): It is not I who's keeping you. You know I can't do anything. Various times I have told you to wait but you . . .

STENOGRAPHER: But I won't wait; what is this about waiting?

OLD MAN: And why not? To wait is to believe and to live.

STENOGRAPHER: I don't wait, because I don't feel like it, because I don't want to, and, nevertheless, I cannot move from here.

YOUNG MAN: You always wind up not giving any reasons.

STENOGRAPHER: What reasons can I give you? There's only one reason and that is—that I love you. The same old reason. When he was a child—(*To the Old Man*) I used to watch him play from my balcony. One day he fell down and bled at the knee—do you remember? (*To the Young Man*) I still have that live blood like a red serpent trembling between my breasts.

OLD MAN: That isn't right. Blood dries and what is past is past.

STENOGRAPHER: Is that my fault, sir? (*To the Young Man*) I beg you to give me my pay. I want to leave this house.

If Five Years Pass

YOUNG MAN: Very well. It's not my fault, either. Besides you know perfectly well that it doesn't concern me. You can go.

STENOGRAPHER (*To the Old Man*): Do you hear him? He orders me out of his house. He doesn't want to have me here. (*She weeps. She leaves.*)

OLD MAN (*Gravely, to the Young Man*): That woman is dangerous.

YOUNG MAN: I wish I could love her as when I am thirsty before a fountain. I wish.

OLD MAN: By no means. What would you do tomorrow, eh? Think, tomorrow.

FRIEND (*Entering noisily*): What a lot of silence there is in this house, and what for? Give me some water with anise and ice.

(*The Old Man leaves.*)

Or a cocktail.

YOUNG MAN: I suppose you will not break my furniture.

FRIEND: Lone man, serious man—and with this heat.

YOUNG MAN: Couldn't you sit down?

FRIEND (*He puts his arms around him and whirls him*):
   Teen, teen, tahn,
   Little flame of St. John.

YOUNG MAN: Let me go. I don't feel like playing games.

FRIEND: Wheee! Who was that old man? A friend of yours? And where's the room you keep the pictures of the girls you sleep with? Look— (*He comes near.*) I'm going to take you by the lapels, and I'm going to paint those waxen cheeks with red . . . or scrub 'em, like this.

YOUNG MAN (*Irritated*): Let me go.

FRIEND: And with a cane I'm going to drive you out into the street.

YOUNG MAN: And what am I going to do there? Just whatever you please, you think? It's already too much for me to hear it full of cars and people who don't know what they want.

FRIEND (*Sitting down and stretching on sofa*): Ay, whee! I on the other hand . . . yesterday I made three conquests, day before yesterday—two, and today—one. Why . . . the result is . . . I'm left without any because I don't have the time. I was with a girl—Ernestina—Do you want to know her?

YOUNG MAN: No.

FRIEND: No-o-o. Signed and sealed. But you ought to see her; she has a figure . . . no, even though Matilda has a much better figure— (*Impetuously*) Oh, Lord! (*He leaps and falls outstretched on the sofa.*) Look, a figure made to measure for all arms, and so fragile you'd like to take a tiny silver hatchet in your hand and cut it up!

YOUNG MAN (*Distracted, apart from the conversation*): Well then, I'd better go upstairs.

FRIEND (*Stretching himself face downwards on the sofa*): I don't have time; I don't have time for anything; everything goes wrong. Just imagine, I make an engagement with Ernestina. (*He rises.*) Her braids here, tight and very black and then . . . Ernesti-ti-ti-tina. I tell her so many sweet things with her name that her breasts fill with tea and since that's harmful to her I have to remove it with my lips, my fingers, my eyes. . . .

(*The Young Man drums impatiently with his fingers on the table.*)

YOUNG MAN: You don't let me think.

FRIEND: But you ought not to think. I'll be going. Even though—(*He looks at the clock.*) the hour is past; it's horrible—the same thing always happens. I don't have time and I feel it. I was going with a very ugly but admirable woman. One of those dark ones you miss at noon on summer days. And I like her—(*He throws a cushion into the air*)—because she's like a horse tamer.

If Five Years Pass

YOUNG MAN: That's enough.

FRIEND: Yes, old man, don't be angry. But a woman can be very ugly and a horse tamer can be beautiful. And otherwise and . . . what do we know about it? (*He fills a glass with a cocktail.*)

YOUNG MAN: Nothing.

FRIEND: Don't you want to tell me what's the matter with you?

YOUNG MAN: Nothing. You know my temperament, don't you?

FRIEND: I can't understand it. But neither can I be serious. (*He laughs.*) I shall greet you like the Chinese. (*He rubs his nose against the Young Man's.*)

YOUNG MAN (*Smiling*): Get away.

FRIEND: Laugh. (*He tickles him.*)

YOUNG MAN (*Laughing*): Barbarian!

FRIEND: A hold.

YOUNG MAN: I can beat you.

FRIEND: I've got you. (*He holds his head between his legs and beats him.*)

OLD MAN (*Entering gravely*): With your permission . . . (*To them as they stand.*) Excuse me. (*Reprovingly, looking at the Young Man.*) I shall forget my hat.

FRIEND: What?

OLD MAN (*Furious*): Yes, sir. I shall forget my hat. (*Under his breath*) That is to say, I have forgotten my hat.

FRIEND: Oh.

(*The clash of shutters is heard.*)

YOUNG MAN (*Loudly*): Juan! Shut the windows!

FRIEND: A bit of a storm. I hope it's a strong one.

YOUNG MAN: Well, I don't care to find out. (*Loudly.*) All of them well closed!

FRIEND: It's thunder; you'll have to hear it.

YOUNG MAN: Oh, no.

FRIEND: Oh, yes.

YOUNG MAN: I don't care what happens outside. This is my house and no one can come in here.

OLD MAN (*To the Friend, indignantly*): That is a truth that cannot possibly be refuted.

(*A distant thunderclap is heard.*)

FRIEND: Any one in the world who wants to can not only come in here but even under your bed.

(*A thunderclap is heard nearer.*)

YOUNG MAN (*Shouting*): But not now, not now!

OLD MAN: Bravo!

FRIEND: Open the window. I'm warm.

OLD MAN: It'll be opened.

YOUNG MAN: Sometime.

FRIEND: But let us go see. . . .

(*Another thunderclap is heard. The light dims and a bluish storm-glow invades the stage. The three persons hide behind a black screen embroidered with stars.*

Through the left door appears the dead Child with the Cat. The Child is dressed in white first-communion robes with a crown of white roses on his head. Upon his painted wax face stand out eyes and lips like a dead lily. In his hand he holds a painted candle and a thick cord with gilded flowers.

The Cat is blue and has two enormous bloodstains on its small gray-white chest and on the head. They advance toward the audience. The Child has the Cat by a leg.)

THE CAT:

Meow.

THE CHILD:

Shh . . .

THE CAT:

Meow!

THE CHILD:

Take my pure white linen.

If Five Years Pass

Take my pure white crown.
But cry no more.

THE CAT:
The wounds are hurting me,
where I was hurt upon the back by the children.

THE CHILD:
My heart is also hurting me.

THE CAT:
Why is it hurting, child, say?

THE CHILD:
Because it doesn't go.
A day ago it slowly, slowly stopped,
nightingale of my cradle.
So much noise; if you had seen . . . they put me
with these roses there before the window.

THE CAT:
And what did you feel then?

THE CHILD:
Why I felt
fountains and bees in the parlor.
They bound my two hands. That was very mean.
The children looked at me there through the windows,
and then a man was nailing with his hammer
some stars made out of paper on my coffin.

(Crossing his hands.)

The angels did not come. No, Tom.

THE CAT:
Don't call me "Tom" any more.

THE CHILD:
No?

THE CAT:
I'm a lady cat.

THE CHILD:
Are you a lady cat?

THE CAT (*Coyly*):

You should have been able to tell.

THE CHILD:

How?

THE CAT:

By my silvery voice.

THE CHILD (*Gallantly*):

Would you like to sit down?

THE CAT:

Yes, I'm hungry.

THE CHILD:

I'll see if I can find you a rat.

(*He begins to look under the chairs. The Cat, seated upon a small stool, trembles.*)

Don't eat it whole. Just a little paw,
because you're very sick.

THE CAT:

It was ten stones
the children threw at me.

THE CHILD:

They're heavy like the roses
That last night wounded my throat.
Do you want one? (*He pulls a rose from his head.*)

THE CAT (*Pleased*):

Yes, I do.

THE CHILD:

With your waxen stains, rose so white,
eye of a crumpled moon, you seem to me
a gazelle among glasses there fainting.

THE CAT:

You, what did you do?

THE CHILD:

Play, and you?

THE CAT:

Play.

I walked upon the rooftops, snub-nosed cat,
little tin nostrils, made so flat,
in the morning
I would go catch the fishes in the water
and at noonday
I would sleep under the wall by the rosebush.

   THE CHILD:

And at night?

   THE CAT (*Emphatically*):

I would walk alone.

   THE CHILD:

With no one.

   THE CAT:

Through the woods.

   THE CHILD (*Happily*):

I walked also, snub-nosed cat, cheap as that,
little tin nostrils, made so flat,
to eat mulberries and apples.

   (*Distant thunderclap.*)

Oh, please wait! Are they coming? I'm afraid,
Do you know? I escaped from my house.
I don't want to go to be buried.
Still, lilies and glasses make pretty my coffin;
but it's better to fall asleep
among the water rushes.
I don't want to go be buried. Let's go quickly.

   (*He takes her by the paw.*)

   THE CAT:

And are we going to be buried? But when?

   THE CHILD:

   Tomorrow,
in two holes in the darkness.
All will cry. All fall silent.
But they'll leave. I have seen it—
oh, but then, do you know?

THE CAT:
What happens then?

THE CHILD:
They'll come to eat us.

THE CAT:
Who?

THE CHILD:
The he-lizard and she-lizard
with their tiny children, who are many.

THE CAT:
And what will they eat?

THE CHILD:
        Our faces
with our fingers—(*Lowering his voice*)—and the *cuca*.

THE CAT (*Offended*):
I don't have a *cuca*.

THE CHILD (*Sternly*):
        Cat,
they will eat your little feet and the whiskers.

(*Thunderclap very distantly.*)

Let us go; from house to house
until we come where will be grazing
little horses of the water.
It's not the sky. It's firmest land
with many crickets there that sing,
with all the sea herbs there that sway
and with the clouds that will be rising,
and slingshots that hurl stones,
and wind just like a sword.
I want to be a boy, a boy.

(*Goes toward door at right.*)

THE CAT:
The door is closed.
Let's take the stairs.

THE CHILD:
They'll see us on the stairs.

THE CAT:
Then wait.

THE CHILD:
They're coming now to bury us.

THE CAT:
Let's go by the window.

THE CHILD:
We'll never see the light again
nor the clouds that will be rising,
nor the crickets in the grasses,
nor the wind just like a sword.

(*Crossing his hands.*)

Oh, sunflower,
Oh, sunflower made of fire.
Oh, sunflower.

THE CAT:
Oh little pink of the sun.

THE CHILD:
The sky has lost its light.
Only oceans and mountains of carbon,
and a dove lying dead on the seashore,
with her pinions shattered and a flower in her bill.

(*He sings.*)

And in the flower an olive,
and in the olive a lemon . . .
What comes next? I don't remember; what comes next?

THE CAT:
Oh sunflower,
Oh sunflower of the morn.

THE CHILD:
Oh little pink of the sun.

(*The light is tenuous. The Child and the Cat, holding on to each other, feel their way about.*)

THE CAT:
There's no light. Where are you?

THE CHILD:
Be still.

THE CAT:
Are the lizards coming, child?

THE CHILD:
No.

THE CAT:
Did you find a door?

(*The Cat walks near the door on the right; a hand comes out and pulls it offstage.*)

THE CAT (*Offstage*):
Child, child, child—(*With anguish*) Child! child!

(*The Child advances terrified, pausing at each step.*)

THE CHILD (*In a low voice*):
He has sunk.
He was taken by a hand.
It must be the hand of God.
Please don't bury me. Wait a few minutes.
Just while I pick off these petals.

(*Takes a rose from his head and picks off the petals.*)

I'll go alone, but very slowly,
and then you'll let me see the sun . . .
just a little; just one ray.

(*Plucking off the petals.*)

Yes, no, yes, no, yes.

VOICE: No.

(*A hand comes out and pulls away the Child, who faints. The light, when the Child disappears, reassumes its first color. From behind the screen, the three characters quickly reappear. They give evidence of heat and lively agitation. The Young Man carries a blue fan. The Old Man a black one, and the Friend an aggressive red one. They fan themselves.*)

If Five Years Pass

OLD MAN: It will be even worse.

YOUNG MAN: Yes, later.

FRIEND: It has been bad enough. I don't believe you'll be able to escape this storm.

VOICE (*Outside*): My son, my son.

YOUNG MAN: Lord, how late. Juan, who's shouting like that?

JUAN (*Entering, and always in a soft tone, and walking on tiptoe*): The child of the porter died and they are going to bury him today. His mother is weeping.

FRIEND: As is natural.

OLD MAN: Yes, yes, but what is past is past.

FRIEND: But what if it is still passing?

(*They argue. The servant, Juan, crosses the stage and is about to go out by the door left.*)

JUAN: Master, will you please leave me the key to the bedroom?

YOUNG MAN: What for?

JUAN: The children have thrown a cat they killed on the garden shed and it must be removed.

YOUNG MAN (*With annoyance*): Take it. (*To the Old Man*) He was more than a match for you.

OLD MAN: It doesn't interest me.

FRIEND: That isn't true. It does interest him. I'm the one it doesn't interest, for I know positively snow is cold and fire burns.

OLD MAN (*Ironically*): That depends.

FRIEND (*To the Young Man*): He's deceiving you.

(*The Old Man looks sternly at the Friend, shaking his hat.*)

YOUNG MAN (*With vigor*): That doesn't influence my character in the slightest. I am I. But you cannot understand what it is to wait for a woman five years filled and burning with a love that increases every day.

FRIEND: There's no need to wait.

YOUNG MAN: Do you believe that I can surmount material things, the obstacles that rise and increase upon the way, without causing pain to others?

FRIEND: You come before the others.

YOUNG MAN: With waiting, the knot is loosened and the fruit ripens.

FRIEND: I prefer to eat it green, or better still, I like to pluck its flower to put in my lapel.

OLD MAN: That isn't true.

FRIEND: You're too old to know.

OLD MAN (*Severely*): I have struggled all my life to light a light in the darkest places. And when a person has tried to twist the dove's neck I have stayed his hand, and have helped the dove to fly.

FRIEND: And, naturally, the hunter has starved to death.

YOUNG MAN: Blessed be hunger.

(*The Second Friend appears through the door on the left. He is dressed in white in a faultless woollen suit, and wears shoes and gloves of the same color. If it is not possible for a very young actor to play this role, it may be played by a girl. The suit must be of a most exaggerated cut; it should have enormous blue buttons and the vest and cravat should be of ruffled lace.*)

SECOND FRIEND: Blessed be when there is toast, oil and sleep afterwards. Much sleep. Let it never be exhausted. I heard you.

YOUNG MAN (*With surprise*): How did you come in?

SECOND FRIEND: Anywhere. Through the window. Two children, very good friends of mine, helped me. I knew them when I was very small and they pushed me up by the feet. A cloudburst is going to fall . . .; but last year's cloudburst was a pretty one. There was so little light that my hands became yellow. (*To the Old Man*) Do you remember?

OLD MAN (*Acidly*): I don't remember anything.

If Five Years Pass

SECOND FRIEND (*To the First Friend*): And you?

FRIEND: Neither do I.

SECOND FRIEND: I was very small but I remember each detail.

FIRST FRIEND: Look . . .

SECOND FRIEND: That's why I don't want to believe you. The rain is beautiful. At the school it came in through the patio and splashed on the walls some naked women, very tiny, which were in each drop. Haven't you ever seen them? When I was five years old, no, when I was two . . . that isn't so, one—when I was only one. That's beautiful, isn't it? One year I caught one of these tiny rain-women and I kept her two days in an aquarium.

FIRST FRIEND (*With apathy*): And did she grow?

SECOND FRIEND: No, each day she became smaller. More like a child, as should be, as is just, until nothing was left of her but a raindrop. And she used to sing a song.

> I return for my wings;
> oh, let me return.
> I want to die being morning,
> I want to die being yesterday.
> I return for my wings,
> oh, let me return.
> I want to die being a fountain.
> Let me die.
> Out of the sea . . .

Which is exactly what I sing all the time.

OLD MAN (*Irritated, to the Young Man*): He's completely insane.

SECOND FRIEND (*Who has heard it*): Insane? Because I don't want to be full of wrinkles and pains like you? Because I want to enjoy what's mine, and they're taking it away from me? I don't know you. I don't want to look at people like you.

FIRST FRIEND (*Drinking*): All of that is nothing but fear of death.

SECOND FRIEND: No, just now, before I came in here, I saw a child that they were taking to be buried just as the first raindrops fell. That's how I want to be buried. In a box this small and then the rest of you can go battle the storm. But my face is mine and they're stealing it from me. I used to be tender and I used to sing, but now there is a man, a gentleman (*To the Old Man*), who walks within me with two or three false faces ready. (*He brings out a mirror and looks at himself.*) But not yet, I can still see myself high in the cherry trees ... with that gray suit ... a gray suit that had some silver anchors.... Oh, my God. (*He covers his face with his hands.*)

OLD MAN: The suits tear, the anchors tarnish and we go on.

SECOND FRIEND: Oh, please, don't talk like that.

OLD MAN (*With enthusiasm*): The houses sink.

FIRST FRIEND (*Sternly and in a defensive attitude*): The houses do not sink.

OLD MAN (*Undaunted*): The eyes lose their light and a sickle reaps the reeds along the shores.

SECOND FRIEND: Of course, all that happens later on.

OLD MAN: On the contrary. That has already happened.

SECOND FRIEND: The past all becomes quiet; how is it possible you don't know that? You only have to go on wakening things softly. On the other hand, four or five years ahead there is a pit into which we shall all fall.

OLD MAN (*Furious*): Silence!

YOUNG MAN (*Trembling, to the Old Man*): Did you hear that?

OLD MAN: Too well. (*He leaves rapidly through the door on the right.*)

YOUNG MAN: Where are you going? Why do you leave like this? Wait! (*He goes out after him.*)

SECOND FRIEND (*Shrugging his shoulders*): Well, he had to grow old. You, on the other hand, have not protested.

If Five Years Pass

FIRST FRIEND (*Who is drinking ceaselessly*): No.

SECOND FRIEND: Drinking is enough for you.

FIRST FRIEND (*Seriously and with honesty*): I do what I like, what seems right to me. I didn't ask your opinion.

SECOND FRIEND (*With fright*): Yes, yes. I didn't say anything. (*He sits down on an armchair with his legs folded up.*)

(*The First Friend drinks rapidly, downing the glasses to the last drop, then, striking himself on the forehead, as if he remembered something, he leaves quickly by the door on the left. The Second Friend bows down his head on the armchair. The Servant appears on the right, always silent, on tiptoe. It begins to rain.*)

SECOND FRIEND: The cloudburst. (*He looks at his hands.*) But what an ugly light. (*He goes to sleep.*)

YOUNG MAN (*Entering*): He will return tomorrow. I need him. (*He sits.*)

(*The Stenographer appears. She is carrying a bag. She crosses the stage and in the middle of it turns quickly.*)

STENOGRAPHER: Did you call me?

YOUNG MAN (*Closing his eyes*): No.

(*The Stenographer leaves looking anxiously and waiting for him to call.*)

STENOGRAPHER (*At the door*): Do you need me?

YOUNG MAN (*Closing his eyes*): No, I don't need you.

(*The Stenographer leaves.*)

    SECOND FRIEND (*In his sleep*):
        I return for my wings;
        Oh, let me to return.
        I want to die being
        yesterday
        I want to die being
        the dawning.

(*It begins to rain.*)

YOUNG MAN: It's very late. Juan, light the lights. What time is it?

JUAN (*Meaningfully*): Six o'clock exactly, sir.

YOUNG MAN: Very well.

    SECOND FRIEND (*In his sleep*):
        I return for my wings,
        oh, let me to return.
        I want to die being
        the fountain.
        I want to die out of
        the sea.

(*The Young Man drums softly on the table with his fingers.*)

SLOW CURTAIN

ACT TWO

(*A bedroom in the style of 1900. Strange furniture. Great curtains full of folds and tassels. On the walls, painted clouds and angels. At the center, a bed with hangings and plumes. To the left, a dresser held up by cherubs with branches of electric lights in their hands. The balconies are open and through them the moonlight enters. An automobile horn is heard sounding insistently. The Betrothed leaps from her bed wearing a splendid robe trimmed with laces and enormous rose-colored ribbons. The robe has a long train; her hair is covered with curls.*)

BETROTHED (*Looking out the window*): Come up. (*Horn is heard.*) You must. My fiancé is coming—the old man, the lyric one—and I need your support.

(*The Football Player enters through the balcony; he wears his knee pads and helmet. He has a pocket full of cigars which he lights and butts without ceasing.*)

BETROTHED: Come in. I haven't seen you for two days. (*They embrace.*)

(*The Football Player does not speak. He only smokes and mashes the cigars on the floor. He gives evidence of great vitality and embraces the Betrothed passionately.*)

BETROTHED: Today you kiss me in a different way. You always change, my love. Do you know that I didn't see you yesterday? But I went to look at the horse. He was beautiful. White, with gilded hooves in the paddock straw. (*They sit on a sofa at the foot of the bed.*) But you are more beautiful, because you're like a dragon. (*Embraces him.*) I think you're going to break me between your arms because I'm weak . . . because I'm tiny . . . because I am like the white frost . . . because I am like a tiny guitar burnt by the sun and you can break me.

(*Football Player blows smoke in her face.*)

BETROTHED (*Passing her hands over his body*): Behind all this shadow there is something like a network of silver bridges to enclose me and to defend me who am tiny like a button; tiny, like a bee who will enter the throneroom. Isn't that so? It's true, isn't it? I shall go with you. (*She leans her head upon the Player's chest.*) Dragon, my dragon. How many hearts have you? In your breast there is something like a torrent in which I shall drown. I shall drown . . . (*Looks at him.*) and then you will run away (*Weeps*) and leave me dead on the shore.

(*Player puts another cigar to his mouth and Betrothed lights it for him.*)

BETROTHED: Oh! (*Kisses him.*) What white heat! What ivory fire your teeth spill! My fiancé had icy teeth; he would kiss me and his lips would get covered with tiny dead leaves—they were like dried lips. I cut off my braids because he liked them so much; just as now I go barefoot because you like it. Isn't that so? Isn't it? (*Player kisses her.*) We must go. My fiancé will be coming.

VOICE (*At the door*): Miss.

BETROTHED: Go. (*Kisses him.*)

VOICE: Miss!

BETROTHED (*Disengaging herself from the Player and adopting a distracted attitude*): I'm coming. (*In a low voice.*) Good-bye.

(*Player returns from the window and kisses her, lifting her in his arms.*)

VOICE: Open!

BETROTHED (*In an affected voice*): What lack of patience!

(*The Player leaves through the balcony, whistling.*)

MAIDSERVANT (*Entering*): Oh, Miss!

BETROTHED: Miss what?

MAIDSERVANT: Miss.

If Five Years Pass

BETROTHED: What? (*She lights the ceiling light. It is a bluer light than that which comes in through the balcony.*)

MAID: Your fiancé has arrived.

BETROTHED: All right. Why do you act like that?

MAID (*Weepily*): No reason.

BETROTHED: Where is he?

MAID: Downstairs.

BETROTHED: With whom?

MAID: With his father.

BETROTHED: Nobody else?

MAID: A man with gold-rimmed glasses. They talk a lot.

BETROTHED: I'm going to dress. (*She sits before dresser and begins her toilette, helped by Maid.*)

MAID (*Weepily*): Oh, Miss!

BETROTHED (*Irritated*): Miss what?

MAID: Miss.

BETROTHED (*Acidly*): What?

MAID: Your fiancé is very handsome.

BETROTHED: You marry him.

MAID: He is very happy.

BETROTHED: Yes?

MAID: He brought a bouquet of flowers.

BETROTHED: You know I don't like flowers. Throw them out the balcony.

MAID: They're so beautiful . . . Freshly cut.

BETROTHED (*Imperiously*): Throw them out!

(*The Maid throws out the window some flowers that were in a vase.*)

MAID: Oh, Miss.

BETROTHED (*Furious*): Miss what?

MAID: Miss.

BETROTHED: Wha-a-at?

MAID: Think well what you're going to do. Consider. The world is large. But the people in it like us are tiny.

BETROTHED: What do you know about it?

MAID: Yes, but I do know. My father was in Brazil twice; yet he was so little you could put him in a suitcase. Things are forgotten, but the bad remains.

BETROTHED: I told you to shut up.

MAID: Oh, Miss.

BETROTHED (*Sternly*): My clothes!

MAID: What are you going to do?

BETROTHED: Whatever I can.

MAID: Such a good man. Such a long time waiting for you . . . With so many dreams. (*Hands her the clothes.*)

BETROTHED: Did he give you his hand?

MAID (*Happily*): Yes, he gave me his hand.

BETROTHED: And how did he give you his hand?

MAID: Very delicately. Almost without pressure.

BETROTHED: You see? He didn't squeeze you.

MAID: I had a soldier sweetheart once who would cut me with my rings and make me bleed. That's why I got rid of him.

BETROTHED: Yes?

MAID: Oh, Miss!

BETROTHED: What dress shall I wear?

MAID: You're lovely in the red one.

BETROTHED: I don't want to look nice.

MAID: The green one.

BETROTHED: No.

MAID: The orange one?

BETROTHED (*Strongly*): No!

MAID: The tulle one?

BETROTHED (*More strongly*): No!

MAID: The autumn-leaves one?

If Five Years Pass

BETROTHED (*Greatly irritated*): I said no! I want a dirt-colored dress . . . a barren-rock dress with a hemp cord at the waist. (*Car horn is heard. Betrothed turns up her eyes, and, changing her expression, continues speaking.*) But with a wreath of jasmin at my throat . . . and with all my flesh bound in a veil wet by the sea. (*Goes toward the balcony.*)

MAID: Don't let your fiancé find out.

BETROTHED: He has to find out sometime. (*Choosing a simple every-day dress.*) This one. (*Puts it on.*)

MAID: You're wrong.

BETROTHED: Why?

MAID: Your fiancé was looking for something else. In my town there was a boy who used to climb the church tower to get a closer look at the moon; his girl got rid of him.

BETROTHED: She did right.

MAID: He used to say that he saw his girl's likeness in the moon.

BETROTHED: And do you think that's right? (*She finishes at the dresser and lights the cherub's lights.*)

MAID (*Surprised*): Oh, Miss!

BETROTHED: What?

MAID: When I broke up with the bellboy.

BETROTHED: Have you gone and broken up with the bellboy? He was so handsome . . . so handsome . . . so handsome.

MAID: Naturally. I gave him a handkerchief, embroidered by me, which said: "Love, Love, Love"—and he lost it.

BETROTHED: Please go.

MAID: Shall I close the balcony doors?

BETROTHED: No.

MAID: The wind is going to burn your skin.

BETROTHED: I like that. I want to be dark—darker than a boy. And if I fall, not to bleed. And if I pick a berry, not to prick myself. They are all walking on the wire with their eyes closed. I want to have lead in my feet. Last night I dreamt that all young children grow by accident . . . that the strength behind a kiss is enough to kill them all. A dagger, some scissors, last forever—yet my bosom lasts only a moment.

MAID (*Listening*): Here comes your father.

BETROTHED: Put all my colored dresses in a suitcase.

MAID (*Trembling*): Yes.

BETROTHED: And have the key to the garage ready.

MAID (*With fright*): Very well.

(*The Father of the Betrothed enters. He is a distracted old man. He has some binoculars hanging at his throat. White wig. Pink face. He carries white gloves and wears a black suit. He shows signs of being slightly near-sighted.*)

FATHER: Are you ready?

BETROTHED (*Irritated*): What am I supposed to be ready for?

FATHER: He's come.

BETROTHED: What of it?

FATHER: Well, since you are betrothed and this concerns your whole life, your happiness, it's natural that you should be happy and decided.

BETROTHED: Well, I'm not.

FATHER: What's that?

BETROTHED: I'm not happy. And you?

FATHER: But, child . . . what is this man going to say?

BETROTHED: Let him say anything he wants.

FATHER: He's coming to marry you. You've written him during the five years this journey has lasted. You haven't danced with any one on the steamers . . . haven't taken any interest in any one else. What is this change?

BETROTHED: I don't want to see him. I have my own life to live. He talks too much.

If Five Years Pass

FATHER: Oh, why didn't you say this before?

BETROTHED: I didn't exist before either. The land and sea existed but I just slept sweetly on the train pillows.

FATHER: That man will insult me, and with reason. Oh, my Lord, and everything was ready! He had given you the wedding dress.

BETROTHED: Don't talk to me about it. I don't want to.

FATHER: What about me? Don't I have a right to rest? Tonight there is an eclipse of the moon. Now I won't be able to look at it from the terrace. Whenever I'm irritated, the blood comes to my eyes and I can't see. What shall we do with this man?

BETROTHED: Anything you say. I don't want to see him.

FATHER (*Sternly*): You must control yourself. You have to carry out your promise.

BETROTHED: I won't.

FATHER: You must.

BETROTHED: No.

FATHER: Yes. (*He makes as if to strike her.*)

BETROTHED (*Strongly*): No!

FATHER: Every one's against me. (*He looks at the sky through the open balcony windows.*) The eclipse is beginning. (*He goes toward the balcony.*) They have turned out the street lamps. (*With anguish.*) It will be beautiful. I've been waiting a long time for it. And now I can't see it. Why have you deceived him?

BETROTHED: I haven't deceived him.

FATHER: Five years day after day, oh my God . . .

(*The Maid enters precipitously and runs toward the balcony; outside voices are heard.*)

MAID: They're arguing.

FATHER: Who?

MAID: Now he's come in. (*She goes out quickly.*)

FATHER: What's happening?

BETROTHED: Where are you going? Shut the door. (*With anguish.*)

FATHER: But why?

BETROTHED: Ah . . .

(*The Young Man enters. He wears street clothes. He is pushing his hair back. At the moment of his entrance all the stage lights go on and the branches of lights which the cherubs carry in their hands. The three characters are left looking at each other not moving or speaking.*)

YOUNG MAN: Pardon. (*Pause.*)

FATHER (*With embarrassment*): Sit down.

(*The Maid enters nervously, with her hands at her bosom.*)

YOUNG MAN (*Giving his hand to the Betrothed*): It has been such a long trip.

BETROTHED (*Regarding him fixedly and without letting go his hand*): Yes. A cold journey. It has snowed much these last years. (*She drops his hand.*)

YOUNG MAN: You must excuse me, but I am excited from running, from climbing the stairs. And then . . . in the street I beat some children who were stoning a cat to death.

(*The Father offers him a chair.*)

BETROTHED (*To the Maid*): A cold hand. An amputated, waxen hand.

MAID: He'll hear you!

BETROTHED: And an old look. A look that breaks in two like the wing of a dry butterfly.

YOUNG MAN: No, no I can't sit. I prefer to talk. Suddenly, while I was climbing the stairs there came to my mind all the songs I had forgotten and I wanted to sing them all at the same time. (*He goes near to the Betrothed.*) Your braids.

BETROTHED: I never had any braids.

If Five Years Pass

YOUNG MAN: It must have been the moonlight. It must have been the air compressed into lips to kiss your head.

(*The Maid retires to a corner. The Father walks about on the balcony and gazes through the binoculars.*)

BETROTHED: And weren't you taller?

YOUNG MAN: No, no.

BETROTHED: Didn't you have a violent smile which spread like a mushroom over your face?

YOUNG MAN: No.

BETROTHED: And didn't you ever play football?

YOUNG MAN: Never.

BETROTHED (*With passion*): And didn't you hold a horse by the mane and in one day kill three thousand pheasants?

YOUNG MAN: Never.

BETROTHED: Then . . . why do you come looking for me? My hands are full of rings. Where is there a drop of blood?

YOUNG MAN: I'll spill some if that pleases you.

BETROTHED (*Sternly*): It's not your blood. It's mine.

YOUNG MAN: Now no one will be able to take my arms from about your neck.

BETROTHED: They aren't your arms; they're mine. I am the one who wants to burn in another fire.

YOUNG MAN: There isn't any other fire but mine. (*He embraces her.*) Because I have waited for you and now I reach my dream. And your braids are not a dream because I will make them myself out of your hair; nor is your waist where my blood sings a dream because this blood is mine, flowing slowly across a rain and this dream is mine.

BETROTHED (*Tearing herself away*): Let me go. You should have said everything except the word "dream." Here you can't dream. I don't want to dream . . .

YOUNG MAN: But you can love.

BETROTHED: Neither can you love. Go.

YOUNG MAN: What are you saying? (*Terrified.*)

BETROTHED: Look for another woman whom you can braid.

YOUNG MAN (*As if awakening*): No.

BETROTHED: How could I allow you to enter my bedroom when another has already entered?

YOUNG MAN: Oh! (*He covers his face with his hands.*)

BETROTHED: Just two days have been enough to make me feel weighted down with chains. In the mirrors and among the laces of the bed I already hear the cry of a child that pursues me.

YOUNG MAN: But my house is already built. With walls I myself have touched. Am I going to let only the wind live there?

BETROTHED: Is that my fault? Do you want me to go with you?

YOUNG MAN (*Seating himself in a chair, dejected:*) Yes, yes, come.

BETROTHED: A mirror, a table, would be closer to you than I.

YOUNG MAN: What am I going to do now?

BETROTHED: Love.

YOUNG MAN: Whom?

BETROTHED: Search. In the streets, in the fields.

YOUNG MAN (*Sternly*): I don't have to search. I have you. You're here, between my hands, this very moment, and you can't close your door on me because I come wet from a rain five years long. Because then there's nothing; then I can't love; then everything's finished.

BETROTHED: Let me go.

YOUNG MAN: It isn't your deceit that hurts me. You're not evil. You mean nothing. It's my lost treasure. It's my purposeless love. But you will come with me.

BETROTHED: I will not go.

YOUNG MAN: So that I won't have to start all over again. I feel I'm forgetting even my A, B, C's.

If Five Years Pass

BETROTHED: I will not go.

YOUNG MAN: So that I won't die. Do you hear that? So that I won't die.

BETROTHED: Let me go.

MAID (*Entering*): Miss.

(*The Young Man lets go of the Betrothed.*)

BETROTHED: There is some one who must not find out what you have done.

MAID: Sir.

FATHER (*Entering*): Who's shouting?

BETROTHED: No one.

FATHER (*Looking at the Young Man*): Sir.

YOUNG MAN (*Dejected*): We were talking.

BETROTHED (*To the Father*): I must return his gifts.

(*The Young Man makes a movement.*) All of them. It would be unjust. . . . All except the fans . . . because they're broken.

YOUNG MAN (*Remembering*): Two fans . . .

BETROTHED: One blue . . .

YOUNG MAN: With three sunken gondolas . . .

BETROTHED: And another white . . .

YOUNG MAN: With a tiger's head in the center. And they're broken?

MAID: The coalman's child took the last sticks of them.

FATHER: They were good fans, but come . . .

YOUNG MAN (*Smiling*): It doesn't matter that they were lost. Right now they stir a breeze that is burning my skin.

MAIE (*To the Betrothed*): Your wedding dress too?

BETROTHED: Naturally.

MAID (*Weepily*): It's inside there.

FATHER (*To the Young Man*): I wish that . . .

YOUNG MAN: It doesn't matter.

FATHER: Nevertheless, you must consider this your home.

YOUNG MAN: Thank you.

FATHER (*Always glancing towards the balcony*): It ought to be beginning now. Excuse me. (*To the Betrothed*) Are you coming?

BETROTHED: Yes. (*To the Young Man*) Good-bye.

YOUNG MAN: Good-bye.

(*They leave.*)

VOICE (*Outside*): Good-bye.

YOUNG MAN: Good-bye. . . . And what else? What shall I do with this hour that comes and that I do not recognize? Where shall I go?

(*The stage lights darken. The globes of the cherubs take on a blue light. Through the balconies there flows again moonshine which increases until the end. A groan is heard.*)

YOUNG MAN (*Looking at the door*): Who is that?

(*The Manikin, wearing the wedding dress, enters the stage. This character has a grave face and golden eyebrows and lips like a manikin out of a luxurious shop window. She wears with a certain embarrassment a splendid white wedding dress with a large veil and train.*)

MANIKIN (*Sings and weeps*):
Who will use now the good silver
of the bride so tiny and dark?
My train is lost in the sea
and the moon wears orange blossoms meant for me.
My ring, sir, my ring of old gold
has sunk through the sands of the mirror cold.
Who will wear my gown? Who will wear it?
The broad river will put it on to marry the sea.

YOUNG MAN:
What are you singing; tell me?

If Five Years Pass

MANIKIN:
I am singing
of death which I never had,
of the sorrow of the unused veil,
a sorrow of silk and of feathers.
Underclothes that must remain
frozen by the dark snow,
so that the laces can never
be the rivals of the foam.
Fabrics that should clothe the flesh
shall be for the restless water
and in the place of warm murmuring,
a torso broken in the rain.
Who will wear the good clothes
of the bride so tiny and dark?

YOUNG MAN:
They will be worn by the darkened wind
playing at daybreak in its cavern;
garters of satin the marsh reeds,
stockings of pure silk the moon.
Give the veil to the spiders,
so that they may eat and cover
the doves, by it enmeshed
in its threads of loveliness.
No one now will wear your gown,
form so white, and light confused,
to whom the silk and foam were
lightest architecture.

MANIKIN:
My train disappears in the sea.

YOUNG MAN:
And the moon wears on high your orange blossom wreath.

MANIKIN (*Angry*):
I don't want that. My silks,
thread by thread and one by one,
desire the warmth of marriage.

And my robe is asking
where are the warm hands
to tighten about the waist.

                YOUNG MAN:

I also ask. Be still.

                MANIKIN:

You lie. It's all your fault.
You could have been to me
a stallion of lead and foam,
the wind against the bit broken
and the ocean bound to your crupper.
You could have been a soft neighing,
you are a lagoon asleep,
full of dead leaves and mosses
where this gown will rot.
My ring, sir, my ring of ancient gold

                YOUNG MAN:

Has sunk through the sands of the mirror cold.

                MANIKIN:

She was waiting naked
like a serpent of the wind
dismayed by the arrows.

                YOUNG MAN (*Rising*):

Silence! Leave me. Go,
or I shall shatter with fury
the initials of sweet blossoms
which the white silk hides.
Go out in the street to search for
the shoulders of a night time virgin
or guitars that will cry you
six long wails of music.
No one will wear your gown.

                MANIKIN:

I'll follow you forever.

YOUNG MAN:
> Never.

MANIKIN:
Let me speak to you.

YOUNG MAN:
> It's useless. I don't want to know.

MANIKIN:
But listen. Look.

YOUNG MAN:
> What?

MANIKIN:
> A tiny dress
that I stole from the sewing room.

(*She shows a pink child's dress.*)
The fountains of white milk
are staining my silk robes with anguish
and a bee's white sorrow
covers my head with lightning.
My child. I want my child.
Through my skirt it is outlined
by these cords that are bursting
with joy at my waist.
And he's your son.

YOUNG MAN:
> Yes, my son:
where meet and come together
birds of insane dreaming
and jasmins of sanity.

(*Anguished.*)
And if my son does not come?
Bird that crosses the wind
cannot sing.

MANIKIN:
> Cannot.

YOUNG MAN:
And if my son does not come?
Sailboat that plows the sea
cannot float.

MANIKIN:
                Cannot.

YOUNG MAN:
Quiet now the rain-harp;
a sea turned stone laughs
its last dark waves.

MANIKIN:
Who will wear my gown? Who will wear it?

YOUNG MAN (*Enthusiastic and jovial*):
The woman who waits at the edge of the sea will wear it.

MANIKIN:
She waits for you always, remember?
She was hidden in your house.
She loved you and she went away.
Your child sings in its cradle
and being but a child of snow
he waits for your warm blood.
Run quickly to find her
and bring her to me naked
so that my silks may then
thread by thread and one by one,
make the rose bloom that hides
her womb of rosy flesh.

YOUNG MAN:
I must live.

MANIKIN:
              Without delay.

YOUNG MAN:
My son sings in his cradle
and since he's but a child of snow
he waits for warmth and help.

MANIKIN:
Give me the dress.

YOUNG MAN (*Sweetly*):
No.

MANIKIN (*Snatching the dress from him*):
I want it.
While you conquer and search
I shall sing it a song
over its tender folds. (*Kisses it.*)

YOUNG MAN:
Quickly! Where is she?

MANIKIN:
In the street.

YOUNG MAN:
Before the scarlet moon
cleanses with the blood of an eclipse
the perfection of her curve
I shall bring trembling with love
my own woman naked.

(*The light is of an intense blue. The Maidservant enters, left, with a candelabrum and the stage softly takes on its natural light without affecting the blue light of the wide open balconies that are at the rear.*

At the moment the servant enters the Manikin grows rigid with a department-store-window pose—the head inclined and the hands lifted in an attitude most delicate. The maid leaves the candelabrum upon the dressing table. Always in a remorseful attitude and looking at the Young Man.

At this moment the Old Man appears through the door, right. The light increases.)

YOUNG MAN (*Surprised*): You.

OLD MAN (*He shows signs of great excitement and puts his handkerchief to his chest. He has a silk handkerchief in his hand*): Yes, I.

(*The Maid leaves quickly.*)

YOUNG MAN (*Bitterly*): I don't need any one.

OLD MAN: More than ever. Oh, you have wounded me! Why did you come up? I knew what was going to happen. Oh . . . !

YOUNG MAN (*Sweetly*): What's the matter?

OLD MAN (*Sternly*): Nothing, nothing's the matter with me. A wound but . . . blood dries, and what's past is past.

(*The Young Man starts to leave.*)

Where are you going?

YOUNG MAN (*With joy*): To search.

OLD MAN: For whom?

YOUNG MAN: For the woman who loves me. You saw her in my house. Don't you remember?

OLD MAN: I don't remember her. But wait . . .

YOUNG MAN: No. Right now.

(*The Old Man takes him by the arm.*)

FATHER (*Entering*): Daughter. Where are you? Daughter!

(*A car horn is heard.*)

SERVANT (*At the balcony*): Miss! Miss!

FATHER (*Going to the balcony*): Daughter! Wait. Wait! (*Exits.*)

YOUNG MAN: I'm going too. Like her I am looking for the new flower of my blood. (*Goes out running.*)

OLD MAN: Wait. Wait. Don't leave me wounded. Wait. Wait! (*Exits. Their voices are lost.*)

MAID (*Enters quickly, takes the candelabrum and leaves through balcony*): Oh, my mistress. Oh Lord, my mistress!

(*The car horn is heard distantly.*)

MANIKIN:

My ring, sir, my ring of ancient gold,
(*Pause*)

Has sunk through the sands of the mirror cold.
Who will wear my gown? Who will wear it?
(*Pause, weeping*)
The broad stream will wear it in marriage with the sea.
(*She faints and lies stretched on the sofa.*)
VOICE (*Outside*): W-a-a-ait!

QUICK CURTAIN

ACT THREE

SCENE ONE

(*A forest. Great treetrunks. In the center a theatre surrounded by baroque hangings with the curtain drawn. A small set of stairs unites the little scaffold with the stage. When the curtain rises, two figures dressed in black, with white plaster of Paris faces and hands, cross among the treetrunks. Distant music sounds. Harlequin enters. He is dressed in black and green. He carries two masks, one in each hand, hidden behind his back. He enters gesturing in a plastic manner like a dancer.*)

HARLEQUIN:
A dream goes out over time
afloat like a sailboat gleaming
and no one can harvest seeds
within the heart of dreaming.

(*He puts on a mask with a very gay expression.*)
Oh how the dawn is singing, how it sings!
What icy mountains colored blue it brings!

(*Removes the mask.*)
But time flies over the dream
sunk to the roots of its hair.
Yesterday and tomorrow eat
dark flowers of despair.

(*He puts on a mask with an expression of slumber.*)
Oh how the night is singing, how it sings!
What richness of anemones it brings!

(*He takes off the mask.*)
Upon the very same column
time and the dream intertwine

If Five Years Pass   117

with the cry of the child
and the old man's babbling tongue.
(*With one mask.*)
Oh how the dawn is singing, how it sings!
(*With the other.*)
What richness of anemones it brings!

(*From this moment and during all the act, deep hunting horns are heard offstage, in gradually lengthening intervals.*)

(*A Girl appears, dressed in black, with a Greek tunic. She enters leaping, carrying a garland.*)

GIRL:
Who will say it;
oh who will tell me?
My love awaits for me
there deep below the sea.

HARLEQUIN (*Charmingly*):
It's a lie.

GIRL:
It's the truth.
I lost my wish,
I lost my thimble—then
I searched among the trees
and found them once again.

HARLEQUIN (*Ironically*):
A very long cord.

GIRL:
A cord that's long enough
to lower sharks and fishes
and coral branches rough.

HARLEQUIN:
He is below.

GIRL:
      He's deep below.

HARLEQUIN:
Asleep he is.

GIRL:
>So deep below.
Banners green as water
to sea shall make him go.

HARLEQUIN (*In a voice high and charming*):
It's a lie.

GIRL (*In a high voice*):
It's the truth.
I lost my crown
I lost my thimble—then
by turning half around
I found them both again.

HARLEQUIN:
This very day.

GIRL:
>Today?

HARLEQUIN:
You'll see your lover fair
in half a turn again
of ocean and of air.

GIRL (*Frightened*):
It's a lie.

HARLEQUIN:
It's the truth.
I'll give him back to you.

GIRL (*Uneasy*):
You won't bring him to me.
No one returns who lies
so deep below the sea.

HARLEQUIN (*Shouting, in the manner of a circus barker*):
>Mister man, attend.

(*A splendid Clown, covered with sequins, appears. His powdered head gives the feeling of a skull. He laughs in great peals.*)

HARLEQUIN:
It's up to you to free
this girl's love who lies
so deep below the sea.

CLOWN (*Draws back his sleeves*):
I'll need a ladder then.

GIRL (*Frightened*):
Truly?

CLOWN (*To the girl*):
To descend.
(*To the audience.*)
Good evening, sirs.

HARLEQUIN:
Bravo!

CLOWN (*To Harlequin*):
You look the other way.
(*Harlequin, laughing, turns.*)
Now, sir, it's time to play. (*Claps.*)
The Harlequin plays a white violin with two gold strings. It must be large and plain. He nods in rhythm to the music.*)
Now can you see him there?

HARLEQUIN (*Disguising his voice*):
Through the seaweed cool
in a sea cave's vault
I shall hunt great shells
and lilies of salt.

GIRL (*Afraid of reality*):
I don't want this.

CLOWN:
Silence. (*Harlequin laughs.*)

GIRL (*Frightened, to the Clown*):
I shall run away
Through the tallest ferns.

HARLEQUIN (*Jestingly*):
It's a lie.

GIRL (*To the Clown*):
It's true.
Afterwards we'll go.
where sea-water churns.

(*Starts to leave, weeping.*)

Who shall say it?
Oh who will tell me?
I lost my crown,
I lost my crown.

HARLEQUIN (*Melancholy*):
In a half a turn again
of the wind and sea.

(*Girl leaves.*)

CLOWN (*Pointing*):
Look there.

HARLEQUIN:
Look where? At what?

CLOWN:
What we'll act out now
concerns a little boy.
This story tells you how
he changed his bread for steel
in flowers on his brow.

HARLEQUIN:
It's a lie.

CLOWN (*Severely*):
It's the truth.

HARLEQUIN (*Adopting a circus attitude, and as if the child could hear them*):
Mister man, attend.

(*Starts to leave.*)

If Five Years Pass

CLOWN (*Shouting, looking toward the forest, and heading Harlequin off*):
Not so much shouting.
Good day.
(*In a low voice*):
Come.
Play.

HARLEQUIN:
Shall I play?

CLOWN:
A waltz.

(*Harlequin begins to play.*)

CLOWN (*Shouting*):
Quickly!
Gentlemen
I shall demonstrate to you . . .

HARLEQUIN:
How in the ivory clouds
she came on them anew.

CLOWN:
I shall demonstrate to you . . . (*Leaves.*)

HARLEQUIN (*Leaving*):
The wheel that ever turns
the wind and ocean through.

(*The trumpets are heard. The Stenographer enters. She wears a tennis frock and a tam of an intense color. Over the dress a long cape. She comes with the First Mask. This Mask wears a dress in the style of 1900 with a long train of poisonous yellow, yellow silk hair falling like a shawl, and white plaster of Paris mask; gloves up to the elbow of the same color. She carries a yellow hat and her whole bosom is embroidered with golden sequins. The effect of this character should be that of a flame upon the background of blue moons and nocturnal tree-trunks. She speaks with a slight Italian accent.*)

FIRST MASK (*Laughing*): How enchanting!

STENOGRAPHER: I left his house. I remember that on the afternoon of my departure there was a great summer storm. The doorkeeper's child had died and he said to me: "Did you call me?" To which I answered, closing my eyes: "No." And then when I was at the door he said to me: "Do you need me?" And I said to him: "No, I don't need you."

FIRST MASK: Charming.

STENOGRAPHER: He would wait all night standing until I should look out my window.

FIRST MASK: And you, Miss Stenographer?

STENOGRAPHER: I wouldn't look out. But . . . I would look out through the cracks . . . quiet, (*She pulls out a handkerchief*) with such eyes. . . . The wind would come in like a knife, but I couldn't talk to him.

FIRST MASK: Why not, Miss?

STENOGRAPHER: Because he loved me too much.

FIRST MASK: O, *mio Dio!* He was just like the Count Arturo of Italia. . . . Oh, love!

STENOGRAPHER: Yes?

FIRST MASK: In the foyer of the Paris opera there are some enormous balustrades that go down to the sea. The Count Arturo, with a camellia between his lips, would come in a tiny boat with his child—both of them by me abandoned. But I would draw the curtains and throw them a diamond. Oh, what sweet torment, my friend! (*Weeps.*) The Count and his child would suffer hunger and sleep among the branches with a greyhound which a Russian gentleman had given me. (*Sternly and begging.*) Don't you have a little piece of bread for me? Don't you have a little piece of bread for my child? For the child that the Count Arturo allowed to die among the rushes? (*Excited.*) And afterwards I went to the hospital and there I learned that

If Five Years Pass

the Count had married a great Roman lady; and since then I have begged and shared my bed with the men who unload coal at the docks.

STENOGRAPHER: What are you saying? Why do you speak?

FIRST MASK (*Becoming calmer*): I say that the Count Arturo loved me so much that he used to cry behind the curtains with his child, while I was like a silver halfmoon among the opera glasses and the gas lights that glittered underneath the cupola of the grand Paris opera.

STENOGRAPHER: Delightful. And when will the Count come?

FIRST MASK: And when will your friend come?

STENOGRAPHER: He will be a long time.

FIRST MASK: Arturo will be a long time also. He has on his right hand a scar where he was stabbed by a dagger . . . over me, of course. (*Showing her hand.*) Can't you see it? (*Pointing to her throat.*) And another one here. Do you see it?

STENOGRAPHER: Yes, but why?

FIRST MASK: Why? What should I do without my wounds? Whose are my Count's wounds?

STENOGRAPHER: Yours, it's true. He has been waiting for me for five years but . . . how beautiful it is to wait with certainty for the moment of being loved.

FIRST MASK: And it is certain.

STENOGRAPHER: Certain. That is why we are going to laugh. When I was a child I saved the sweets to eat them later.

FIRST MASK: Ha-ha-ha! Yes, isn't it true? They taste better.

(*The trumpets are heard.*)

STENOGRAPHER (*Starting to leave*): If my friend should come—tall, with all his hair curling, but curling in a special way—you pretend that you don't know him.

FIRST MASK: Naturally, my friend. (*She gathers up her train.*)

(*The Young Man appears. He wears a gray field suit with blue checked hose.*)

HARLEQUIN (*Entering*): Eh?

YOUNG MAN: What?

HARLEQUIN: Where are you going?

YOUNG MAN: To my house.

HARLEQUIN (*Ironically*): Yes?

YOUNG MAN: Certainly. (*He begins to walk.*)

HARLEQUIN: Hey! You can't go through there.

YOUNG MAN: Have they closed the walk?

HARLEQUIN: The circus is that way.

YOUNG MAN: All right. (*He turns.*)

HARLEQUIN: Full of spectators. (*Softly.*) Doesn't the gentleman want to go in?

YOUNG MAN: No.

HARLEQUIN (*Emphatically*): The poet Virgil constructed a golden fly and all the flies that poisoned the air of Naples died. Inside there, in the circus, there is soft gold, enough to make a statue the same size . . . that you—

YOUNG MAN: Is the street of the poplar trees also closed?

HARLEQUIN: The wagons are there and the cages for the serpents . . .

YOUNG MAN: Then I shall go back. (*Starting to leave.*)

CLOWN (*Appearing on the other side*): But where are you going? Ha-ha-ha!

HARLEQUIN: He says he's going to his house.

CLOWN (*Giving a circus blow to Harlequin*): Take that, house.

(*Harlequin falls to the floor shouting.*)

HARLEQUIN: Oh, it hurts. It hurts.

CLOWN (*To the Young Man*): Come.

YOUNG MAN (*Irritated*): But will you please tell me what kind of a joke this is? I was going to my house, that is, not to my house; to another house, to . . .

CLOWN (*Interrupting him*): To search . . .

If Five Years Pass

YOUNG MAN: Yes; because I must. To search.

CLOWN (*Happy*): Do a half-turn and you will find it.

VOICE OF THE STENOGRAPHER (*Singing*):
Where do you wander now, my love,
my love, where go,
with all the wind in a water glass
while under a glass the oceans show?

(*The Harlequin has now risen. The Young Man has his back turned and the Clown and Harlequin go out without turning their backs, on tiptoes, performing a dance step, holding a finger to their lips.*)

YOUNG MAN (*Wonderingly*):
Where do you wander now, my love,
my life, my love, where do you go,
with all the wind in a water glass
while under a glass the oceans show?

STENOGRAPHER (*Appearing*):
Oh where? Where am I called?

YOUNG MAN:
My life!

STENOGRAPHER:
To go with you!

YOUNG MAN:
Naked I will carry you,
ill-used flower and cleanest body,
to the place where all the silks
await and tremble with the cold.
The whitest sheets wait there for you.
But let us quickly go. But now.
Before within the branches weep
the yellow nightingales.

STENOGRAPHER:
Yes; for the sun is like a kite,
better; a falcon made of glass.
No: for the sun's a large treetrunk,

and you are like a river's shade.
How, if you embrace me, say,
rise lilies not, nor rushes here?
And why your arms about me now
have not my dress discolored then?
Love, leave me on the mountainside
     of clouds and dew,
that I may see you great and sad,
    a sky asleep.

    YOUNG MAN:
Don't speak like that, my child. Come.
What use is time, if it is lost?
The purest blood, the deepest warmth
are taking me some other place.
I want to live.

    STENOGRAPHER:
      With whom?

    YOUNG MAN:
      With you.

    STENOGRAPHER:
But what is sounding far away?

    YOUNG MAN:
Love,
the day returning,
my love.

STENOGRAPHER (*Happy and as if in a dream*):
It is a nightingale that sings,
a nightingale of evening gray
upon the branch of wind,
upon the cable's lyre.
Oh, nightingale, it's you I've felt.
I want to live.

    YOUNG MAN:
      But live with whom?

STENOGRAPHER:
With the shadow of a river.
(*Anguished, and taking refuge on the Young Man's chest*):
But what is sounding far away?

YOUNG MAN:
Love,
the blood at my throat,
my love.

STENOGRAPHER:
Always like this, always,
awake or asleep.

YOUNG MAN:
Never like this, never, never.
We must go from here.

STENOGRAPHER:
Please wait.

YOUNG MAN:
But love can never wait.

STENOGRAPHER (*Moves away from the Young Man*):
Where do you wander now, my love,
with all the wind in a water glass,
while under a glass the oceans show?
(*Goes toward stairs.*)

(*The curtains of the little stage are drawn. The Library of the first act set appears, reduced, and in pale tones. On the small stage the Yellow Mask appears. She has a lace handkerchief in her hand and smells continually a vial of smelling salts.*)

FIRST MASK (*To the Stenographer*): Just now I have abandoned the Count forever. He has stayed back there with his child. (*She descends the stairs.*) I'm sure that he will die. But he loved me so much, so much. (*She weeps.*) (*To the Stenographer.*) Didn't you know that? His child will die under the white frost. I have abandoned it. Don't you see how happy I am? Don't you see how I laugh?

(*Weeping.*) Now he will look for me everywhere. (*On the lower stage.*) I'm going to hide in the blackberry bushes. (*In a loud voice.*) In the blackberry bushes! I speak like this because I don't want Arturo to hear me. (*In a loud voice*): I don't want him to! I have told you I don't love you! (*She goes, weeping.*) You me, yes; but not I you. I don't love you.

(*Two Servants dressed in blue livery and with very pale faces appear. They leave two white stools at left stage.*)

(*The Servant of the first act crosses the stage, walking, as always, on tiptoe.*)

STENOGRAPHER (*To the Servant, and climbing the steps of the little stage*): If your master comes, show him in. (*On the little stage*): Although he won't come till he must.

(*The Young Man begins to climb the stairs slowly.*)

YOUNG MAN (*On the little stage, passionately*): Are you happy here?

STENOGRAPHER: Have you written the letters?

YOUNG MAN: It's better upstairs. Come.

STENOGRAPHER: I have loved you so much.

YOUNG MAN: I love you so much.

STENOGRAPHER: I will love you so much.

YOUNG MAN: It seems to me that I die without you. Where shall I go if you leave me? I don't remember anything. The other one does not exist, but you do because you love me.

STENOGRAPHER: I have loved you, love. I will love you forever.

YOUNG MAN: Now . . .

STENOGRAPHER: Why do you say 'now'?

(*The Old Man appears on the stage. He is dressed in blue and carries in his hand a large bloodstained handkerchief which he puts to his chest and face. He gives signs of excitement and slowly becomes conscious of what is happening on the little stage.*)

If Five Years Pass

YOUNG MAN: I waited and was dying.

STENOGRAPHER: I was dying because I waited.

YOUNG MAN: But the blood pounded at my temples with its little knots of fire, and now at last I have you here.

VOICE (*Outside*): My child! My child!

(*The Dead Child crosses the little stage. He comes alone and leaves through a door left.*)

YOUNG MAN: Yes, my son. Run with me like a little ant alone in a closed box. (*To the Stenographer.*) A little bit of light for my son. Please. He's so small. He pushes his little nose against the crystal of my heart but, nevertheless, he has no air.

FIRST MASK (*Appearing on the large stage*): My child.

(*Two other Masks which witness the scene appear.*)

STENOGRAPHER (*Dryly, with authority*): Have you written the letters? It isn't your son; it's I. You waited and you let me go, but you always thought yourself loved. Is what I say a lie?

YOUNG MAN (*Impatiently*): No, but . . .

STENOGRAPHER: I, on the other hand, knew that you would never love me, and, nevertheless, I have nurtured my love and I have changed you and I have seen you at the corners of my house. (*Passionately.*) I love you, but far beyond you. I have fled so much that I must look at the sea to notice the trembling of your mouth.

OLD MAN: But if he is twenty years old he can be twenty moons.

STENOGRAPHER (*Logically*): Twenty roses. Twenty norths of snow.

YOUNG MAN (*Irritated*): Be quiet. You will come with me because you love me and because I must live.

STENOGRAPHER: Yes, I love you, but much more. You don't have eyes to see me naked, nor a mouth that never stops kissing my body. Leave me. I love you too much to be able to look at you.

YOUNG MAN: Not a minute more. Let us go. (*He takes her by the wrists.*)

STENOGRAPHER: You hurt me, love.

YOUNG MAN: That way you feel me.

STENOGRAPHER: Wait . . . I will go . . . always. (*She embraces him.*)

OLD MAN: She'll go. Sit down, my friend.

YOUNG MAN (*Anguished*): No.

STENOGRAPHER: I feel very tall. Why did you leave me? I was going to die of cold and I had to seek your love where there were no people. But I'll go with you. Let me come down to you little by little.

(*The Clown and Harlequin appear. The Clown carries a curtain and the Harlequin his white violin. They sit on the white stools.*)

CLOWN:
Some music.

HARLEQUIN:
Of years.

CLOWN:
Moons and seas unopened.

HARLEQUIN:
What stays behind?

CLOWN:
The wind's winding sheet,
and the music of your violin.

YOUNG MAN (*Coming out of a dream*): Let us go.

STENOGRAPHER: Yes . . . but can it be possible that this is you? Like this, suddenly, without having tried out slowly this beautiful idea. It will be tomorrow? Aren't you sorry for me?

If Five Years Pass

YOUNG MAN: It's like a nest upstairs. We can hear the nightingales sing . . . and even though we couldn't hear, even though the bat should dash against the windows . . .

STENOGRAPHER: Yes, yes, but . . .

YOUNG MAN (*Sternly*): Your mouth. (*He kisses her.*)

STENOGRAPHER: Later.

YOUNG MAN (*Passionately*): It's better at night.

STENOGRAPHER: I'll go.

YOUNG MAN: Without delay.

STENOGRAPHER: I want . . . listen . . .

YOUNG MAN: Let us go.

STENOGRAPHER: But . . .

YOUNG MAN: Tell me.

STENOGRAPHER: I will go with you . . .

YOUNG MAN: Love.

STENOGRAPHER: . . . if five years pass.

YOUNG MAN: Oh! (*He puts his hand to his forehead.*)

OLD MAN (*In a low voice*): Bravo.

(*The Young Man begins to descend the stairs slowly. The Stenographer remains in an ecstatic attitude on the little stage. The Servant tiptoes in and covers her with a great white cloak.*)

CLOWN:
Some music.

HARLEQUIN:
Of years.

CLOWN:
Moons and seas unopened.
What stays behind?

HARLEQUIN:
The wind's winding sheet.

CLOWN:
And the music of your violin.

(*They play.*)

FIRST MASK: The Count kisses.

OLD MAN: We are not going to arrive, but we are going to go.

YOUNG MAN (*Desperately, to the Clown*): The exit, where?

STENOGRAPHER (*On the small stage and as if dreaming*): Love, love.

YOUNG MAN (*Shaken*): Show me the door.

CLOWN (*Ironically, pointing to the left*): That way.

HARLEQUIN (*Pointing to the right*): That way.

STENOGRAPHER: I wait for you, love. I wait; come back soon.

HARLEQUIN (*Ironically*): That way.

YOUNG MAN (*To the Clown*): I'll break your cages and your webs. I know how to leap the wall.

OLD MAN (*Anguished*): This way.

YOUNG MAN: I want to go back. Let me go.

HARLEQUIN:
The wind is left.

CLOWN:
And the music of your violin.

CURTAIN

SCENE TWO

(*The same Library as in the first act. To the left, the wedding gown on a manikin without head or hands. Several open suitcases. To the right, a table. The Servant, Juan, and the Maid enter.*)

MAID (*Astonished*): Yes?

SERVANT: She is a porter now, but before that she was a great lady. She lived a long time with a very rich Italian count. The father of the child they have just buried.

If Five Years Pass

MAID: Poor little thing. He looked so beautiful.

SERVANT: Her delusions of grandeur date from that time. That is why she spent everything she had on the clothes for the child and on the coffin.

MAID: And on the flowers. I sent him a little bunch of roses, but it was so small that they didn't even put them in the room.

YOUNG MAN (*Entering*): Juan.

SERVANT: Sir?

(*The Maid leaves.*)

YOUNG MAN: Give me a glass of cold water.

(*The Young Man shows signs of despair and physical exhaustion. The Servant attends him.*)

Wasn't this window much larger?

SERVANT: No.

YOUNG MAN: It's astonishing that it should be so narrow. My house had an enormous patio where I played with my hobby horses. At twenty years, when I saw it again, it was so tiny that it seemed to me incredible that I should have been able to fly about in it so.

SERVANT: Is the gentleman all right?

YOUNG MAN: Is a fountain spouting water all right? Answer!

SERVANT: I don't know.

YOUNG MAN: Is the weathercock turning in the wind all right?

SERVANT: Sir, you give me such examples that . . . but I'd like to ask, if the master will permit me, is the wind all right?

YOUNG MAN (*Dryly*): I'm all right.

SERVANT: Did you rest enough after your trip?

YOUNG MAN: Yes.

SERVANT: I'm very glad. (*The Servant starts to leave.*)

YOUNG MAN: Juan, are my clothes ready?

SERVANT: Yes sir, they're in the bedroom.

YOUNG MAN: What suit?

SERVANT: Your frock coat. I put it on the bed.

YOUNG MAN (*Excited*): Well, take it away. I don't want to go up and find it stretched out on a bed so large, so empty. I don't know who thought of buying it. I had another bed, a small one before. Do you remember?

SERVANT: Yes, sir. The carved walnut one.

YOUNG MAN: That's right. The carved walnut one. How well I slept in it. I remember when I was a child seeing an enormous moon rise behind the slats of its footboard. Or was it behind the balcony railing? I don't know. Where is it?

SERVANT: You gave it away, sir.

YOUNG MAN (*Thinking*): To whom?

SERVANT (*Gravely*): To your old stenographer.

(*The Young Man remains pensive. Pause.*)

YOUNG MAN (*Gesturing toward the Servant, who is leaving*): That's all right.

(*The Servant leaves.*)

YOUNG MAN (*With anguish*): Juan!

SERVANT (*Sternly*): Sir.

YOUNG MAN: I suppose you put out patent-leather shoes.

SERVANT: Those with black-silk laces.

YOUNG MAN: Black silk . . . yes. Look for some others. (*Rising.*) Can it be the air in this house is always rarefied? I'm going to cut all the flowers in the garden—above all those damned rosebays that leap the wall, and that weed that springs by itself at midnight . . .

SERVANT: They say the windflowers and poppies make one's head ache at certain hours of the day.

YOUNG MAN: That may be. Take that also. (*Pointing to his overcoat.*) Put it in the clothespress.

SERVANT: Very well. (*Starts to leave again.*)

YOUNG MAN (*Timidly*): And leave the patent-leather shoes. But change the laces.

(*A bell rings.*)

SERVANT (*Entering*): It is the gentlemen who are coming to play.

YOUNG MAN (*Bored*): Oh.

SERVANT (*At the door*): The master will have to dress.

YOUNG MAN (*Leaving*): Yes.

(*He leaves almost like a shadow. The Players enter. They are three. They wear formal clothes and long capes of white satin reaching to their feet.*)

FIRST PLAYER: It was in Venice. A bad year for playing, but that boy really played. He was pale, so pale that on the last card he couldn't do anything but throw in the ace of hearts. His own heart full of blood. He threw it in . . . and, on trying to recover it—(*Lowering his voice and looking to the sides*)—he had an ace of hearts running over at the brim and fled drinking from it down the Grand Canal with two girls.

SECOND PLAYER: Pale people are not to be trusted—or those that are sated. They play but hold something back.

THIRD PLAYER: In India I played with an old man who, when he had not a drop of blood left on the cards and I was waiting for the moment to throw myself on him, stained all the hearts red with a special dye and was able to escape through the trees.

FIRST PLAYER: We play and we win, but after so much work! The cards drink in rich blood from the hands and it is difficult to cut the cord that binds them.

SECOND PLAYER: But I think with this one we aren't mistaken.

THIRD PLAYER: I don't know.

FIRST PLAYER (*To the Second*): Will you never learn to know your clients? This one? His life escapes him through his eyes wetting the slit of his lips and staining his shirtfront blue.

SECOND PLAYER: Yes, but remember the boy who played with us in Sweden—almost breathing his last—and then almost blinding the three of us with a gush of blood that spurted at us.

THIRD PLAYER: So it goes. (*Draws a card.*)

SECOND PLAYER: We must go easy with him so that he won't recover.

THIRD PLAYER: Even though neither of the other ones, nor the Stenographer, will think to come here until five years pass. That is, if they should ever come. (*Laughing.*) If they should ever come! Ha-ha-ha!

FIRST PLAYER: It won't be amiss to be quick in our playing.

SECOND PLAYER: He has one ace.

THIRD PLAYER: A young heart where likely the arrows will glance off.

FIRST PLAYER (*Happy and profound*): It's just like placing arrows in a shooting match.

SECOND PLAYER (*With curiosity*): Where?

FIRST PLAYER: In a shooting match. Arrows that stick not only to the hardest steel but to the finest gauze. And that's really difficult.

(*They laugh.*)

SECOND PLAYER: Well, we shall see.

(*The Young Man appears dressed in a frock coat.*)

YOUNG MAN: Gentlemen. (*Gives them his hand.*) You have come early. It's too hot.

FIRST PLAYER: Not so very.

SECOND PLAYER (*To the Young Man*): Elegant as ever.

FIRST PLAYER: So elegant that he should never disrobe again.

THIRD PLAYER: There are times when clothes become us so that we would not like to . . .

SECOND PLAYER (*Interrupting*): That we cannot remove them from the body.

If Five Years Pass

YOUNG MAN (*Distastefully*): You are too kind.

(*The Servant appears with a tray of glasses which he leaves at the table.*)

Shall we begin?

(*The three sit down.*)

FIRST PLAYER: We are ready.

SECOND PLAYER (*In a low voice*): Look sharp.

THIRD PLAYER: Aren't you going to sit down?

YOUNG MAN: No, I prefer to play standing.

FIRST PLAYER: Standing?

SECOND PLAYER (*In a low voice*): You'll have to dig down pretty far.

FIRST PLAYER (*Dealing cards*): How many?

YOUNG MAN: Four.

(*The First Player deals them to the others.*)

THIRD PLAYER (*In a low voice*): No play.

YOUNG MAN: What cold cards. Nothing. (*He leaves them on the table.*) And you . . .

FIRST PLAYER (*In a low voice*): Nothing. (*He deals them cards again.*)

SECOND PLAYER (*Looking at his cards*): Magnificent.

THIRD PLAYER (*Looking uneasily at his cards*): Let's see . . .

FIRST PLAYER (*To the Young Man*): Your play.

YOUNG MAN (*Happily*): I play. (*He throws a card on the table.*)

FIRST PLAYER (*Sternly*): And I.

SECOND PLAYER: And I.

THIRD PLAYER: And I.

YOUNG MAN (*Excitedly, with one card*): And now?

(*The Three Players show their cards. The Young Man holds back and hides his in his hand.*)

YOUNG MAN (*Anguished*): Juan, serve some wine to these gentlemen.

FIRST PLAYER: The card, if you will be so kind.

YOUNG MAN (*Desperately*): What would you like to drink?

SECOND PLAYER (*Sweetly*): The card?

YOUNG MAN (*To the Third Player*): Surely you would like some anise. It's a drink that . . .

THIRD PLAYER: If you please, the card.

YOUNG MAN (*To the Servant, who enters*): What, is there no whisky?

(*At the moment the Servant enters, the Players fall silent, with their cards in their hands.*)

Nor cognac?

FIRST PLAYER (*In a low voice, so as not to be heard by the Servant*): The card.

YOUNG MAN (*Anguished*): Cognac is a drink for men who know how to resist.

SECOND PLAYER (*Sternly, but in a low voice*): The card.

YOUNG MAN: Or do you prefer chartreuse?

(*The Servant leaves.*)

FIRST PLAYER (*Standing, sternly*): Have the kindness to play.

YOUNG MAN: Right away. But let us drink.

THIRD PLAYER (*Strongly*): You have to play.

YOUNG MAN (*Breathing his last*): Yes, yes. A little bit of chartreuse. It's like night with a great green moon inside a castle where there's a young man with golden she-goats.

FIRST PLAYER (*Strongly*): You must give us your ace.

YOUNG MAN (*Aside*): My heart.

SECOND PLAYER: Because one must win or lose. Come, your card.

THIRD PLAYER: Let us have it.

FIRST PLAYER: Play.

YOUNG MAN (*With sorrow*): My card.

FIRST PLAYER: The last one.

If Five Years Pass

YOUNG MAN: I play.

(*He places the card on the table. At this moment, there appears, illuminated on the library shelves, the ace of hearts. The First Player whips out a pistol and shoots an arrow noiselessly. The ace of hearts disappears and the Young Man places his hands over his heart.*)

FIRST PLAYER: We must flee.

SECOND PLAYER: No, we must wait.

THIRD PLAYER: Cut now. Cut well.

(*The First Player cuts in the air with some scissors.*)

FIRST PLAYER (*In a low voice*): Let us go.

SECOND PLAYER: Quickly.

(*They leave.*)

YOUNG MAN: Juan. Juan.

ECHO: Juan. Juan.

YOUNG MAN (*Dying*): I've lost it all.

ECHO: I've lost it all.

YOUNG MAN: My love.

ECHO: Love.

YOUNG MAN (*On the sofa*): Juan.

ECHO: Juan.

YOUNG MAN: Isn't there?

ECHO: Isn't there?

SECOND ECHO (*More distant*): Isn't there?

YOUNG MAN: Any one here?

ECHO: Here . . .

SECOND ECHO: Here . . .

(*The Young Man dies. The Servant appears with a lighted candelabrum. The clock strikes twelve.*)

CURTAIN

Yerma

*A Tragic Poem in
Three Acts and Six Scenes*

CHARACTERS

Yerma
María
Pagan Crone
Dolores
First Laundress
Second Laundress
Third Laundress
Fourth Laundress
Fifth Laundress
Sixth Laundress
First Young Girl
Second Young Girl
The Female Mask
First Sister-in-law
Second Sister-in-law
First Woman
Second Woman
The Child
Juan
Victor
The Male Mask
First Man
Second Man
Third Man

ACT ONE

SCENE ONE

(When the curtain rises Yerma is asleep with an embroidery frame at her feet. The stage is in the strange light of a dream. A Shepherd enters on tiptoe looking fixedly at Yerma. He leads by the hand a Child dressed in white. The clock sounds. When the Shepherd leaves, the light changes into the happy brightness of a spring morning. Yerma awakes.)

VOICE (*Within, singing*):
For the nursey, nursey, nursey,
For the little nurse we'll make
A tiny hut out in the fields
And there we'll shelter take.

YERMA: Juan, do you hear me? Juan!

JUAN: Coming.

YERMA: It's time.

JUAN: Did the oxen pass?

YERMA: They've passed.

JUAN: Good-bye (*He starts to leave.*)

YERMA: Won't you drink a glass of milk?

JUAN: What for?

YERMA: You work a lot and don't have the strength for it.

JUAN: When men grow thin they become strong as steel.

YERMA: But not you. When we were married you were another person. Now your face is white as if the sun had never shone on it. I wish you'd go to the river and swim and climb up to the roof when the rain beats down on our house. Twenty-four months married and you only get sadder, thinner, as if you grew backwards.

JUAN: Are you through?

YERMA (*Rising*): Don't be offended. If I were sick I'd want you to take care of me. "My wife is sick. I'm going to butcher this lamb and fry her a good piece of meat." "My wife is sick. I'm going to keep this chicken-fat to relieve her chest; I'm going to take her this sheepskin to protect her feet from the snow." That's the way I am. That's why I take care of you.

JUAN: I'm grateful.

YERMA: But you don't let me take care of you.

JUAN: There's nothing wrong with me. All these things are just ideas of yours. I work hard. Each year I'll just be so much older.

YERMA: Each year. You and I will just keep on each year . . .

JUAN (*Smiling*): Naturally. And well content. Things on the farm go well. We have no children to use them up.

YERMA: No children . . . Juan!

JUAN: What?

YERMA: Don't I love you?

JUAN: You love me.

YERMA: I know many girls who trembled and cried before getting into bed with their husbands. Did I cry the first time I slept with you? Didn't I sing as I turned back the holland-cloth sheets? Didn't I say, "How these bed-clothes smell of apples"?

JUAN: That's what you said!

YERMA: My mother cried because I wasn't sorry to be separated from her. And it was true! No one ever got married with more happiness. And yet . . .

JUAN: Hush! It's enough to hear it said every moment that . . .

YERMA: Don't. Don't repeat what they say. My own eyes tell me that can't be. The rain just by the force of its falling on the stones softens them and makes weeds grow—weeds which people say aren't good for anything. "Weeds aren't good for anything." Yet I see them move their yellow flowers in the wind.

JUAN: We must wait.

YERMA: Yes; loving. (*Yerma embraces and kisses her husband. She takes the initiative.*)

JUAN: If you need something, tell me and I'll bring it. You know I don't like you to go out.

YERMA: I never go out.

JUAN: You're better off here.

YERMA: Yes.

JUAN: The street is for idle people.

YERMA (*Darkly*): Of course.

(*The husband leaves and Yerma walks toward her sewing. She passes her hand over her belly, lifts her arms in a beautiful sigh, and sits down to sew.*)

YERMA:
From where do you come, my love, my baby?
"From the mountains of icy cold."
What do you lack, sweet love, my baby?
"The woven warmth in your dress."

(*Threads the needle.*)

Let mighty branches rake the sun
and teeming fountains leap all around!

(*As if she spoke to a child.*)

In the courtyard the dog barks,
In the trees the wind sings.
The oxen low for the ox-herd,
and the moon curls up my hair.
What want you, boy, from so far away?

(*Pause.*)

"The mountains white upon your chest."
Let mighty branches rake the sun
and teeming fountains leap all around!

(*Sewing.*)
> I shall say to you, child, yes,
> for you I'll torn and broken be.
> How painful is this belly now,
> where first you shall be cradled!
> When, boy, when will you come to me?

(*Pause.*)
> "When sweet your flesh of jasmin smells."
> Let mighty branches rake the sun
> and teeming fountains leap all around.

(*Yerma continues singing. María enters through the door carrying a bundle of clothes.*)

YERMA: From where are you coming?

MARÍA: From the store.

YERMA: From the store so early?

MARÍA: For my part, I would have waited outside the door until they opened. Can you guess what I have bought?

YERMA: Probably coffee for breakfast, sugar, bread.

MARÍA: No. Laces. Three skeins of thread, bands, and colored wool to make tassels. My husband had some money and he gave it to me without my even asking for it.

YERMA: You're going to make yourself a blouse?

MARÍA: No, it's because . . . can you guess?

YERMA: What?

MARÍA: Because it's come. (*She lowers her head.*)

(*Yerma rises and looks at her with surprise.*)

YERMA: In just five months!

MARÍA: Yes.

YERMA: And can you tell it?

MARÍA: Naturally.

YERMA (*With curiosity*): And what do you feel?

MARÍA: I don't know. Anguish.

YERMA: Anguish? (*Holding her.*) But when did he arrive? Tell me. You weren't expecting him.

MARÍA: No, I wasn't expecting him.

YERMA: You might have been singing; isn't that so? I sing. You . . . tell me . . .

MARÍA: Don't ask me. Have you never held a live bird pressed in your hand?

YERMA: Yes.

MARÍA: Well, it's the same—but more within the blood.

YERMA: How beautiful! (*Looks at her, beside herself.*)

MARÍA: I'm confused. I don't know anything.

YERMA: About what?

MARÍA: About what I must do. I shall ask my mother.

YERMA: What for? She's old and may have forgotten these things. Don't walk very much, and when you breathe, breathe as softly as if you had a rose between your teeth.

MARÍA: You know, they say that later he kicks you softly with his little legs.

YERMA: And then is when one loves him best, when one already says: "My child!"

MARÍA: In the midst of it all, I'm ashamed.

YERMA: What did your husband say?

MARÍA: Nothing.

YERMA: Does he love you very much?

MARÍA: He doesn't tell me, but when he comes near me his eyes tremble like two green leaves.

YERMA: Did he know that you . . . ?

MARÍA: Yes.

YERMA: And how did he know?

MARÍA: I don't know. But the night we married he spoke of it constantly with his mouth pressed against my cheek; so much so that now it seems to me my child is a dove of fire he made slip in through my ear.

YERMA (*With joy*): Ah, yes!

MARÍA: But you know more about these things than I.

YERMA: What good does it do me?

MARÍA: That's true! Why should it be so? Of all the brides of your time you are the only one . . .

YERMA: That's the way it is. Of course, there's still time. Helena was three years, and long ago some in my mother's time were much longer, but two years and twenty days—like me—is too long to wait. I don't think it's right for me to burn myself out here. Many nights I go out barefooted to the patio to walk on the ground. I don't know why. If I keep on like this, I'll end by becoming bad.

MARÍA: But come now, you child. You speak as if you were an old woman. What am I saying? No one can complain of these things. A sister of my mother's had one after fourteen years. And you should have seen what a beauty of a child!

YERMA (*With eagerness*): What would he do?

MABÍA: Bellow like a little bull with the force of a thousand locusts buzzing at once, and wet us, and pull our braids, and when he was four months old scratch our faces all up.

YERMA: But those things don't hurt.

MARÍA: Let me tell you . . .

YERMA: Bah! I've seen my sister feed her child with her breast full of very painful wounds, and it hurt her, but that was a fresh pain—good, and necessary for the health.

MARÍA: They say one suffers a lot with children.

YERMA: That's not true. It's what weak, complaining mothers say. What do they have them for? Having a child is not a bouquet of roses. We must suffer to see them grow. I sometimes think half our blood must go. But that is good, healthy, beautiful. Every woman has blood for four or five children, and when she doesn't have them it turns into poison . . . as it will in me.

Yerma

MARÍA: I don't know how I feel.

YERMA: I've always heard say that the first time one is frightened.

MARÍA (*Timidly*): We'll see. And since you sew so well . . .

YERMA (*Taking the bundle*): Give that to me. I'll cut you two little gowns. And this . . . ?

MARÍA: For the diapers.

YERMA: Very well. (*Sits.*)

MARÍA: Good-bye, then.

(*As she comes near, Yerma lovingly presses her hands against her belly.*)

YERMA: Don't run on the cobble streets.

MARÍA: Good-bye. (*She kisses her and leaves.*)

YERMA: Come back soon. (*Yerma is in the same attitude as at the beginning. She takes scissors and starts to cut. Victor enters.*) Victor. Good-bye. (*To María.*)

VICTOR (*He is deep looking and has a firm gravity about him*): And Juan?

YERMA: In the field.

VICTOR: What are you sewing?

YERMA: I'm cutting some diapers.

VICTOR (*Smiling*): Come now!

YERMA (*Laughs*): I'm going to border them with lace.

VICTOR: If it's a girl, give her your name.

YERMA (*Trembling*): What?

VICTOR: I'm happy for you.

YERMA (*Almost choking*): No, they aren't for me. They're for María's child.

VICTOR: Well. Let's see if her example will encourage you. A child is needed in this house.

YERMA (*With anguish*): Needed!

VICTOR: Well, forward. Tell your husband to think less of work. He wants to make money and he will, but to whom is he going to leave it when he dies? I'm going to watch the sheep. Tell Juan to take out the two he bought from me. And about this other—try harder! (*He leaves, smiling.*)

YERMA: That's it! Try . . .!
>I shall say to you, child, yes,
>for you I'll torn and broken be.
>How painful is this belly now,
>where first you shall be cradled!
>When, boy, when will you come to me?

(*Pause.*)
>"When sweet your flesh of jasmin smells."
>Let mighty branches rake the sun
>And teeming fountains leap all around!

(*Yerma, who has risen thoughtfully, goes to the place where Victor stood, and breathes deep as one who breathes mountain air. Then she goes to the other side of the room as if looking for something, and after that sits down and takes up the sewing again. She begins to sew. Her eyes remain fixed on one point.*)

CURTAIN

SCENE TWO

(*A field. Yerma enters carrying a basket. The First Old Woman enters.*)

YERMA: Good morning!

FIRST OLD WOMAN: Good morning to a beautiful girl! Where are you going?

YERMA: I'm coming from taking dinner to my husband who works in the olive groves.

FIRST OLD WOMAN: Have you been married long?

YERMA: Three years.

Yerma

FIRST OLD WOMAN: Have you any children?

YERMA: No.

FIRST OLD WOMAN: Bah! You'll have them!

YERMA (*Eagerly*): Do you think so?

FIRST OLD WOMAN: Why not? (*Sits down.*) I also come from taking my husband his food. He's old. He still has to work. I have nine children like nine suns but, since not one of them is a girl, here you have me going from one side to the other.

YERMA: You live at the other side of the river?

FIRST OLD WOMAN: Yes. In the mills. From what family are you?

YERMA: I'm the daughter of Enrique, the shepherd.

FIRST OLD WOMAN: Ah! Enrique the shepherd. I knew him. Good people. Get up, sweat, eat some bread and die. No playing, no nothing. The fairs for somebody else. Silent creatures. I could have married an uncle of yours. But, then . . .! I've been a woman with her skirts to the wind. I have run like an arrow to melon cuttings, to parties, to sugar cakes. Many times at dawn I have stood in the doorway thinking I heard the music of a band going along and coming near, but it was only the wind. (*Laughs.*) You're going to laugh at me. I've had two husbands, fourteen children—five of them dead—and yet I'm not sad, and I would like to live much longer. That's what I say! The fig trees, how they last! The houses, how they last! And only we poor bedeviled women turn to dust for any reason.

YERMA: I'd like to ask you a question.

FIRST OLD WOMAN: Let's see. (*Looks at her.*) I know what you're going to say. About those things one can't say a word. (*She rises.*)

YERMA (*Holding her*): Why not? Hearing you talk has given me confidence. For some time I've been wanting to talk to an older woman—because I want to find out. Yes. You can tell me . . .

FIRST OLD WOMAN: What?

YERMA (*Lowering her voice*): What you already know. Why am I barren? In the prime of my life shall I merely have to take care of birds, or iron little curtains to hang at my windows? No. You must tell me what I have to do, because I'll do anything, even if you should send me to stick needles in the weakest part of my eyes.

FIRST OLD WOMAN: Me? I don't know anything. I lie down face up and begin to sing. Children come like water. Oh, who can say that your body is not beautiful? You take a step and at the end of the street a horse whinnys. Ay! Leave me, girl; don't let me speak. I think a lot of things which I don't want to say.

YERMA: Why? I don't talk of anything else with my husband.

FIRST OLD WOMAN: Listen. Does your husband please you?

YERMA: What?

FIRST OLD WOMAN: Do you love him? Do you want to be with him?

YERMA: I don't know.

FIRST OLD WOMAN: Don't you tremble when he comes near you? Don't you feel something like a dream when he puts his lips near yours? Tell me.

YERMA: No. No, I've never felt that.

FIRST OLD WOMAN: Never? Not even when you dance?

YERMA (*Remembering*): Perhaps. Once, Victor . . .

FIRST OLD WOMAN: Go on.

YERMA: He took me by the waist and I wasn't able to say anything to him because I couldn't speak. Another time this same Victor when I was fourteen years old—he was a shepherd then—took me in his arms to leap a ditch and I started trembling so that my teeth chattered. But it's just that I've always been shy.

FIRST OLD WOMAN: And with your husband . . .

Yerma

YERMA: My husband was something else. My father gave him to me and I accepted him. With happiness. That's the pure truth. Why, the first day I was engaged to him I already thought about our children, and I could see myself in his eyes. Yes, but it was to see myself reflected very small, very manageable, as if I were my own daughter.

FIRST OLD WOMAN: It was just the opposite with me. Maybe that's why you haven't had a child. Men must please us much, girl. They must unbraid our hair and give us water out of their own mouths. So runs the world.

YERMA: Your world, not mine. I think of many things. Many. And I'm sure that the things I think about will come true in my son. I gave myself to my husband because of him. And I go on giving to see if he will be born—but never just for pleasure.

FIRST OLD WOMAN: And the result is that you are empty!

YERMA: No, not empty, because I am filling with hate. Tell me; is it my fault? Is it necessary to want in a man only the man? Then, what are you going to think when you lie in bed looking at the ceiling with sad eyes and he turns and goes to sleep? Should I go on thinking of him or of what can come shining out of my breast? I don't know; but you tell me. Out of charity! (*She kneels.*)

FIRST OLD WOMAN: Oh, what an open flower! What a beautiful creature you are. Leave me. Don't make me say any more. I don't want to talk to you any more. These are matters of honor. And I don't burn any one's honor. You'll know. But anyway you should be less innocent.

YERMA (*Sadly*): Girls like me who grow up in the fields have all doors closed to them. Everything becomes half-words, gestures, because they all say that these things must not be known. And you, too; you, too, are silent and leave with the air of a doctor—knowing everything, but denying it to one who dies of thirst.

FIRST OLD WOMAN: To a calmer woman, I could speak, but not to you. I am an old woman and I know what I am saying.

YERMA: Then, may God help me.

FIRST OLD WOMAN: Not God; I have never liked God. When will you realize he doesn't exist? It's men who'll have to help you.

YERMA: But, why do you tell me that, why?

FIRST OLD WOMAN (*Leaving*): Although there should be a God, even a tiny one, to send his lightning against those men of rotted seed who make puddles out of the happiness of the fields.

YERMA: I don't know what you're trying to tell me.

FIRST OLD WOMAN: Well, I know. Don't be unhappy. Be firm, and wait. You're still very young. What do you want me to do? (*She leaves.*)

(*Two girls appear.*)

FIRST GIRL: Everywhere we go we meet people.

YERMA: With all the work, the men have to be in the olive groves, and we must take them their food. No one's left at home but the old people.

SECOND GIRL: Are you returning to the village?

YERMA: I'm going toward there.

FIRST GIRL: I'm in a great hurry. I left my baby asleep and there is no one at home.

YERMA: Then hurry, woman. Babies can't be left alone. Are there any pigs in your house?

FIRST GIRL: No. But you're right. I must hurry.

YERMA: Go on. That's how things happen. You have probably locked him in.

FIRST GIRL: Naturally.

YERMA: Yes, but you don't realize how tiny a child is. The thing that seems most harmless to you might finish him off. A needle. A drink of water.

FIRST GIRL: You're right. I must run. I just don't think of those things.

YERMA: Hurry.

SECOND GIRL: If you had four or five, you wouldn't talk like that.

YERMA: Why not? Even if I had forty.

SECOND GIRL: Anyway, you and I, not having any, live more calmly.

YERMA: Not I.

SECOND GIRL: I do. What a bother! My mother, on the other hand, does nothing but give me herbs so that I may have them, and in October we shall go to the saint who is said to give them to women who ask for them eagerly. My mother will ask for them. Not I.

YERMA: Then, why did you marry?

SECOND GIRL: Because they made me marry. We all get married. If we keep on like this, the only unmarried ones will be the little girls. Well, and furthermore . . . one marries in reality long before she goes to the church. But old women keep worrying about all these things. I'm nineteen and I don't like to cook or wash. Well, all day I have to be doing what I don't like. And for what? What need does my husband have of being my husband? As sweethearts, we used to do the same things we do now. Just old people's foolishness.

YERMA: Be quiet; don't say those things.

SECOND GIRL: You'll call me wild, too. The wild one, the wild one! (*Laughs.*) I can tell you the only thing I've learned in life: all people are stuck inside their houses doing what they don't like to do. How much better it is in the middle of the street. Now I go to the stream, now I climb up to ring the bells, now I take a drink of wine.

YERMA: You're a child.

SECOND GIRL: Yes, but I'm not crazy (*Laughs.*)

YERMA: Your mother lives at the tallest door in the village?

SECOND GIRL: Yes.

YERMA: In the last house?

SECOND GIRL: Yes.

YERMA: What is her name?

SECOND GIRL: Dolores. Why do you ask?

YERMA: No reason.

SECOND GIRL: Could you have some reason?

YERMA: I don't know . . . there's a saying . . .

SECOND GIRL: Well, that's up to you. Look, I'm going to take my husband his food. (*Laughs.*) Look at that. It's too bad I can't say my sweetheart, isn't it? (*Laughs.*) Now the wild girl's going! (*Leaves, laughing happily.*) Good-bye!

> VICTOR'S VOICE (*Singing*):
> Why, shepherd, sleep alone?
> Why, shepherd, sleep alone?
> On my wool-quilt deep
> you'd finer sleep.
> Why, shepherd, sleep alone?
>
> YERMA (*Listening*):
> Why, shepherd, sleep alone?
> On my wool-quilt deep
> you'd finer sleep.
> Your quilt of shadowed stone,
> shepherd,
> and your shirt of frost,
> shepherd,
> gray rushes of the winter
> on the night-tide of your bed.
> The oak-roots weave their needles,
> shepherd,
> Beneath your pillow silently,
> shepherd,
> sleepless, haunted by a woman's voice,

> know it was the stream that sighed.
> Shepherd, shepherd.
> What does the hillside want of you,
> Shepherd?
> Hillside of bitter weeds
> what lad is killing you?
> A thorn the broom-tree bore!

(*She starts to leave and meets Victor as he enters.*)

VICTOR (*Happily*): Where is all this beauty going?

YERMA: Was it you singing?

VICTOR: I.

YERMA: How well you sing! I had never heard you.

VICTOR: No?

YERMA: And what a vibrant voice! It's like a stream of water that fills all your mouth.

VICTOR: I'm happy.

YERMA: That's true.

VICTOR: Just as you are sad.

YERMA: I'm not usually sad. It's just that I have reasons for being that way.

VICTOR: And your husband's sadder than you.

YERMA: He, yes. He is a dry sort.

VICTOR: He was always the same. (*Pause. Yerma is seated.*) Did you come to bring his supper?

YERMA: Yes. (*Looks at him. Pause.*) What have you here? (*Points to his face.*)

VICTOR: Where?

YERMA (*Rises and stands near Victor*): Here . . . on your cheek. Like a burn.

VICTOR: It isn't anything.

YERMA: I thought it was. (*Pause.*)

VICTOR: It must be the sun . . .

YERMA: Perhaps . . . (*Pause. The silence is accentuated and without the slightest gesture, a struggle between the two begins.*)

YERMA (*Trembling*): Do you hear?

VICTOR: What?

YERMA: Don't you hear a crying?

VICTOR (*Listening*): No.

YERMA: I thought I heard a child crying.

VICTOR: Yes?

YERMA: Very near. And he cried as though drowning.

VICTOR: There are always a lot of children around here who come to steal fruit.

YERMA: No, it's the voice of a small child. (*Pause.*)

VICTOR: I don't hear anything.

YERMA: I probably just imagined it.

(*She looks at him fixedly. Victor also looks at her, then slowly shifts his gaze as if afraid. Juan enters.*)

JUAN: Still here? What are you doing?

YERMA: I was talking.

VICTOR: Good health to you! (*He leaves.*)

JUAN: You should be at home.

YERMA: I was delayed.

JUAN: I don't understand what has kept you.

YERMA: I heard the birds sing.

JUAN: That's all very well. But this way you'll give people something to talk about.

YERMA (*Strongly*): Juan, what are you thinking?

JUAN: I don't say it because of you. I say it because of other people.

YERMA: Other people be damned!

JUAN: Don't curse. That's ugly in a woman.

YERMA: I wish I were a woman.

JUAN: Let's stop talking. Go on home. (*Pause.*)

YERMA: Very well. Shall I expect you?

JUAN: No. I'll be out all night with the irrigating. There's very little water; it's mine until the sun rises, and I have to defend it against thieves. You go to bed and sleep.

YERMA (*Dramatically*): I'll sleep! (*Leaves.*)

END OF FIRST ACT

ACT TWO

SCENE ONE

(*Song before the curtain.*)

SONG:
>In the icy current
>I wash your lace,
>like a jasmine glowing
>is your laughing face.

(*A stream where the village women wash their clothes. The laundresses are at various heights.*)

FIRST LAUNDRESS: I don't like to talk.
SECOND LAUNDRESS: Well, we talk here.
FOURTH LAUNDRESS: And there's no bad in it.
FIFTH LAUNDRESS: Whoever wants a good name, let her earn it.
FOURTH LAUNDRESS (*Sings*):
>I planted thyme,
>it grew up fine.
>Who longs for honor
>must hew the line.

(*They laugh.*)

FIFTH LAUNDRESS: That's how we talk.
FIRST LAUNDRESS: But really we never know anything.
FOURTH LAUNDRESS: What is true is that the husband has taken his two sisters to live with him.
FIFTH LAUNDRESS: The spinsters?
FOURTH LAUNDRESS: Yes. They used to watch the church, and now they watch their sister-in-law. I couldn't live with them.
FIRST LAUNDRESS: Why?

Yerma

FOURTH LAUNDRESS: Because they give me the creeps. They're like those big leaves that suddenly spring up on graves. They're covered with wax. They grow inwards. I imagine they fry their food with lamp oil.

THIRD LAUNDRESS: And they're already at the house?

FOURTH LAUNDRESS: Since yesterday. The husband is going back to the fields.

FIRST LAUNDRESS: But, does any one know what happened?

FIFTH LAUNDRESS: Night before last, she spent all night sitting on her doorstep—in spite of the cold.

FIRST LAUNDRESS: But why?

FOURTH LAUNDRESS: It's hard work for her to stay at home.

FIFTH LAUNDRESS: These mannish creatures are like that. When they should be making laces, or apple cakes, they like to climb the roof, or wade barefoot in the river.

FIRST LAUNDRESS: Who are you to say those things? She doesn't have any children, but that's not her fault.

FOURTH LAUNDRESS: The one who wants children has them. The spoiled ones, the lazy ones, the soft ones, aren't made to have a wrinkled belly.

(*They laugh.*)

THIRD LAUNDRESS: And they put on face powder and rouge, and pin on branches of rosebay, looking for some other man who is not their husband.

FIFTH LAUNDRESS: Nothing could be truer!

FIRST LAUNDRESS: But have you seen her with anybody?

FOURTH LAUNDRESS: We haven't, but other people have.

FIRST LAUNDRESS: Always other people!

FIFTH LAUNDRESS: Twice, they say.

SECOND LAUNDRESS: And what were they doing?

FOURTH LAUNDRESS: Talking.

FIRST LAUNDRESS: Talking isn't a sin.

FOURTH LAUNDRESS: In this world just a glance can be something. My mother always said that. A woman looking at roses isn't the same as a woman looking at a man's thighs. And she looks at him.

FIRST LAUNDRESS: But whom?

FOURTH LAUNDRESS: Some one. Don't you hear? You find out. Do you want me to say it louder? (*Laughter.*) And when she doesn't look at him—because she's alone, because he's not with her—his image is in her eyes.

FIRST LAUNDRESS: That's a lie.

(*Excitement.*)

FIFTH LAUNDRESS: And the husband?

THIRD LAUNDRESS: Her husband is like a deaf man. Standing—like a lizard in the sun.

(*Laughter.*)

FIRST LAUNDRESS: All this would take care of itself if they had children.

SECOND LAUNDRESS: All this comes of people not being contented with their lot.

FOURTH LAUNDRESS: Every hour that passes, the hell in that house increases. She and her sisters-in-law, without opening their lips, scrub the walls all day, polish the copper, clean the windows with steam, and oil the floor: but the more that house shines, the more it seethes inside.

FIRST LAUNDRESS: It's all his fault; his. When a father doesn't give children, he should look after his wife.

FOURTH LAUNDRESS: The fault is hers because she has a rock quarry for a tongue.

FIRST LAUNDRESS: What devil has got into your hair that you should talk like that?

FOURTH LAUNDRESS: And who has given your mouth leave to give me advice?

SECOND LAUNDRESS: Silence!

Yerma

FIRST LAUNDRESS: I'd take a knitting needle and run it through all gossiping tongues.

SECOND LAUNDRESS: Hush!

FOURTH LAUNDRESS: And I the breasts of hypocrites.

SECOND LAUNDRESS: Silence! Don't you see that here come the sisters-in-law?

(*Whispering. Yerma's two sisters-in-law enter. They are in mourning. They start washing in the midst of silence. Sheep bells are heard.*)

FIRST LAUNDRESS: Are the shepherds leaving already?

THIRD LAUNDRESS: Yes, all the flocks leave today.

FOURTH LAUNDRESS (*Breathing*): I like the smell of sheep.

THIRD LAUNDRESS: Yes?

FOURTH LAUNDRESS: And why not? The odor of what one has for his own. Just as I like the odor of the red mud the river carries in winter.

THIRD LAUNDRESS: Whims!

FIFTH LAUNDRESS (*Looking*): All the flocks are together.

FOURTH LAUNDRESS: It's a flood of wool. They carry everything before them. If the green wheat had eyes it would tremble to see them coming.

THIRD LAUNDRESS: Look how they run! What a band of devils!

FIRST LAUNDRESS: They're all out now, no flock is missing.

FOURTH LAUNDRESS: Let's see. No. Yes, yes. One is missing.

FIFTH LAUNDRESS: Which one?

FOURTH LAUNDRESS: Victor's.

(*The two Sisters-in-law sit up and look at each other.*)

FOURTH LAUNDRESS (*Sings*):

In the icy current
I wash your lace.
Like a jasmin glowing
is your laughing face.
Now let me live

in the tiny snowstorm
that jasmins give.

FIRST LAUNDRESS:

Alas for the barren wife:
For her whose breasts hold only sand!

FIFTH LAUNDRESS:

Tell me if your husband
has fertile seed
so water through your clothes
will sing indeed.

FOURTH LAUNDRESS:

Your petticoat to me
is silvery boat and breeze
that sweep along the sea.

FIRST LAUNDRESS:

I wash my baby's clothes
in water of the stream
that he may learn to know
clear water's crystal gleam.

SECOND LAUNDRESS:

Down the hillside he comes
At lunchtime to me,
my husband with *one* rose
and I to him give three.

FIFTH LAUNDRESS:

Through the meadows at dusk comes
my husband to eat.
The live-coals he brings me
I cover with myrtle sweet.

FOURTH LAUNDRESS:

Through the night skies he comes,
my husband, to bed.
He like red rosebays
and I rosebay red.

FIRST LAUNDRESS:
But flower to flower one must wed
when summer dries the reaper's blood so red.

FOURTH LAUNDRESS:
And open one's womb to birds without sleep
when winter tries the door and cold's to keep.

FIRST LAUNDRESS:
The bedclothes must receive our tears.

FOURTH LAUNDRESS:
But we must sing in bed!

FIFTH LAUNDRESS:
When a faithful husband nears
to bring the wreath and bread.

FOURTH LAUNDRESS:
Because our arms must intertwine.

SECOND LAUNDRESS:
Because in our throats the light is rent.

FOURTH LAUNDRESS:
Because the leaf-stem becomes fine,

FIRST LAUNDRESS:
And the hill is covered with a breeze's tent.

SIXTH LAUNDRESS (*Appearing at the highest part of the stream*):
So that a tiny child may weld
great shards for dawn to see.

FIRST LAUNDRESS:
And our bodies then may hold
torn stems of coral tree.

SIXTH LAUNDRESS:
And there'll be no lack of oarsmen bold
in waters of the sea.

FIRST LAUNDRESS:
A tiny child, one.

SECOND LAUNDRESS:
And when the doves stretch wing and beak
THIRD LAUNDRESS:
an infant weeps, a son.
FOURTH LAUNDRESS:
And men like deer advance,
who, wounded, shelter seek.
FIFTH LAUNDRESS:
Joy! joy, joy!
of swollen womb beneath the dress!
SECOND LAUNDRESS:
Joy, joy, joy!
The waist can miracles possess!
FIRST LAUNDRESS:
Alas for the barren wife!
For her whose breasts hold only sand!
THIRD LAUNDRESS:
Let her work for her pain!
FOURTH LAUNDRESS:
Let her run!
FIFTH LAUNDRESS:
Let her work once again!
FIRST LAUNDRESS:
Let her sing!
SECOND LAUNDRESS:
Let her hide!
FIRST LAUNDRESS:
Sing again for the peace it will bring.
SECOND LAUNDRESS:
Let her sing of the dawn that my boy
sends in his clothes to the spring.
FIRST AND SECOND LAUNDRESS (*They sing together*):
In the icy current
I wash your lace.

> Like a jasmin glowing
> is your laughing face.
> Ha! ha! ha!

(*They move the clothes in rhythm and beat them.*)

CURTAIN

SCENE TWO

(*Yerma's house. It is twilight. Juan is seated. The two Sisters-in-law are standing.*)

JUAN: You say she went out a short while ago? (*The Older sister answers with a nod.*) She must be at the fountain. But you know I don't like her to go out alone. (*Pause.*) You can set the table. (*Younger sister enters.*) The bread I eat is hard enough earned! (*To his sister.*) I had a hard day yesterday. I was pruning the apple trees, and when evening fell I began to wonder why I should be working so much when I could not even put an apple in my mouth. I'm tired. (*Passes his hand over his face. Pause.*) She doesn't come. One of you ought to go out with her always, because that's why you're here eating at my table and drinking my wine. My life is in the fields, but my honor is here. And my honor is yours too. (*The Sister bows her head.*) Don't take that the wrong way. (*Yerma enters carrying two pitchers. She stands at the door.*) Have you been to the fountain?

YERMA: So that we should have fresh water for supper. (*Other Sister enters.*) How are the fields?

JUAN: Yesterday I pruned the trees. (*Yerma sets down the pitchers. Pause.*)

YERMA: Will you stay here?

JUAN: I have to watch the flocks. You know that's an owner's duty.

YERMA: I know it very well. Don't repeat it.

JUAN: Each man has his life to lead.

YERMA: And each woman hers. I'm not asking you to stay. I have everything I need here. Your sisters guard me well. Soft bread and cheese and roast lamb I eat here, and in the field your cattle eat grass softened with dew. I think you can live in peace.

JUAN: In order to live in peace one must be at ease.

YERMA: And you are not?

JUAN: No I am not.

YERMA: Don't say what you were going to.

JUAN: Don't you know my way of thinking? The sheep in the fold and women at home. You go out too much. Haven't you always heard me say that?

YERMA: Justly. Women in their homes. When those homes are not tombs. When the chairs break and the linen sheets wear out with use. But not here. Each night, when I go to bed, I find my bed newer, more shining, as if it had recently been brought from the city.

JUAN: You yourself realize that I have reason to complain. That I have reason to be on the alert!

YERMA: Alert? For what? I don't offend you in any way. I live obedient to you, and what I suffer I keep close in my flesh. And every day that passes will be worse. Let's be quiet now. I'll learn how to bear my cross as best I can, but don't ask me anything. If I could suddenly turn into an old woman and have a mouth like a withered flower, I could smile and share my life with you. But now, now leave me with my thorns.

JUAN: You speak in a way I don't understand. I don't deprive you of anything. I send to nearby towns for the things you like. I have my faults, but I want peace and quiet with you. I want to be sleeping outside, thinking that you are sleeping too.

YERMA: But I don't sleep. I can't sleep.

JUAN: Is it because you need something? Tell me. Answer me!

YERMA (*Deliberately, looking fixedly at her husband*): Yes, I need something. (*Pause.*)

JUAN: Always the same thing. It's more than five years. I am almost forgetting about it.

YERMA: But I'm not you. Men get other things out of life: their cattle, the trees, their conversations, but women have only their children and the care of their children.

JUAN: All the world is not the same. Why don't you bring one of your brother's children here? I do not oppose that.

YERMA: I don't want to take care of the children of others. I think my arms would freeze from holding them.

JUAN: You brood on this one idea until you're half crazy—instead of thinking about other things—and you're determined to push your head into a stone.

YERMA: A stone, yes, and it's an infamy that it should be one, because it ought to be a basket of flowers and sweet scents.

JUAN: At your side one feels nothing but uneasiness, dissatisfaction. As a last resort you should resign yourself.

YERMA: I have come to these four walls determined not to resign myself. When a cloth binds my head so that my mouth will not drop open, and my hands are tight tied within the coffin, in that hour I will have resigned myself.

JUAN: Then, what do you want to do?

YERMA: I want to drink water and there's neither water nor a glass. I want to climb the hill and I have no feet. I want to embroider my skirts and I cannot find a thread.

JUAN: What's happening is that you're not a real woman and you're looking to ruin a man whose will is weak.

YERMA: I don't know who I am. Let me move about; get myself in hand again. I have in no way failed you.

JUAN: I don't like people to point me out. That's why I want to see this door closed and each person in his house.

(*The First Sister enters slowly and walks towards some shelves.*)

YERMA: Speaking with people is not a sin.

JUAN: But it may seem one.

(*The other Sister enters and goes towards the water jars, from one of which she fills a pitcher.*)

JUAN (*Lowering his voice*): I don't have the strength for these things. When you are offered conversation close your mouth and remember that you are a married woman.

YERMA (*With surprise*): Married!

JUAN: And that families have honor. And that honor is a burden that rests on all. (*The Sister leaves slowly with the pitcher.*) But that it is both dark and weak in the same channels of the blood. (*The other Sister leaves with a platter in almost a processional manner. Pause.*) Forgive me. (*Yerma looks at her husband. He raises his head and his glance catches hers.*) Even though you look at me so that I ought not to say to you: "Forgive me," but force you to obey me, lock you up, because that's what I'm the husband for.

(*The two Sisters appear at the door.*)

YERMA: I beg you not to speak. Let the matter rest.

JUAN: Let's go eat.

(*The two Sisters leave.*)

JUAN: Do you hear me?

YERMA (*Sweetly*): You eat with your sisters. I'm not hungry yet.

JUAN: As you wish. (*Leaves.*)

> YERMA (*As though dreaming*):
> Oh, what a field of sorrow!
> Oh, this is a door to beauty closed:
> to beg a son to suffer, and for the wind

>   to offer dahlias of a sleeping moon!
>   These two teeming springs I have
>   of warm milk are in the closeness
>   of my flesh two rhythms of a horse's gallop
>   to make vibrate the branch of my anguish.
>   Oh, breasts, blind beneath my clothes!
>   Oh, doves with neither eyes nor whiteness!
>   Oh, what pain of imprisoned blood
>   is nailing wasps at my brain's base!
>   But you must come, sweet love, my baby,
>   because water gives salt, the earth fruit,
>   and our womb guards tender infants,
>   just as a cloud is sweet with rain.

YERMA (*Looks toward the door*): María! Why do you hurry so past my door?

MARÍA (*Enters with a child in her arms*): I hurry by whenever I have the child—since you always weep!

YERMA: Yes, you are right. (*Takes child and sits down.*)

MARÍA: It makes me sad that you should be envious.

YERMA: It's not envy; it's poverty.

MARÍA: Don't complain.

YERMA: How am I not going to complain when I see you and the other women full of flowers from within, and me useless in the middle of so much beauty!

MARÍA: But you have other things. If you would listen to me you could be happy.

YERMA: A field woman who bears no children is as useless as a handful of thorns, and even bad—even though I may be a part of that waste abandoned by the hand of God. (*María makes a gesture as if to take the child.*) Take him; he's more content with you. I must not have the hands of a mother.

MARÍA: Why do you tell me that?

YERMA (*Rises*): Because I'm tired. Because I'm tired of having them and not being able to use them on something of my own. For I am offended, offended and humiliated to the last degree, seeing the wheat ripening, the fountains never ceasing to give water, the sheep bearing hundreds of lambs, the she-dogs; until it seems that the whole countryside rises to show me its tender sleeping young while I feel two hammer-blows here, instead of the mouth of my child.

MARÍA: I don't like what you're saying.

YERMA: You women who have children can't think about us who don't! You stay always fresh, ignorant, just as any one swimming in fresh water has no idea of thirst.

MARÍA: I don't want to tell you what I've always said.

YERMA: Each time I have more desire and less hope.

MARÍA: That's evil.

YERMA: I shall end by thinking that I am my own son. Many nights I go down to feed the oxen,—which I never did before, because no woman does it, and when I pass through the darkness of the shed my footsteps sound to me like the footsteps of a man.

MARÍA: Each one of us reasons things out for himself.

YERMA: And in spite of all, I go on loving myself. You see how I live!

MARÍA: And your sisters-in-law?

YERMA: Dead may I be, and without a shroud, if ever I speak a word to them.

MARÍA: And your husband?

YERMA: They are three against me.

MARÍA: What do they think?

YERMA: Fantastic things. Like all people who don't have a clear conscience. They think I may like another man, and they don't know that even if I should like another, to those of my caste honor comes first. They are stones in front of me. But they don't know that I, if I want to, can be a stream of water to carry them along before me.

(*One Sister enters and leaves carrying a piece of bread.*)

Yerma

MARÍA: Even so, I think your husband still loves you.

YERMA: My husband gives me bread and a house.

MARÍA: What troubles you have to go through! What troubles! But remember the wounds of Our Lord.

(*They are at the door.*)

YERMA (*Looking at the child*): He's awake.

MARÍA: In a little while he'll begin to sing.

YERMA: The same eyes as you. Did you know that? Have you noticed them? (*Weeping.*) He has the same eyes that you do! (*Yerma pushes María gently and she leaves silently. Yerma walks toward the door through which her husband left.*)

SECOND GIRL: Sst!

YERMA (*Turning*): What?

SECOND GIRL: I waited until she left. My mother is expecting you.

YERMA: Is she alone?

SECOND GIRL: With two neighbors.

YERMA: Tell them to wait a little.

SECOND GIRL: But are you going? Aren't you afraid?

YERMA: I'm going.

SECOND GIRL: That's up to you!

YERMA: Wait for me even if it's late!

(*Victor enters.*)

VICTOR: Is Juan here?

YERMA: Yes.

SECOND GIRL (*Acting the accomplice*): Well then, I'll bring the blouse later.

YERMA: Whenever you like.

(*The Girl leaves.*)
    Sit down.

VICTOR: I'm all right.

YERMA: (*Calling*): Juan!

VICTOR: I have come to say good-bye. (*He trembles a little, but his composure returns.*)

YERMA: Are you going with your brother?

VICTOR: That's what my father wants.

YERMA: He must be old now.

VICTOR: Yes. Very old. (*Pause.*)

YERMA: You're right to change fields.

VICTOR: All fields are alike.

YERMA: No. I'd like to go far away.

VICTOR: It's all the same. The same sheep have the same wool.

YERMA: For men, yes; but it's a different thing with women. I never heard a man eating say "How good these apples are!" You go to what is yours without bothering over trifles. But for myself, I can say I have grown to hate the water from these wells.

VICTOR: That may be.

(*The stage is in a soft shadow.*)

YERMA: Victor.

VICTOR: Yes?

YERMA: Why are you going? The people here like you.

VICTOR: I have always behaved myself.

YERMA: You have always behaved well. When you were a boy, you carried me once in your arms. Don't you remember? One never knows what is going to happen.

VICTOR: Everything changes.

YERMA: Some things never change. There are things shut up behind walls that cannot change because nobody hears them.

VICTOR: That's how it is.

(*The Second Sister appears and goes slowly towards the door, where she remains fixed, illuminated by the last light of evening.*)

YERMA: But if they should suddenly come out and shout, they would fill the world.

VICTOR: There would be nothing gained by that. The ditch in its place, the sheep in the fold, the moon in the sky, and the man with his plow.

YERMA: What a great pity, not to be able to feel the teaching of the old ones!

(*The long and melancholy sound of the shepherds' conchshell horns is heard.*)

VICTOR: The flocks.

JUAN (*Enters*): Are you on your way?

VICTOR: I want to get through the pass before daybreak.

JUAN: Have you any complaint against me?

VICTOR: No. You were always a good payer.

JUAN (*To Yerma*): I bought his flocks.

YERMA: Yes?

VICTOR (*To Yerma*): They're yours.

YERMA: I didn't know that.

JUAN (*Satisfied*): It's so.

VICTOR: Your husband will see his lands overflowing.

YERMA: The harvest comes to the worker who seeks it.

(*The Sister at the door leaves.*)

JUAN: We no longer have room for so many sheep.

YERMA (*Darkly*): The earth is large. (*Pause.*)

JUAN: We'll go together to the river.

VICTOR: I wish the greatest happiness for this house. (*Gives Yerma his hand.*)

YERMA: May God hear you! Good luck!

(*Victor is about to leave, but, at an imperceptible movement from Yerma, turns.*)

VICTOR: Did you say something?

YERMA: Luck, I said.

VICTOR: Thank you.

(*They leave. Yerma stands, anguished, looking at her hand that she gave to Victor. She goes quickly to the left and takes up a shawl.*)

SECOND GIRL (*Silently, covering her head*): Come.

YERMA: Come.

(*They leave cautiously. The stage is almost in darkness. The First Sister enters with a lamp that must not give the stage any light other than its own. She goes to one side of the stage looking for Yerma. The shepherds' conchshell horns sound.*)

SISTER-IN-LAW (*In a low voice*): Yerma!

(*The other Sister enters. They look at each other and go toward the door.*)

SECOND SISTER-IN-LAW (*Louder*): Yerma!

FIRST SISTER-IN-LAW (*Going to the door, and in an imperious voice*): Yerma!

(*The bells and horns of the shepherds are heard. The stage is quite dark.*)

END OF ACT TWO

ACT THREE

SCENE ONE

(The house of Dolores, the sorceress. Day is breaking. Enter Yerma with Dolores and two Old Women.)

DOLORES: You have been brave.

FIRST OLD WOMAN: There is no force in the world like desire.

SECOND OLD WOMAN: But the cemetery was terribly dark.

DOLORES: Many times I have said these prayers in the cemetery with women who wanted to have a child, and they have all been afraid. All except you.

YERMA: I came because I want a child. I believe you aren't a deceitful woman.

DOLORES: I am not. May my mouth fill with ants, as do the mouths of the dead, if I have ever lied. The last time, I said a prayer with a beggar woman who had been drier than you, and for a longer time, and her womb sweetened in such a beautiful manner that she had two children there below at the river because she didn't have time to reach the house, and she carried them herself in a diaper for me to take care of them.

YERMA: And was she able to walk from the river?

DOLORES: She came with her skirts and shoes drenched with blood but her face shining.

YERMA: And nothing happened to her?

DOLORES: What could happen to her? God is God.

YERMA: Naturally, God is God. Nothing could happen to her. She had only to take up the children and wash them in pure water. Animals lick them, don't they? A child of mine would cause me no repulsion. I have an idea that women who have recently given birth are as though illumined from within and the children sleep hours and hours on them, hearing the stream of warm milk that is filling the breasts for them to suckle, for them to play in until they don't want any more, until they lift their heads "a little more, child . . ."—and their faces and chests are covered with white drops.

DOLORES: Now you'll have a child. I can assure you.

YERMA: I will have one because I must. Or else I don't understand the world. Sometimes, when I'm certain that I'll never, never . . . a tide of fire sweeps up through me from my feet and everything seems empty. The men walking in the streets, the cattle, and the stones seem to be made of cotton. And I ask myself: "Why are they placed here?"

FIRST OLD WOMAN: It's all right for a married woman to want children, but if she doesn't have them, why this hungering for them? The important thing in this world is to let the years carry you along. I'm not criticizing you. You've seen how I have helped at the prayers. But what land do you expect to give your son, or what happiness, or what silver chair?

YERMA: I'm not thinking of tomorrow; I'm thinking of today. You are old and see everything like a book already read. I think that I am thirsty and have no liberty. I want to hold my son in my arms and so sleep peacefully. Listen well and don't be frightened at what I say: even if I knew that my son was later going to torture me and hate me and drag me by the hair through the streets, I would still receive his birth with joy, because it is much better to weep for a live man who stabs us than for this ghost sitting year after year upon my heart.

FIRST OLD WOMAN: You are much too young to listen to advice. But while you wait for God's grace, you ought to take refuge in your husband's love.

YERMA: Ah! You have put your finger in the deepest wound my flesh has.

Yerma

DOLORES: Your husband is a good man.

YERMA (*Rises*): He's good! He's good! But what else? I wish he were bad. But no. He goes out with his sheep over the trails, and counts his money at night. When he covers me, he's doing his duty, but I feel a cold waist as if he were dead, and I, who have always hated passionate women, would like to be in that instant a mountain of fire.

DOLORES: Yerma!

YERMA: I'm not a shameless married woman, but I know that children are born of a man and a woman. Oh, if I could have them myself alone!

DOLORES: Remember that your husband also suffers.

YERMA: He doesn't suffer. What happens is he's not anxious for children.

FIRST OLD WOMAN: Don't say that!

YERMA: I can tell that in his glance, and, since he doesn't want them, he doesn't give them to me. I don't love him; I don't love him, and yet he's my only salvation. By honor and by blood. My only salvation.

FIRST OLD WOMAN (*With fear*): Day will soon begin to break. You ought to go to your own house.

DOLORES: Before you know it, the flocks will be out, and it wouldn't do for you to be seen alone.

YERMA: I needed this relief. How many times do I repeat the prayers?

DOLORES: The laurel prayer, twice, and at noon, St. Anne's prayer. When you feel pregnant, bring me the bushel of wheat you promised me.

FIRST OLD WOMAN: It's beginning to lighten over the hills. Go.

DOLORES: They will soon start opening the gates; you'd best go around by the ditch.

YERMA (*Discouraged*): I don't know why I came!

DOLORES: Are you sorry?

YERMA: No!

DOLORES (*Disturbed*): If you're afraid, I'll go with you to the corner.

FIRST OLD WOMAN (*Uneasy*): It will be the first light of day when you reach home.

(*Voices are heard.*)

DOLORES: Quiet!

(*They listen.*)

FIRST OLD WOMAN: It's no one. God go with you.

(*Yerma starts toward the door, but at this moment a knock is heard. The three women are standing.*)

DOLORES: Who is it?

VOICE: It's me.

YERMA: Open the door. (*Dolores is reluctant.*) Will you open or not?

(*Whispering is heard. Juan enters with the two Sisters.*)

SECOND SISTER-IN-LAW: Here she is.

YERMA: Here I am.

JUAN: What are you doing in this place? If I could shout, I would awaken the whole village so they could see where my house's honor goes; but I have to swallow it all and be silent because you're my wife.

YERMA: If I could shout, I too would do it so that even the dead would rise to see the innocence that covers me.

JUAN: No, not that! I can bear everything except that. You deceive me; you trick me, and since I am a man who tills the fields, I am no match for your sharpness.

DOLORES: Juan!

JUAN: You, not a word out of you!

DOLORES (*Strongly*): Your wife has done nothing bad.

JUAN: She has been doing it from the very day of the wedding. Looking at me with two needles, passing wakeful nights with her eyes open at my side, and filling my pillows with evil sighs.

YERMA: Be quiet!

JUAN: And I can't bear any more. Because one would have to be made of bronze to put up with a woman who wants to stick her fingers in your heart and who goes out of her house at night. In search of what? Tell me! Looking for what? The streets are full of men. There are no flowers to pick in the streets.

YERMA: I won't allow you to say another word. Not another word more. You and your people imagine you are the only ones who look out for honor, and you don't know that my people have never had anything to conceal. Go on now. Come near and smell my clothes. Come near! See if you can find an odor that is not yours, that is not of your body. Stand me naked in the middle of the square and spit on me. Do what you want with me, since I'm your wife, but take care not to put a man's name on my breast.

JUAN: It's not I who put it there. You do it with your conduct, and the town is beginning to say so. It's beginning to say it openly. When I come on a group, they all fall silent; when I go to weigh the flour, they all fall silent, and even at night, in the fields, when I awaken it seems to me that the branches of the trees become silent too.

YERMA: I don't know why the evil winds that soil the wheat begin—but look you and see if the wheat is good!

JUAN: Nor do I know what a woman is looking for outside her house at all hours.

YERMA (*Bursting out, embracing her husband*): I'm looking for you. I'm looking for you. It's you I look for night and day without finding a shade where to draw breath. It's your blood and help that I want.

JUAN: Stay away from me.

YERMA: Don't put me away—love me!

JUAN: Get away!

YERMA: Look how I'm left alone! As if the moon searched for herself in the sky. Look at me! (*She looks at him.*)

JUAN (*Looks at her and draws away roughly*): Let me be once and for all!

DOLORES: Juan!

(*Yerma falls to the floor.*)

YERMA (*Loudly*): When I went out looking for my flowers, I ran into a wall. Ay! Ay! It's against that wall I'll break my head.

JUAN: Be quiet. Let's go.

DOLORES: Good Lord!

YERMA (*Shouting*): Cursed be my father who left me his blood of a father of a hundred sons. Cursed be my blood that searches for them knocking against walls.

JUAN: I told you to be quiet!

DOLORES: People are coming! Speak low.

YERMA: I don't care. At least let my voice go free, now that I'm entering the darkest part of the pit. (*She rises.*) At least let this beautiful thing come out of my body and fill the air.

(*Voices are heard.*)

DOLORES: They're going to pass by here.

JUAN: Silence.

YERMA: That's it! That's it! Silence. Never fear.

JUAN: Let's go. Quick!

YERMA: That's it! That's it! And it's no use for me to wring my hands! It's one thing to wish with one's head . . .

JUAN: Be still.

YERMA (*Low*): It's one thing to wish with one's head and another for the body . . . cursed be the body! . . . not to respond. It's written, and I'm not going to raise my arms against the sea. That's it! Let my mouth be silent! (*Leaves.*)

QUICK CURTAIN

SCENE TWO

(*Near a chapel in the mountains. Downstage are the wheels of a cart and some canvas forming the rustic tent where Yerma is. Some women enter carrying offerings for the shrine. They are barefoot. On the stage is the happy Old Woman of the first act.*)

SONG (*Heard while the curtain is still closed*):
> I could never see you
> when you were unmarried,
> but now you're married
> I shall find you.
> And I'll undress you,
> married and a pilgrim,
> when through the darkness
> twelve o'clock sounds.

OLD WOMAN (*Lazily*): Have you already drunk the holy water?

FIRST WOMAN: Yes.

OLD WOMAN: And now to see this thing.

FIRST WOMAN: We believe in him.

OLD WOMAN: You come to ask the saint for children and it so happens that every year more lone men come on this pilgrimage too; what is it that's going on here? (*Laughs.*)

FIRST WOMAN: Why do you come, if you don't believe?

OLD WOMAN: To see. I'm crazy to see. And to watch out for my son. Last year two men killed themselves for a barren wife and I want to be on guard. And, finally, I come because I feel like it.

FIRST WOMAN: May God forgive you! (*Leaves.*)

OLD WOMAN (*With sarcasm*): May he forgive you. (*She leaves. María enters with the First Girl.*)

FIRST GIRL: Has she come?

MARÍA: There's the cart. It was hard work to make them come. She has been a month without rising from her chair. I'm afraid of her. She has some idea I don't understand, but it's a bad idea.

FIRST GIRL: I came with my sister. She has been coming here eight years in vain.

MARÍA: The one who must have children, has them.

FIRST GIRL: That's what I say.

(*Voices are heard.*)

MARÍA: I have never liked these pilgrimages. Let's get down to the farms where there are people about.

FIRST GIRL: Last year, when it got dark, some boys pinched my sister's breasts.

MARÍA: For four leagues round nothing is heard but these terrible stories.

FIRST GIRL: I've seen more than forty barrels of wine carried to the hermitage.

MARÍA: A river of single men comes down these mountains.

(*They leave. Voices are heard. Yerma enters with six Women who are going to the chapel. They are barefooted and carry decorated candles. Night begins to fall.*)

MARÍA:
Lord, make blossom the rose,
leave not my rose in shadow.

SECOND WOMAN:
Upon her barren flesh
make blossom the yellow rose.

MARÍA:
And in your servants' wombs
the dark flame of the earth.

CHORUS OF WOMEN:
Lord, make blossom the rose,
leave not my rose in shadow.
(*They kneel.*)

YERMA:
The sky must have such gardens

with rosetrees of its joy,
between the rose and the rose,
one rose of all the wonder.
Bright flash of dawn appears,
and an archangel guards,
his wings like storms outspread,
his eyes like agonies.
While sweet about its leaves
the streams of warm milk play,
play and wet the faces
of the tranquil stars.
Lord, make that rosetree bloom
upon my barren flesh. *(They rise.)*

SECOND WOMAN:
Lord, with your own hand soothe
the thorns upon her cheek.

YERMA:
Hark to me, penitent
in holy pilgrimage.
Open your rose in my flesh
though thousand thorns it have.

CHORUS:
Upon my barren flesh
one rose of all, the wonder.

(They leave.)

(Girls running with long garlands in their hands appear at the left. On the right, three others looking backward. On the stage there is something like a crescendo of voices and harness bells, and bellringers' collars. Higher up appear the Seven Girls who wave the garlands toward the left. The noise increases and the two traditional Masks appear. One is Male and the other Female. They carry large masks. They are not in any fashion grotesque, but of great beauty and with a feeling of pure earth. The Female shakes a collar of large bells. The back of the stage fills with people who shout and comment on the dance. It has grown quite dark.)

CHILDREN: The devil and his wife! The devil and his wife!

FEMALE:
In the wilderness stream
the sad wife came to bathe.
About her body crept
the little water shells.
The sand about the banks,
and a breeze that trailed the morn
gave fire to her laughter
and trembling to her back.
Ah, how naked stood
the maiden in the stream!

BOY:
Ah, how the maiden wept!

FIRST MAN:
Oh barren one of love
who stood in wind and water!

SECOND MAN:
Let her say for whom she longs!

FIRST MAN:
Let her say for whom she waits!

SECOND MAN:
Ah, with her withered womb
and her color shattered!

FEMALE:
When night-tide falls I'll tell,
when night-tide glowing falls.
In the night-tide of the pilgrimage
I'll tear my ruffled skirt.

BOY:
Then quickly night-tide fell.
Oh, how the night was falling!
See how dark becomes
the mountain's waterfall.

(*Guitars begin to sound.*)

MALE (*Rises and shakes the horn*):
Ah, how white
the sorrowing wife!
Ah, how she sighs in the branches!
Poppy and carnation to be
when the male unfolds his cape.
(*Approaches.*)
If you've come to the pilgrimage
to pray your womb may flower
don't wear a mourning veil
but a gown of holland cloth.
Walk slow behind the walls
where fig trees thickest grow
and bear my earthly body
until the white dawn wails.
Ah, how she shines!
How she was shining,
Ah, how the sad wife sways!

FEMALE:
Ah, but love will give her
wreathes and coronets,
and darts of living gold
are nailed upon her breast.

MALE:
Seven times she wept
and nine she rose,
fifteen times they joined
jasmins with oranges.

THIRD MAN:
Strike her now with the horn!

SECOND MAN:
With both the rose and the dance!

FIRST MAN:
Ah, how the wife is swaying!

MALE:
Among the pilgrims

the man commands.
The men are bulls,
the women, flowers,
for him who gains them.

BOY:
Strike her now with the wind!

SECOND MAN:
Strike her now with the branch!

MALE:
Come and see the fire
of the one who bathed!

FIRST MAN:
Like a reed she curves.

FEMALE:
And like a flower is wearied.

MEN:
Let young girls draw away!

MALE:
Let the dance burn.
And the shining body
of the immaculate wife.

(*They disappear dancing amidst smiles and the sound of beating palms. They sing.*)

The sky must have such gardens
with rose trees of its joy,
between the rose and the rose
one rose of all the wonder.

(*Two Girls pass again, shouting. The happy Old Woman enters.*)

OLD WOMAN: See that you let us sleep, then. But later it will be the other. (*Yerma enters.*) You. (*Yerma is downcast and does not speak.*) Tell me; what did you come for?

YERMA: I don't know.

Yerma

OLD WOMAN: Are you not convinced? And your husband?

(*Yerma gives signs of fatigue and acts like a person whose head is bursting with a fixed idea.*)

YERMA: He's there.

OLD WOMAN: What is he doing?

YERMA: Drinking. (*Pause. Putting her hands to her forehead.*) Ay!

OLD WOMAN: Ay, ay! Less, "ay!" and more soul. I couldn't tell you anything before, but now I can.

YERMA: And what are you going to tell me that I don't already know?

OLD WOMAN: What can no longer be hushed up. What shouts from all the rooftops. The fault is your husband's. Do you hear? He can cut off my hands if it isn't. Neither his father, nor his grandfather, nor his great-grandfather behaved like men of good blood. For them to have a son heaven and earth had to meet—because they're nothing but spit. But not your people. You have brothers and cousins for a hundred miles around. Just see what a curse has fallen on your loveliness.

YERMA: A curse. A puddle of poison on the wheat heads.

OLD WOMAN: But you have feet to leave your house.

YERMA: To leave?

OLD WOMAN: When I saw you in the pilgrimage, my heart gave a start. Women come here to know new men. And the saint performs the miracle. My son is there behind the chapel waiting for me. My house needs a woman. Go with him and the three of us will live together. My son is made of blood. Like me. If you enter my house, there will still be an odor of cradles. The ashes from your bedcovers will be bread and salt for your children. Come. Don't let what people will say matter to you. And as for your husband, in my house there is courage and there are weapons so that he will not even cross the street.

YERMA: Hush, hush! it's not that. I would never do it. Do you think I could know another man? Where would that leave my honor? Water cannot turn back, nor does the full moon rise at noonday. Go. I am walking where I must, and I shall continue. Did you really imagine that I could give myself to another man? Ask him for what is mine like a slave? Know me, so that you'll never speak to me again. I am not looking for any one.

OLD WOMAN: When one is thirsty, one is grateful for water.

YERMA: I am like a dry field where a thousand pairs of oxen plow, and you offer me a tiny glass of spring water. Mine is a sorrow already beyond the flesh.

OLD WOMAN (*Strongly*): Then stay that way if you want to! Like the thistles in a dry field, pinched, withered.

YERMA (*Strongly*): Barren, yes, I know it! Barren! You don't have to throw it in my face. Nor come to amuse yourself as youngsters do, in the suffering of a tiny animal. Ever since I married I have avoided that word, and this is the first time I have heard it, the first time it's been said to my face. The first time I see it's the truth.

OLD WOMAN: You make me feel no pity. None. I'll find another woman for my son.

(*She leaves. A great chorus is heard distantly, sung by the pilgrims. Yerma goes toward the cart, and from behind it her husband appears.*)

YERMA: Were you there all the time?

JUAN: I was.

YERMA: Spying?

JUAN: Spying.

YERMA: And you heard?

JUAN: Yes.

YERMA: And so? Leave me and go to your singing. (*Sits on the canvases.*)

JUAN: It's time for me to speak, too.

YERMA: Speak!

JUAN: And to complain.

YERMA: Why?

JUAN: I have a bitterness in my throat.

YERMA: And I in my bones.

JUAN: Now the moment has come when I can no longer endure your continual lament for dark things outside of life, for things in the air.

YERMA (*With dramatic surprise*): Outside of life, do you say? In the air, you say?

JUAN: For things that have not happened and that neither you nor I can control.

YERMA (*Violently*): Go on! Go on!

JUAN: For things that don't matter to me. Do you hear that? That don't matter to me. Now I'm forced to tell you. What matters to me is what I can hold in my hands. What my eyes can see.

YERMA (*Rising to her knees, desperately*): Yes, yes. That's what I wanted to hear from your lips . . . the truth is not felt when it's inside us, but how great it is, how it shouts when it comes out and raises its arms! It doesn't matter to him! Now I've heard it!

JUAN (*Approaching*): Tell yourself it had to happen like this. Listen to me. (*Embraces her to help her rise.*) Many women would be glad to have your life. Without children life is sweeter. I am happy not having them. It is not our fault.

YERMA: Then what did you want with me?

JUAN: Yourself!

YERMA (*Excited*): True! You wanted a home, ease, and a woman. But nothing more. Is what I say true?

JUAN: It's true. As it is of all of us.

YERMA: And what about the rest? What about your son?

JUAN (*Strongly*): Didn't you hear me say I don't care? Don't ask me any more! I shout it in your ear so you'll know it and perhaps live in peace now!

YERMA: And you never thought of it, seeing me desire it?

JUAN: Never. (*Both are on the ground.*)

YERMA: And I may not hope?

JUAN: No.

YERMA: Nor you?

JUAN: Nor I. Resign yourself!

YERMA: Barren!

JUAN: And live in peace. Both of us in comfort, in pleasure. Embrace me! (*He embraces her.*)

YERMA: What are you looking for?

JUAN: You. In the moonlight you're beautiful.

YERMA: You want me as you sometimes want a pigeon to eat.

JUAN: Kiss me . . . like this.

YERMA: That I'll never do. Never.

(*She shouts and presses her husband's throat. He falls backward. She chokes him until he dies. The chorus of the pilgrimage begins.*)

Barren, barren, but sure. Now I really know it for sure. And alone. (*She rises. People begin to gather.*) Now I can sleep without waking up anxious to see if I feel in my blood another new blood. My body dry forever! What do you want? Don't come near me, because I have killed my son. I have killed my son myself!

(*A group that remains in the background gathers. The chorus of the pilgrimage is heard.*)

CURTAIN

Doña Rosita, the Spinster
or
The Language of the Flowers

*A Poem of 1900 Granada,
Divided into Various Gardens, with
Scenes of Song and Dance.*

CHARACTERS

Doña Rosita
The Housekeeper
The Aunt
First Manola
Second Manola
Third Manola
First Spinster
Second Spinster
Third Spinster
The Mother of the Spinsters
First Miss Ayola
Second Miss Ayola
The Uncle
The Nephew
The Economics Instructor
Don Martín
The Youth
Two Workmen
A Voice

ACT ONE

(*A room leading to a greenhouse.*)

UNCLE: And my seeds?

HOUSEKEEPER: They were here.

UNCLE: Well, they're not now.

AUNT: Hellebore, fuchsias and the chrysanthemums, violaceous Louis Passy, and silver white altair with heliotrope points.

UNCLE: You must be careful of the flowers.

HOUSEKEEPER: If you say that because of me . . .

AUNT: Quiet. Don't talk back.

UNCLE: I say that because of everybody. Yesterday I found the dahlia bulbs trampled underfoot. (*Enters the greenhouse.*) You do not appreciate my greenhouse; since 1807, the year in which the Countess of Wandes was able to raise a muscous rose, no one in Granada has been able to raise one but me—not even the university botanist. You must have more respect for my plants.

HOUSEKEEPER: Oh, so I don't respect them?

AUNT: Hush! You're the worst.

HOUSEKEEPER: Yes, madam. But I am not the one who says that from so much watering of the flowers and so much water everywhere, toads are going to appear in the sofa.

AUNT: You certainly enjoy smelling them at times.

HOUSEKEEPER: No, madam. To me flowers smell like a child's funeral, a nun's taking holy vows, or a church altar. Of sad things. Where there is an orange or a good quince, let the roses of the world go by. But here . . . roses to the right, basil to the left, anemones, sage, petunias, and those new fashionable flowers, the chrysanthemums, tousle-headed like gypsies. How I long to see planted in this garden a pear tree, a cherry tree, or a persimmon!

AUNT: So you could eat them!

HOUSEKEEPER: That's what I have a mouth for . . . as they used to say in my village:

> The mouth is useful when we eat,
> The legs are useful when we dance,
> And women have a thing quite neat . . .

(*She stops, goes to the Aunt, and whispers.*)

AUNT: Heavens! (*Crosses herself.*)

HOUSEKEEPER: Those are rustic obscenities. (*Crosses herself.*)

ROSITA (*Enters rapidly. She is dressed in rose, in the style of 1900: leg-of-mutton sleeves and braid trimming*): And my hat? Where is my hat? The bells have rung thirty times at San Luis!

HOUSEKEEPER: I left it on the table.

ROSITA: Well, it isn't there.

(*They search. The Housekeeper leaves.*)

AUNT: Have you looked in the clothespress? (*The Aunt leaves.*)

HOUSEKEEPER (*Enters*): I cannot find it.

ROSITA: Can it be possible that you do not know where my hat is?

HOUSEKEEPER: Wear the blue one with the daisies.

ROSITA: You're crazy.

HOUSEKEEPER: Then you're crazier.

AUNT (*Reenters*): Come, here it is!

(*Rosita takes it and goes running out.*)

HOUSEKEEPER: She wants everything in such a hurry. She wishes that today were day after tomorrow. She starts flying and slips through our hands. When she was a child, I used to have to tell her every day the story of when she should be an old lady: "My Rosita is now eighty years old . . ." always something like that. When have you ever seen her sit down to tat or make frivolité or garland points or drawn work to decorate a cap?

AUNT: Never.

HOUSEKEEPER: Always from this to that and that to this; from this to that and that to this.

AUNT: You may be wrong yet!

HOUSEKEEPER: If I'm wrong, you'll never hear another word out of me.

AUNT: It's true that I've never liked to say no to her: who wants to grieve a child who has no father or mother?

HOUSEKEEPER: Neither father nor mother nor a little dog to bark for her, but she does have an uncle and aunt worth a treasure. (*Embraces her.*)

UNCLE (*Within*): This is really too much!

AUNT: Holy Mother!

UNCLE: It's all very well for the seeds to be trampled, but it's simply unbearable for the rose bush I most cherish to have its little leaves bruised. I think more of it than of the muscous, or the hispid, or the pomponiana, the damascene, or even Queen Elizabeth's eglantine. (*To the Aunt*) Come in here; just come in here and you will see.

AUNT: Is it torn?

UNCLE: No, nothing very serious happened to it, but it could have.

HOUSEKEEPER: We'll never hear the end of it!

UNCLE: I ask myself: who turned over the flowerpot?

HOUSEKEEPER: Don't you look at me.

UNCLE: Then was it I?

HOUSEKEEPER: Are there no cats or dogs, or a sudden gust of wind to blow through the window?

AUNT: Silence now: go sweep the greenhouse.

HOUSEKEEPER: It's easy to see that in this house one is not permitted to speak.

UNCLE (*Enters*): It's a rose you never have seen: a surprise I prepared for you. It's unbelievable. The rosa declinata with its fallen buds, and the inermis without thorns—a marvel isn't it? Not a thorn! . . . and the mirtiflora which comes from Belgium, and the sulfurata, which blooms in the darkness. But this one surpasses them all in rarity. The botanists call it Rosa Mutabile; that is to say: it changes. . . . This book has its description and its picture; look! It is red in the morning—(*Opens the book*)—in the evening it changes to white, and at night it shatters.

> When it opens in the morning
> red as blood it is.
> The dew does not dare touch her
> for fear that it will burn.
> Full-blown in the noonday,
> hard as coral then she is.
> The sun looks in against the panes
> that it may see her glow.
> When the birds begin
> to sing among the branches
> and the afternoon is fainting
> on the violets of the sea,
> she turns pale, with the pallor
> of a cheek that's made of salt.
> And when the night is touched
> by a soft metallic horn
> and the stars advance
> while the winds retreat,
> on the very edge of darkness
> her petals begin to fall.

AUNT: And has it a bud yet?

UNCLE: One that is just beginning to open.

AUNT: Does it last only one day?

UNCLE: Only one. But I intend to pass all that day by its side to see how it changes white.

ROSITA (*Entering*): My parasol.

UNCLE: Her parasol.

Doña Rosita

AUNT (*Shouting*): The parasol!

HOUSEKEEPER (*Appearing*): Here's the parasol!

(*Rosita takes the parasol and kisses her Aunt and Uncle.*)

ROSITA: How do I look?

UNCLE: A beauty!

AUNT: Not another like you.

ROSITA (*Opening the parasol*): And now?

HOUSEKEEPER: Heavens! Close the parasol! It shouldn't be opened in the house! It's bad luck!
> By the wheel of Saint Bartholomew
> and Saint Joseph's staff that grew,
> by the holy laurel too,
> enemy, retreat and rue
> Jerusalem's four corners through.

(*All laugh. The Uncle leaves.*)

ROSITA (*Closing the parasol*): There, then!

HOUSEKEEPER: Never do that again . . . ji-miny!

ROSITA: Goodness!

AUNT: What were you going to say?

HOUSEKEEPER: Well, I didn't really say it!

ROSITA (*Exits laughingly*): Until later!

AUNT: Who is going with you?

ROSITA (*Looking in*): I'm going with the Manola* girls.

HOUSEKEEPER: And with your sweetheart.

AUNT: Her sweetheart, I think, was busy.

HOUSEKEEPER: I don't know which one I like better: her sweetheart, or her.

(*The Aunt sits down to make lace with bobbins.*)

A pair of cousins fit to put in a showcase! And if they

---

*Manola: the high-spirited young coquette, conscious of her charms, and able to accentuate them through the witchery lent by flowers, high combs, a lace mantilla, or a fan—and usually all of these. We have come to think of the *Manola* as typically Spanish, and, indeed, she has always existed. In Goya's day she was called the *Maja*.

should die, heaven forbid, embalm them and put them in a niche of crystals and snow. Which one do you like most? (*She starts dusting.*)

AUNT: Both. I love them as niece and nephew.

HOUSEKEEPER: One for the upper sheet and one for the lower sheet, but . . .

AUNT: Rosita grew up with me . . .

HOUSEKEEPER: Naturally. And I don't believe in blood ties. This is what I think. The blood runs down in the veins, but you can't see it. So one loves a second cousin more that one sees every day, than a brother who is far away. And the reason is this: . . .

AUNT: Keep on with your cleaning, miss.

HOUSEKEEPER: Right away. Here one isn't allowed to even open her mouth. You raise a beautiful little girl for this. Abandon your own children in a hut, trembling with hunger.

AUNT: You mean with cold.

HOUSEKEEPER: Trembling with everything. Just to be told—shut up! And, as I'm a servant, there's nothing to do but shut up. So I do that and don't dare answer back and say . . .

AUNT: And say what?

HOUSEKEEPER: And say—drop those bobbins with all that clicking. My head is going to burst with that clicking.

AUNT (*Laughing*): Go see who's calling.

(*The stage is silent and only the clicking of the bobbins is heard.*)

VOICE: Ca-a-a-mo-o-o-mile, fine ca-a-mo-o-mile from the fo-o-rest!!

AUNT (*Talking to herself*): We should buy some more camomile. There are occasions when one needs it. . . . In just one more day . . . thirty-seven, thirty-eight . . .

PEDLAR'S VOICE (*Distantly*): Ca-a-amo-o-mile, fine ca-a-amomile from the fo-o-rest!

AUNT (*Placing a pin*): And forty.

Doña Rosita

NEPHEW (*Entering*): Aunt . . .

AUNT (*Without looking at him*): Hello. Sit down if you like. Rosita has already left.

NEPHEW: With whom did she go?

AUNT: With the Manolas. (*Pauses, looks at Nephew.*) Something has happened to you.

NEPHEW: Yes.

AUNT (*Disturbed*): I can almost guess what. I hope I'm wrong.

NEPHEW: No. Read this.

AUNT (*Reads*): Well, this is only what was to be expected. That's why I opposed your engagement with Rosita. I knew that sooner or later you would have to go to your parents. And that's where you belong! It's a forty days' journey to Tucuman. If I were a man and young I'd slap your face . . .

NEPHEW: It's not my fault I'm in love with my cousin. Do you imagine I like this? It's precisely because I want to stay that I have come here.

AUNT: Stay? Stay? Your duty is to go. The hacienda is many miles wide and your father is old. I'm the one who must force you to take the boat. But you will embitter my life. I don't even want to think of your cousin. You are going to stick an arrow with purple ribbons in her heart. Now she'll find out that linen isn't merely to embroider flowers on, but also to dry tears.

NEPHEW: What do you advise me to do?

AUNT: To go. Remember that your father is my brother. Here you are only a walker in little gardens—and there you will be a workingman.

NEPHEW: But I should like to . . .

AUNT: Get married? Are you crazy? Only when your future is assured. And take Rosita, no? You would have to leap over the dead bodies of me and your uncle.

NEPHEW: I was just talking. I know very well that I cannot. But I want Rosita to wait for me because I'll be back soon.

AUNT: If you don't take up with a Tucuman girl first. My tongue should have stuck to the roof of my mouth before I consented to your engagement; because my child will be left alone within these four walls and you will go free across the ocean, across those rivers, through those citron groves, and my little girl here, one day just like another— and you over there, with your horse and musket shooting pheasants.

NEPHEW: There's no reason for you to talk to me in this fashion. I gave my word and I will keep it. In order to keep his word my father is in America and you know . . .

AUNT (*Softly*): Quiet.

NEPHEW: I'll be quiet, but don't you confuse respect with lack of honor.

AUNT (*With Andalusian irony*): Pardon! Pardon! I had forgotten you were a man now.

HOUSEKEEPER (*Enters weeping*): If he were a man he wouldn't go.

AUNT (*Sternly*): Silence!

(*The Housekeeper weeps with great sobs.*)

NEPHEW: I will be back very soon. You tell her that.

AUNT: Never mind. The old people are the ones who have to bear the hard times.

(*The Nephew leaves.*)

HOUSEKEEPER: Oh, what a pity about my little girl! What a pity! What a pity! These are the men of today! Even if I had to beg in the streets I would stay by the side of this prize. Once more tears will come to the house. Oh, Madam! (*Recovering.*) I hope the sea-serpent eats him!

AUNT: God will decide that!

HOUSEKEEPER:
By the sesame seed,

> By the three holy questions
> And the cinnamon flower,
> May he have bad nights
> And bad seeding times.
> By the well of St. Nicholas
> May his salt turn to poison.

(*She takes a water jar and makes a cross on the ground.*)

AUNT: Don't curse. Go to your room.

(*Housekeeper leaves. Laughter is heard. The Aunt leaves.*)

FIRST MANOLA (*Entering and closing her parasol*): Ay!

SECOND MANOLA (*Likewise*): Ay, what coolness.

THIRD MANOLA (*Likewise*): Ay!

ROSITA (*Likewise*): For whom are the sighs of my three lovely Manolas?

FIRST MANOLA: For no one.

SECOND MANOLA: For the wind.

THIRD MANOLA: For a gallant who is courting me.

ROSITA: What hands will gather the sighs from your mouths?

FIRST MANOLA: The wall.

SECOND MANOLA: A certain photograph.

THIRD MANOLA: The laces of my counterpane.

ROSITA: I also want to sigh. Ay, friends! Ay, Manolas!

FIRST MANOLA: Who gathers those?

ROSITA:
> Two eyes
> that make the shade seem white,
> whose lashes grapevines are
> where daybreak goes to sleep.
> And even though they're dark—
> two twilights set in poppies.

FIRST MANOLA: Bind that sigh.

SECOND MANOLA: Ay!

THIRD MANOLA: Happy you.

FIRST MANOLA: Happy!

ROSITA: Don't try to deceive me, for I know a certain rumor about you.

FIRST MANOLA: Rumors are yellow flowers.

SECOND MANOLA: And gossipings of the waves.

ROSITA: I'm going to tell it . . .

THIRD MANOLA: Rumors are crowns.

          ROSITA:
    Granada, street of Elvira,
    the home of the Manolas,
    they who go to the Alhambra,
    the three and the four alone.
    One has a dress in green,
    another mauve, and one
    a Scottish corselet
    with ribbons to the train.
    The ones in front are herons,
    the one behind, a dove;
    beneath the trees they spread
    mysterious muslin scarves.
    How dark is the Alhambra!
    Where could they all be going,
    while in the darkness suffer
    the fountain sprays and roses?
    What gallants there await them?
    Reposing 'neath what myrtles?
    What hands will steal perfumes
    from their two flowers round?
    No one goes with them, no one;
    two herons and a dove.
    But this world has gallants
    who hide beneath the leaves.
    Cathedral bells have left
    a bronze the breeze is taking;
    the Genil lulls its oxen,

the Dauro, butterflies.
The night approaches laden
with its darkened hillsides;
one of them shows her shoes
among the lacy ruffles;
the eldest opens her eyes,
but the youngest turns them.
Oh who could be those three,
high-bosomed and long-trained?
Why do their kerchiefs wave?
Where go they at this hour?
Granada, street of Elvira,
the home of the Manolas,
they who go to the Alhambra,
the three and the four alone.

FIRST MANOLA:
Let the rumor spread
its waves over Granada.

SECOND MANOLA: Have we a sweetheart?

ROSITA: Not one of you.

SECOND MANOLA: Am I telling the truth?

ROSITA: Yes, all of it.

THIRD MANOLA:
White frost laces trim
our bridal clothes.

ROSITA: But . . .

FIRST MANOLA: We like the night.

ROSITA: But . . .

SECOND MANOLA: Through darkened streets

FIRST MANOLA:
We climb toward the Alhambra
the three and four alone.

THIRD MANOLA: Ay!

SECOND MANOLA: Hush!

THIRD MANOLA: Why?
SECOND MANOLA: Ay!
FIRST MANOLA: Ay, let no one hear it!

ROSITA:
Alhambra, jasmine of sorrow,
where the moon reposes.

HOUSEKEEPER (*Very sadly*): Child, your aunt is calling you.

ROSITA: Have you been crying?

HOUSEKEEPER (*Controlling herself*): No . . . it's just that . . . something . . .

ROSITA: Don't frighten me. What has happened. (*She leaves quickly, looking towards the Housekeeper.*)

(*When Rosita leaves the Housekeeper begins to cry silently.*)

FIRST MANOLA (*Loudly*): What is the matter?

SECOND MANOLA: Tell us.

HOUSEKEEPER: Hush.

THIRD MANOLA (*In a low voice*): Bad news?

(*The Housekeeper takes them to the door and looks out to where Rosita went.*)

HOUSEKEEPER: She is telling her now!

(*Pause, while all listen.*)

FIRST MANOLA: Rosita is crying. Let's go in.

HOUSEKEEPER: Come and I'll tell you about it. Leave her alone! You can go out through the side gate.

(*They leave. The stage is empty. A very distant piano plays a Czerny étude. Pause. The Nephew enters and on reaching the center of the room stops because Rosita enters. The two stand regarding each other face to face. The Nephew advances. He takes her by the waist. She leans her head on his shoulder.*)

ROSITA:
Why were your treacherous eyes
so to my own welded?
And why did your hands weave,

over my head, flowers?
What sighing of nightingales
you leave within my youth,
since holding my north and health
in your figure and presence,
you break with cruel absence
the strings of my lute!

NEPHEW (*Takes her to a "vis-à-vis" and they sit down*):
Oh, cousin, who are my treasure!
Nightingale of winter snow,
your mouth must be firm closed
against imagined cold;
my departure is not of ice,
for though I cross the sea,
the water must lend to me
gardenias of foam and quiet
that I may contain my fire
when I should fear to burn.

ROSITA:
On a languorous night
from my jasmin balconies
I saw descend two cherubs
to an enamoured rose;
bright scarlet she became
though she had first been white;
but like a tender flower,
her petals all afire,
wounded, began to fall,
by the first kiss of love.
Thus, I, innocent cousin,
within my myrtle garden,
gave the wind my longing,
my whiteness to the fountain.
Tender thoughtless gazelle,
I raised my eyes and saw you,
and straight in my heart felt

needles that trembled there
and open wounds in me
red as the gillyflower.

    NEPHEW:

I must return, my cousin,
to take you by my side
in burnished golden ship
with sails of happiness;
light and shade, night and day,
I'll think only of loving you.

    ROSITA:

But the poison that overflows,
love, on a soul alone,
will weave with land and wave
the garments of my death.

    NEPHEW:

When my stallion slow
eats grasses wet with dew,
when the river's fog
shall cloud the wall of wind;
when the violent summer
with scarlet paints the plain
and seafoam leaves in me,
bright needles from a star,
I tell you, because I love you,
that I will die for you.

    ROSITA:

I long to see you come
some evening through Granada
when all the light's besalted,
nostalgic for the sea;
a yellow lemon grove,
a white-bled jasmin garden,
entangled by the stones
that will impede your way,
and nards like whirlpools

that make insane my roof.
You will return.

NEPHEW:
Yes. I'll return!

ROSITA:
And what refulgent dove
announces your arrival?

NEPHEW:
The dove that is my faith.

ROSITA:
Then see, I will embroider
white sheets for both of us.

NEPHEW:
By the diamonds of the Lord,
and his side's carnation,
I swear I will return.

ROSITA:
Good-bye, cousin!

NEPHEW:
Cousin, good-bye!

(*They embrace in the "vis-à-vis." The piano is heard distantly. The Nephew leaves. Rosita is left weeping. The Uncle appears and crosses the stage toward the greenhouse. When she sees her uncle, Rosita picks up the rose book which is near her hand.*)

UNCLE: What were you doing?

ROSITA: Nothing.

UNCLE: Were you reading?

ROSITA: Yes.

(*The Uncle leaves, reading.*)

ROSITA (*Reads*):
When it opens in the morning
red as blood it is.
The dew does not dare touch her

for fear that it will burn.
Full-blown in the noonday,
she is then as hard as coral.
The sun looks in against the panes
that it may see her glow.
When the birds begin
to sing among the branches
and the afternoon is fainting
on the violets of the sea,
she turns pale, with the pallor
of a cheek that's made of salt.
And when the night is touched
by a soft metallic horn
and the stars advance
while the winds retreat,
on the very edge of darkness
her petals begin to fall.

CURTAIN

ACT TWO

(A room of Doña Rosita's house. The garden in the background.)

MR. X.: Therefore, I always will be of this century.

UNCLE: The century we have just begun will be a century of materialism.

MR. X.: But of much more progress than the one which just passed. My friend, Mr. Longoria, of Madrid, has just bought an automobile with which he can hurl himself along at the fantastic speed of eighteen miles per hour; and the Shah of Persia, who certainly is a most pleasant man, has also bought a Panhard Levasson motor car of twenty-four horsepower.

UNCLE: And I say: where are they going in such a great hurry? Just see what happened in the Paris-Madrid race, which had to be suspended because before they reached Bordeaux all the racers killed themselves.

MR. X.: Count Zboronsky, dead in that accident and Marcel Renault, or Renol, since in both fashions it is wont to be and can be pronounced, dead also in that accident, are martyrs of science who will be enshrined the day a religion of the positive comes. Renault I know quite well. Poor Marcello.

UNCLE: You will not convince me. *(He sits.)*

MR. X. *(One foot on the chair, playing with his cane)*: Superlatively! Although a professor of political economy cannot argue with a cultivator of roses. But in this day of today, believe me, neither quietisms nor obscurantist ideas can rule one. In this day a road is opened by a John the Baptist Sai or Se, since in both fashions it is wont to be and can be pronounced, or a count Leon Tolstwa, vulgarly Tolstoy, as gallant in form as he is profound in concept.

I feel myself in the living cosmos; I am not of the earth, earthy.

UNCLE: Every one lives as he can, or as he best knows how in his daily life.

MR. X.: That's understood. The earth is a mediocre planet, but one must lend aid to civilization. If Santos Dumont, instead of studying comparative meteorology, had dedicated himself to watching roses, the dirigible aerostat would be in the bosom of Brahama.

UNCLE (*Disgusted*): Botany is also a science.

MR. X. (*Disparagingly*): Yes, but an applied one: to study of the juices of the fragrant Anthemis or the rhubarb, or the great Pulsatila, or the narcotic of the Datura Stramonium.

UNCLE (*Innocently*): Do these plants interest you?

MR. X.: I do not possess a sufficient volume of experience concerning them. I'm interested in culture, which is different. *Voila!* (*Pause.*) And Rosita?

UNCLE: Rosita! (*Pause. Shouts.*) Rosita!!

VOICE (*Within*): She's not here.

UNCLE: She's not here.

MR. X.: I regret it.

UNCLE: I also. Since it is her birthday she must have gone to pray the forty credos.

MR. X.: Deliver to her for me this pendant. It is a mother-of-pearl Eiffel Tower over two doves which carry in their bills the wheel of industry.

UNCLE: She will be most grateful.

MR. X.: I almost brought her a little silver cannon through whose mouth one could see the Virgin of Lourdes, or Lordes, or a buckle for a belt made with a serpent and four butterflies, but I chose the first as being in better taste.

UNCLE: Thank you.

MR. X.: I am charmed with your favorable reception.

UNCLE: Thanks.

MR. X.: Place me at the feet of your dear spouse.

UNCLE: Many thanks.

MR. X.: Place me at the feet of your enchanting little niece to whom I wish good fortune in her birthday celebration.

UNCLE: A thousand thanks.

MR. X.: Consider me as your faithful servant.

UNCLE: A million thanks.

MR. X.: Once more I repeat . . .

UNCLE: Thank you, thank you, thank you.

MR. X.: Then, until always! (*He leaves.*)

UNCLE (*Shouting*): Thank you, thank you, thank you!!

HOUSEKEEPER (*Enters laughing*): I don't know how you have the patience. With that man and with the other—Mr. Confucius Montes de Oca, baptized in lodge number forty-three—the house will burn down some day.

UNCLE: I have told you I don't like you to eavesdrop on our conversations.

HOUSEKEEPER: That is what is called ingratitude. I was behind the door, true enough, but it was not to listen, but to place a broom upside down so that the gentleman would leave.

AUNT (*Entering*): Has he left yet?

UNCLE: Yes. (*Exits.*)

HOUSEKEEPER: Is this one also a suitor for Rosita?

AUNT: But why do you speak of suitors? You don't know Rosita!

HOUSEKEEPER: But I do know the suitors.

AUNT: My niece is affianced.

HOUSEKEEPER: Don't make me say it, don't make me say it, don't make me say it.

AUNT: Then be quiet.

HOUSEKEEPER: Does it seem right to you for a man to go away now for fifteen years and leave behind a woman who is the very cream of the crop? She ought to marry. My hands ache from storing away Marseille lace tablecloths and embroidered bed sets and table scarves and gauze bedspreads with raised flowers. It's now she ought to use them and tear them, but she doesn't realize how the time passes. She will have silver hair and still be sewing satin bands on the ruffles of her honeymoon nightgown.

AUNT: But why do you stick your nose in what does not concern you?

HOUSEKEEPER (*With surprise*): It's not that I stick it in, it's already in.

AUNT: I'm sure that she is happy.

HOUSEKEEPER: She just imagines it. Yesterday she had me with her all day at the gate to the circus because she insisted one of the puppeteers resembled her cousin.

AUNT: And did he resemble him really?

HOUSEKEEPER: He was as beautiful as a young priest when he comes to sing his first mass. But your nephew just wishes he had that waist, that white throat, that mustache. They didn't look at all alike. In your family there aren't any good-looking men.

AUNT: Thank you, miss.

HOUSEKEEPER: They are all short and a little stoop-shouldered.

AUNT: Well!

HOUSEKEEPER: That's the real truth, Madame. What happened is that Rosita liked the mountebank, just as I liked him and as you would. But she lays it all on the other one. Sometimes I'd like to throw a shoe at her head. Because from so much looking at the sky she's going to get eyes like a cow's.

AUNT: Very well. Now let it rest. It's all right for the clown to speak but not to bark.

HOUSEKEEPER: You won't throw it in my face that I don't love her.

AUNT: Sometimes I think you don't.

HOUSEKEEPER: I would take the bread from my mouth and the blood from my veins if she wanted them.

AUNT (*Strongly*): Honey-tongued liar! Words!

HOUSEKEEPER (*Strongly*): And deeds! I have proved it, and deeds! I love her more than you.

AUNT: That's a lie.

HOUSEKEEPER (*Strongly*): That's the truth!

AUNT: Don't raise your voice to me!

HOUSEKEEPER (*Loudly*): That's what I have a tongue for.

AUNT: Be quiet, know-nothing!

HOUSEKEEPER: Forty years at your side.

AUNT (*Almost weeping*): You're dismissed!

HOUSEKEEPER (*Very loudly*): Thank goodness I won't have to look at you any more!

AUNT (*Weeping*): To the street at once!

HOUSEKEEPER (*Breaking into tears*): To the street!

(*She goes weeping toward the door and as she steps outside some object falls. Both are weeping. Pause.*)

AUNT (*Drying her tears, sweetly*): What did you drop?

HOUSEKEEPER (*Weeping*): A thermometer case. Louis Quinze style.

AUNT: Yes?

HOUSEKEEPER: Yes, Madame.

(*They weep.*)

AUNT: May I see it?

HOUSEKEEPER: For Rosita's birthday. (*She approaches.*)

AUNT (*Sniffling*): It's a precious thing.

HOUSEKEEPER (*In a tearful voice*): In the middle of the velvet there's a fountain made out of real shells. Over the fountain there is a wire arbor with green roses. The water in the basin is a group of blue sequins and the stream of water is the thermometer itself. The puddles around are painted in oil and upon them a nightingale drinks, all embroidered in golden thread. I wanted it to have a spring and wind up and sing, but that could not be.

AUNT: That could not be.

HOUSEKEEPER: But it doesn't need to sing. In the garden we have live ones.

AUNT: That's true. (*Pause.*) Why have you gone to all this trouble?

HOUSEKEEPER (*Crying*): I'd give everything I have for Rosita.

AUNT: You love her as no one else does!

HOUSEKEEPER: But after you.

AUNT: No. You have given her your blood.

HOUSEKEEPER: You have sacrificed your life.

AUNT: But I have done it through duty and you out of generosity.

HOUSEKEEPER (*Louder*): Don't you say that!

AUNT: You have proved you love her more than any one.

HOUSEKEEPER: I have done what any one would have done in my case. A servant. You pay me and I serve you.

AUNT: We've always considered you one of the family.

HOUSEKEEPER: A humble servant who gives what she has and nothing more.

AUNT: Why do you say "nothing more"?

HOUSEKEEPER: Well, am I anything else?

AUNT: You can't say that here. I'm going so I won't have to listen to you.

HOUSEKEEPER (*Irritated*): Me, too.

(*They go out quickly. Each by a separate door. As the Aunt is going out she stumbles into the Uncle.*)

UNCLE: From so much living together, laces seem like thorns to you.

AUNT: It's just that she always wants to have her way.

UNCLE: Don't explain to me. I know it all by heart. . . . Nevertheless, you can't be without her. Yesterday I heard how you explained to her in complete detail about our account at the bank. You don't know how to keep your place. It doesn't seem to me the most suitable topic for conversation with a servant.

AUNT: She's not a servant.

UNCLE (*With sweetness*): Enough, enough. I don't want to contradict you.

AUNT: But can no one even speak with me?

UNCLE: One can, but I prefer to be quiet.

AUNT: Even though you are left with your words of reproach.

UNCLE: Why should I reply to these high-flown words? In order not to argue, I would make up my bed, clean my suits with soap bark, and change the rugs in my room.

AUNT: It isn't right for you to give yourself this air of a superior man, badly served, when everything in this house is subordinated to your comfort and your likes.

UNCLE (*Sweetly*): On the contrary, child.

AUNT: Completely. Instead of making lace, I prune the plants. What do you do for me?

UNCLE: Forgive me. There comes a moment in which people who have lived together many years make a pretext for ill humor and anxiety out of the smallest things, in order to put intensity and worry into what's definitely dead. When we were twenty years old we didn't have any such conversations.

AUNT: No, when we were twenty years old the windows could break . . .

UNCLE: And the cold was a toy in our hands.

(*Rosita appears. She comes dressed in rose. The styles have changed from leg-o'-mutton sleeves to 1900. Her skirt is like a bell. She crosses the stage quickly with a pair of scissors in her hand. In the center she pauses.)*

ROSITA: Has the postman come?

UNCLE: Has he come?

AUNT: I don't know. (*Loudly*) Has the postman come? (*Pause.*) No, not yet.

ROSITA: He always passes at this hour.

UNCLE: He should have been here some time ago.

AUNT: Well, many times he's delayed.

ROSITA: The other day I met him playing hop-scotch with three children and the whole pile of letters on the ground.

AUNT: He'll come.

ROSITA: Let me know. (*She goes out quickly.*)

UNCLE: But where are you going with those scissors?

ROSITA: I'm going to cut some roses.

UNCLE (*Astounded*): What? And who has given you permission?

AUNT: I did. Today's her birthday.

ROSITA: I want to put some in the jardinière, and in the vase in the front hall.

UNCLE: Every time you cut a rose, it's as if you cut off one of my fingers. It's just exactly like that! (*Looking at his wife.*) I don't want to argue. I know they don't last very long.

(*The Housekeeper enters.*)

So says the Waltz of the Roses, which is one of the prettiest compositions of these times, but I cannot restrain the disgust I feel at seeing them in vases.

ROSITA (*To the Housekeeper*): Did the mail come?

HOUSEKEEPER: Well, the only thing roses are good for is to decorate rooms.

ROSITA (*Irritated*): I asked you if the mail had come.

Doña Rosita

HOUSEKEEPER (*Irritated*): Do I hide the letters when they come?

AUNT: Go on now and cut the flowers.

ROSITA: There's a drop of bitterness for everything in this house.

HOUSEKEEPER: Yes, we find arsenic in the corners. (*Leaves the stage.*)

AUNT: Are you happy?

ROSITA: I don't know.

AUNT: What does that mean?

ROSITA: When I don't see people I'm happy, but since I have to see them . . .

AUNT: Of course. I don't like the life you lead. Your fiancé doesn't demand that you be a stay-at-home. In his letters he always tells me you should go out.

ROSITA: It's just that in the streets I become aware of how time has passed and I don't want to lose my illusions. They've built another new house in the marketplace. I don't want to find out how time goes.

AUNT: Of course. I have many times advised you to write your cousin and marry some one else here. You are very attractive. I know there are boys and mature men in love with you.

ROSITA: But Aunt, my roots are planted very deep, very deep in my feelings. If it were not for seeing people, I could believe that it's just a week since he left. I wait as if it were the first day. Anyway, what is one year, or two, or five? (*A little bell sounds.*) The mail.

AUNT: I wonder what he sent you?

HOUSEKEEPER (*Entering*): Here are those awful old maids.

AUNT: Holy Mary!

ROSITA: Tell them to come in.

HOUSEKEEPER: The mother and the three little girls! Luxury on the outside, but for the mouth, a few stale bread crumbs. How could I beat them on the . . .

(*She leaves. The three awful Girls and their Mother enter. The three Spinsters wear immense hats trimmed with bad feathers, most exaggerated dresses, gloves to the elbow with bracelets over them, and fans hanging from large chains. The Mother wears a faded black dress with a hat of old purple ribbons.*)

MOTHER: Many happy returns! (*They kiss.*)

ROSITA: Thank you. (*Kisses the Spinsters.*) Love! Charity! Clemency!

FIRST SPINSTER: Many happy returns.

SECOND SPINSTER: Many happy returns.

THIRD SPINSTER: Many happy returns.

AUNT (*To the Mother*): How are those feet?

MOTHER: Every day worse. If it weren't for these girls, I'd stay at home always.

(*They sit down.*)

AUNT: Don't you give yourself the lavender water treatments?

FIRST SPINSTER: Every night.

SECOND SPINSTER: And the boiled mallows.

AUNT: No rheumatism can resist it. (*Pause.*)

MOTHER: And your husband?

AUNT: He's very well, thank you. (*Pause.*)

MOTHER: With his roses.

AUNT: With his roses.

THIRD SPINSTER: Flowers are so pretty.

SECOND SPINSTER: We have a Saint Francis rosebush in a pot.

ROSITA: But the Saint Francis roses have no odor.

FIRST SPINSTER: Very little.

MOTHER: The ones I like best are the *celindas*.

THIRD SPINSTER: Violets are also very pretty. (*Pause.*)

MOTHER: Girls, did you bring the card?

THIRD SPINSTER: Yes. It is a little girl in a rose-colored dress, which is, at the same time, a barometer. The monk with

Doña Rosita

his cape is much too common now. According to the humidity, the skirts of the little girl, which are of the finest paper, rise or fall.

ROSITA (*Reading*):
One morning in the field
 the nightingale's breast
was full of song that said:
 "Rosita is the best."
You shouldn't have done it.

AUNT: It's so refined.

MOTHER: I don't lack refinement—what I lack is money.

FIRST SPINSTER: Mama!

SECOND SPINSTER: Mama!

THIRD SPINSTER: Mama!

MOTHER: Now daughters, I'm among friends here. No one can overhear us. But you know very well that since I lost my poor husband I have performed real miracles in order to manage on the pension we have left. I still seem to hear the father of these girls when, generous and gentlemanly as he was, he would say to me: "Henrietta, spend, spend, spend, for I am earning seventy *duros* now!" But those times are gone. In spite of everything, however, we have kept our position in society. And what anguish I've gone through, madam, so that these daughters could continue wearing hats. How many tears; how many pains for a ribbon or a cluster of curls. Those feathers and those wires have cost me many a sleepless night!

THIRD SPINSTER: Mama!

MOTHER: That's the truth, my dear child. We daren't in the least exceed our budget. Many times I ask them, "What do you want, daughters of my soul, eggs for breakfast, or chairs at the promenade?" And the three at once answer: "Chairs!"

THIRD SPINSTER: Mother, don't comment further on that. All Granada knows it.

MOTHER: Naturally, what else could they answer? And there we go, eating potatoes or a bunch of grapes, but with a Mongolian cape or a painted parasol or a poplinette blouse with all the trimmings, because there's nothing else to do. But it's costing me my life, and my eyes fill with tears when I see them competing with those who can do more.

SECOND SPINSTER: Are you going to the park today, Rosita?

ROSITA: No.

THIRD SPINSTER: We always associate there with the Ponce de Leon girls, or with the Herrasti, or the daughters of the Baroness of Saint Matilda of the Papal Benediction. The finest of Granada!

MOTHER: Naturally. They went to Heaven's Gate School together.

AUNT (*Rising*): Will you have something?

(*They all rise.*)

MOTHER: There are no hands like yours for making that paste of pine nut kernels and sugar, or for the Glory Cakes.

FIRST SPINSTER (*To Rosita*): Have you had any news?

ROSITA: The last letter promised me news. We'll see what this one brings.

THIRD SPINSTER: Have you finished the set with the valencienne lace?

ROSITA: Finished it! I have already made another of nainsook with moiré butterflies.

SECOND SPINSTER: The day you marry you are going to have the best household things in the world.

ROSITA: Alas, I think it all too little. They say that men grow tired of us if they see us always with the same dress.

HOUSEKEEPER (*Entering*): Here are those Ayolas, the photographer's daughters.

AUNT: The *Misses* Ayola, you must mean.

Doña Rosita

HOUSEKEEPER: Here by all that is high are the great ladies of Ayola, photographer to his Majesty, and gold medal at the Madrid Exposition.

AUNT: One must put up with her. But sometimes she sets my nerves on edge.

(*The Spinsters are with Rosita looking at some linens.*)

Servants are impossible.

MOTHER: Cheeky. I have a girl who cleans the flat in the afternoons; she used to earn what they have always earned: one peseta a month and leftovers, which is enough in these times. Well, the other day she flew off the handle saying she wanted a dollar, and I simply can't.

AUNT: I don't know where it's all going to end.

(*The Ayola girls enter and greet Rosita gayly. They come in with the greatly exaggerated style of the period and richly dressed.*)

ROSITA: Do you know each other?

FIRST AYOLA: By sight.

ROSITA: The Misses Ayola, Mrs. Scarpini and her daughters.

SECOND AYOLA: We've seen them seated on their chairs at the promenade. (*They conceal their laughter.*)

ROSITA: Please be seated.

(*The Spinsters sit.*)

AUNT (*To the Ayola girls*): Would you care for some sweets?

SECOND AYOLA: No. We ate just a little while ago. Truly, I ate four eggs with tomato sauce and I was almost unable to rise from the chair.

FIRST AYOLA: How charming!

(*They laugh. Pause. The Ayolas begin an uncontrollable laughter that communicates itself to Rosita, who tries to stop them. The Spinsters and their Mother are serious. Pause.*)

AUNT: What children!

MOTHER: Youth.

AUNT: It is the happy age.

ROSITA (*Walking around the stage as if arranging things*): Please. Be quiet.

(*They stop.*)

AUNT (*To the Third Spinster*): And your piano?

THIRD SPINSTER: I study very little just now. I have so much fancy work to do.

ROSITA: It's a long time since I've heard you.

MOTHER: If it were not for me her fingers would have grown stiff. But I am always there with—Practice! Practice!

SECOND SPINSTER: Since poor Father died she doesn't feel like it. He used to like it so much.

SECOND AYOLA (*With humor*): I remember sometimes his tears would fall.

FIRST SPINSTER: When she played Popper's "Tarantella."

SECOND SPINSTER: And the "Virgin's Prayer."

MOTHER: She had so much soul.

(*The Ayolas, who have been containing their laughter, burst out now in great peals. Rosita, turning her back to the Spinsters, also laughs, but controls herself.*)

AUNT: What naughty girls.

FIRST AYOLA: We are laughing because just before we came in here . . .

SECOND AYOLA: This one stumbled and was on the point of doing the Bell turn . . .

FIRST AYOLA: And I . . .

(*They laugh. The Spinsters start a slight faint laugh of a weary and sad complexion.*)

MOTHER: We must go.

AUNT: By no means.

ROSITA (*To all of them*): Well, we are glad you didn't fall. (*To the Housekeeper*) Bring the Saint Kathleen's Bones.

THIRD SPINSTER: They're so rich.

Doña Rosita

MOTHER: Last year we were given a pound of them.

(*The Housekeeper comes in with the Bones.*)

HOUSEKEEPER: Morsels for fine people. (*To Rosita*) The postman is coming through the grove.

ROSITA: Wait for him at the door.

FIRST AYOLA: I don't want to eat. I prefer an anisette cookie.

SECOND AYOLA: And I a brandy cake.

ROSITA: You've always been a little tippler.

FIRST AYOLA: When I was six years old I used to come here and Rosita's sweetheart got me used to eating them. Don't you remember, Rosita?

ROSITA (*Serious*): No.

SECOND AYOLA: Rosita and her sweetheart used to teach me the letters B, C, D. How long ago was that?

AUNT: Fifteen years.

FIRST AYOLA: I almost, almost don't remember your sweetheart's face.

SECOND AYOLA: Didn't he have a scar on his lip?

ROSITA: A scar? Aunt, did he have a scar?

AUNT: Why don't you remember? It was the only thing that detracted a little from his looks.

ROSITA: It wasn't a scar; it was a burn that was a little irritated. Scars are deep.

FIRST AYOLA: Goodness but I want Rosita to get married!

ROSITA: For heaven's sake!

SECOND AYOLA: No more nonsense. So do I!

ROSITA: Why?

FIRST AYOLA: To be in a wedding. As soon as I can, I'm going to get married.

AUNT: Child!

FIRST AYOLA: With any one—just so I'm not left an old maid.

SECOND AYOLA: I think the same way.

AUNT (*To the Mother*): What do you think?

FIRST AYOLA: Ah! And if I'm Rosita's friend, it's because she has a sweetheart. Women without sweethearts are either uncooked or overcooked and all of them . . . (*Looks at the Spinsters.*) well, not all, but some of them . . . No, all of them have hydrophobia!

AUNT: Here! That's enough of that.

MOTHER: Just let her keep on.

FIRST SPINSTER: There are many who don't get married because they don't want to.

SECOND AYOLA: I don't believe that.

FIRST SPINSTER (*Significantly*): I know it for a fact.

SECOND AYOLA: One who doesn't want to get married quits putting powder on her face and wearing false bosoms and doesn't spend all night and all day at her balcony rail waylaying every passer-by.

SECOND SPINSTER: She may like to take the air.

ROSITA: What a childish discussion!

(*They laugh strainedly.*)

AUNT: Well, why don't we play a little?

MOTHER: Go on, child!

THIRD SPINSTER (*Rising*): Play: "Viva Frascuelo!"

SECOND SPINSTER: The barcarolle of the "Numancia Frigate."

ROSITA: And why not: "What the Flowers Say"?

MOTHER: Oh, yes! "What the Flowers Say"! (*To the Aunt*) Have you heard her? She recites and plays at the same time. Precious!

THIRD SPINSTER: I can also recite: "The swallows dark will return, from your balcony their nests to hang."

FIRST AYOLA: That's very sad.

FIRST SPINSTER: Sad things are also beautiful.

Doña Rosita

AUNT: Come! Come!

THIRD SPINSTER (*At the piano*):
Mother, take me to the fields,
in the earliest light of morn,
there to see the flowers bloom
when the branches start to sway.
One thousand flowers a thousand things
to as many girls will say,
and the fountain gossips now
what the nightingales would not.

ROSITA:
Already had the rosebud flowered
in the earliest light of morn,
so scarlet in its tender blood
that the dew would not come near;
so warm it burned upon the stem
that the breeze itself was seared.
So tall!
How it shone!
It was open!

THIRD SPINSTER:
"For you alone my glances are,"
the heliotrope will always mean.
"I will not love you while I live,"
the basil flower is wont to say.
The violet says that she is shy.
"My nature's cold," says the white rose;
the jasmin says, "Have faith in me";
"Impassioned!" the carnation cries.

SECOND SPINSTER:
The hyacinth is bitterness;
the passion flower is for pain.

FIRST SPINSTER:
A yellow flower means disdain;
but lilies ever stand for hope.

AUNT:
Says the gardenia: "I'm your friend";
the passion flower, "I trust in you."
The honeysuckle lulls to sleep;
the purple leek puts you to death.

MOTHER:
Purple leek that stands for death,
flower with hands crossed on its breast,
you best exist whene'er the wind
must sadly weep upon your wreath!

ROSITA:
The rose had early bloomed,
but afternoon was near,
and messengers of all sad snow
began to weigh its branches down;
when the shade returned
the nightingale sang
and like one dead from grief
she pale and lifeless turned;
and when the night a great
metallic horn made sound,
and the winds subdued
slept on the mountainside,
she shattered while she sighed
for crystals of the dawn.

THIRD SPINSTER:
Upon your long soft hair
the flowers unstemmed must weep,
some carry tiny knives,
some water, others fire.

FIRST SPINSTER:
The flowers have a tongue
for maids who are in love.

ROSITA:
Some flowers speak of jealousy;
the dahlia speaks of shy disdain;

> gardenia's but a sigh of love,
> laughter is the fleur-de-lis.
> Amaryllises are hate;
> the scarlet flowers stand for fury;
> the whitest flowers weddings mean,
> the bluest ones, a winding sheet.

THIRD SPINSTER:
> Mother, take me to the fields
> in the earliest light of morn,
> there to see the flowers bloom
> when the branches start to sway.

(*The piano plays a last arpeggio and stops.*)

AUNT: How precious!

MOTHER: They also know the language of the fan, the language of the gloves, the language of the stamps and the language of the hours. I get goose-flesh when they say that about:
> Twelve o'clock tolls o'er the world
> With horrible sounding rigor;
> Now of the hour of your death
> Bethink yourself, poor sinner.

FIRST AYOLA (*With her mouth full of candy*): Why, what an ugly thing!

MOTHER: And when they say:
> At one we are born
> La ra la, la
> And this birth
> la, la, ran,
> is like opening one's eyes,
> lan,
> in a bower,
> bower, bower.

SECOND AYOLA (*To the Sister*): I think the old lady has been bending her elbow. (*To the Mother*) Would you care for another drink?

MOTHER: With consummate pleasure and finest will, as they used to say in my time.

(*Rosita has been watching for the arrival of the postman.*)

HOUSEKEEPER: The postman.

(*General excitement.*)

AUNT: And he's come just in time.

THIRD SPINSTER: He had to pick his days to arrive on this one.

MOTHER: How fitting!

SECOND AYOLA: Open the letter!

FIRST AYOLA: It's more discreet for you to read it alone. Because at best, he may say something daring.

MOTHER: Heavens!

(*Rosita leaves with the letter.*)

FIRST AYOLA: A letter from a sweetheart is not a prayer book.

THIRD SPINSTER: It is a prayer book of love.

SECOND AYOLA: Oh, how refined!

(*The Ayolas laugh.*)

FIRST AYOLA: You can tell she never received one.

MOTHER (*Strongly*): Fortunately for her!

FIRST AYOLA: That's her problem!

AUNT (*To the Housekeeper who starts to go out to Rosita*): Where are you going?

HOUSEKEEPER: Can't one take a step around here?

AUNT: Let her go alone.

ROSITA (*Entering*): Aunt, Aunt!

AUNT: What's the matter, child?

ROSITA (*Excitedly*): Oh, Aunt!

FIRST AYOLA: What?

THIRD SPINSTER: Tell us!

SECOND AYOLA: What?

HOUSEKEEPER: Speak!

AUNT: Do speak!

MOTHER: A glass of water.

SECOND AYOLA: Come.

FIRST AYOLA: Quickly.

(*Excitement.*)

ROSITA (*In a choking voice*): Oh, he's getting married! (*They all look frightened.*)
　　He can't wait any longer, and he wants to marry me, but . . .

SECOND AYOLA (*Embracing her*): Hooray! What happiness!

FIRST AYOLA: Give me a hug.

AUNT: Let her speak.

ROSITA (*Calmer*): But since he's not able to come right now the marriage will be by proxy and he'll come when he can.

FIRST SPINSTER: Congratulations!

MOTHER (*Almost weeping*): May God make you as happy as you deserve to be. (*Embraces her.*)

HOUSEKEEPER: Well, and this proxy? What is it?

ROSITA: Nothing. Just that another person represents the groom in the ceremony.

HOUSEKEEPER: And what else?

ROSITA: Just that one is married then.

HOUSEKEEPER: And at night what?

ROSITA: Heavens!

FIRST AYOLA: Very well said—and at night what?

AUNT: Children!

HOUSEKEEPER: Let him come in person and get married. Proxy! I never heard of it. The bed and its paintings trembling with cold and the chemise of the bride in the darkest part of the trunk. Madam, don't you let those proxies come in this house.

(*They all laugh.*)
　　Madam, I don't want any proxies.

ROSITA: But he will come soon. This is just one more proof of how much he loves me.

HOUSEKEEPER: Very well. Let him come—and let him take you by the arm and stir the sugar in your coffee and taste it first to see if it burns.

(*Laughter. The Uncle comes in bearing a rose.*)

ROSITA: Uncle!

UNCLE: I have heard everything and almost without knowing what I was doing I cut the only Rosa Mutabile that I had in my greenhouse. It was still red,
>Full-blown in the noonday,
>hard as coral then she is.

ROSITA:
>The sun looks in against the panes
>that it may see her glow.

UNCLE: If I had waited two hours longer to cut it, I would have given it to you white.

ROSITA:
>White like the dove,
>like the laughter of the sea;
>white with the cold whiteness
>of a cheek of salt.

UNCLE: But it still has the fire of its youth.

AUNT: Have a little drink with me, husband. This is the day for that.

(*Excitement. The Third Spinster goes to the piano and plays a polka. Rosita is looking at the rose. The First and Second Spinsters dance with the Ayolas and sing:*)

>Because I caught a glimpse
>Of you beside the sea,
>Your languor sweet perceived
>Was reason for my sighs;
>And that most subtle sweetness

Which was my fatal dream,
Within this moonlight pale,
In shipwreck here you saw.

(*The Aunt and Uncle dance. Rosita goes to the Second Spinster and the Ayola. She dances with the Spinster. On seeing the old couple dancing, the Ayola claps her hands; the Housekeeper, upon entering, does likewise.*)

CURTAIN

ACT THREE

(A small living room with green shutters opening on the garden. The stage is silent. A clock strikes six in the evening. The Housekeeper crosses the stage with a box and a suitcase. Ten years have passed. The Aunt appears and sits on a low chair in the center of the stage. Silence. The clock strikes six again. Pause.)

HOUSEKEEPER *(Entering)*: It struck six o'clock twice.

AUNT: And the child?

HOUSEKEEPER: Up there in the tower. And you, where were you?

AUNT: I was taking the last flower pots from the greenhouse.

HOUSEKEEPER: I didn't see you the whole morning.

AUNT: Since my husband died the house is so empty that it seems twice as large, and we even have to search to find each other. Some nights, when I toss on my bed I hear an echo as if I were in a church.

HOUSEKEEPER: It's true that the house is now far too large.

AUNT: And then . . . if he were still alive, with that insight he had, with that talent . . . *(Almost weeping.)*

HOUSEKEEPER *(Singing)*: Lan-lan-van-lan-lan. . . . No, madam. I do not permit crying. He died six years ago and I don't want you to be like the first day. We have cried enough for him! Let us step firmly, madam! Let the sun begin to shine through! May he still wait for us many years cutting roses.

AUNT *(Rising)*: I'm very old, Ama. There is a great ruin weighing down on us.

HOUSEKEEPER: We won't lack for anything. I'm old too!

AUNT: Would that I had your years!

HOUSEKEEPER: There is not much difference between us. But since I have worked a lot I am spry, while your legs have stiffened from so much loafing.

AUNT: You mean to say you think I haven't worked?

HOUSEKEEPER: Just with the tips of your fingers. With threads, with sprouts, with sweetmeats; I, however, have worked with my back, with my knees, with my nails.

AUNT: Then, running a house is not work?

HOUSEKEEPER: It is much more difficult to scrub its floors.

AUNT: I don't want to argue.

HOUSEKEEPER: Well, why not? It will make the time pass. Go ahead. Answer me. But we've grown mute. Before, we used to shout— How about this? How about that? How about the custards? Aren't you going to iron any more? . . .

AUNT: I have resigned myself. . . . One day soup, another day crumbs. My little glass of water and my rosary in my purse; I could wait for death with dignity . . . but when I think of Rosita.

HOUSEKEEPER: That's the wound.

AUNT (*Aroused*): When I think of the wrong done against her and of the terrible deceit kept up and of the falsity in the heart of that man, who was not of my family nor deserves to be of my family, I would like to be twenty years old to take a boat to Tucaman, snatch up a lash and . . .

HOUSEKEEPER (*Interrupting her*): And take a sword and cut off his head and crush it with two stones and cut off that hand with its false vows and lying letters of affection.

AUNT: Yes, yes! To make him pay with blood what has cost blood, even though it should all be my blood. And afterwards . . .

HOUSEKEEPER: . . . To scatter the ashes over the sea.

AUNT: To revive him and bring him to Rosita so that I can draw a breath with my honor satisfied.

HOUSEKEEPER: Now, you will admit I was right.

AUNT: I admit it.

HOUSEKEEPER: Over there he found the rich woman he was looking for and married her, but he ought to have said it in time. Because who wants this woman now? She's faded. Madam, couldn't we send him a poisoned letter? So that he would die the instant he opened it?

AUNT: What nonsense! Eight years married and until last month the villain didn't write me the truth. I noticed something in the letters; the power of attorney that didn't come, an air of doubtfulness. . . . He didn't dare . . . but finally he did it. Naturally, after his father had died! And this creature . . .

HOUSEKEEPER: Shh . . .

AUNT: And remove the two urns.

(*Rosita appears. She wears a light dress of rose color in the style of 1900. She wears long curls. She has aged much.*)

HOUSEKEEPER: Child!

ROSITA: What are you doing?

HOUSEKEEPER: Criticizing a little bit. And you, where are you going?

ROSITA: I'm going to the greenhouse. Have they taken the plants already?

AUNT: A few are left.

(*Rosita leaves. The two women wipe away their tears.*)

HOUSEKEEPER: And that's all? You sit down and I sit down? And do we just wait to die? And is there no law? And no justice to make dust out of him?

AUNT: Hush. Don't go on!

HOUSEKEEPER: I don't have the patience to stand these things without my heart running through my breast as if it were a dog being chased. When I buried my husband, I was very sorry, but at the bottom I had a great happiness . . . not happiness, but surges, great surges to see that I was not the one who was buried. When I buried my little daughter—do you understand me?—when I buried my little girl it was as if my entrails had been trampled—but the dead are the dead. They're dead—so let's go cry. The door closes, and we keep on living! But this about my Rosita is the worst. It's to love some one and not be able to hold him; it's to cry and not to know for whom one weeps; it's to sigh for some one that one knows doesn't deserve those sighs. It is an open wound that gives off without ceasing a little thread of blood and there is no one, no one in the whole world, to bring the bandages, or the precious piece of ice.

AUNT: What do you want me to do?

HOUSEKEEPER: Let the river carry us along.

AUNT: Everything turns its back on old age.

HOUSEKEEPER: While I have arms you won't lack for anything.

AUNT (*Pause. Very low as though with shame*): Ama, I'm not able to pay you any more. You will have to leave us.

HOUSEKEEPER: Wheee! What a blast comes in through the windows! Wheee! Or maybe I'm growing deaf? Well . . . Why do I feel like singing? Just like children coming out of school! (*Children's voices are heard.*) Do you hear that, madam? My mistress, more my mistress than ever. (*Embraces her.*)

AUNT: I hear.

HOUSEKEEPER: I'm going to fry a pan of seafish flavored with fennel.

AUNT: Listen!

HOUSEKEEPER: And a snow mountain! I'm going to make you a mountain snowed over with colored sugar-plums . . .

AUNT: But, woman! . . .

HOUSEKEEPER (*Loudly*): I have spoken! Why, here's Don Martín! Don Martín, come in! Come! Entertain my mistress a little while.

(*She leaves quickly. Don Martín enters. He is an old man with red hair. He carries a crutch with which he supports a withered leg. A noble type of great dignity with a definite air of sadness.*)

AUNT: Happy the eyes that see you!

DON MARTÍN: When is the definite moving day?

AUNT: Today.

DON MARTÍN: So you're really going!

AUNT: The new house isn't this one. But it has good views and a little patio with two fig trees where we may have flowers.

DON MARTÍN: It's better like that.

(*They sit down.*)

AUNT: And you?

DON MARTÍN: Same old life. I've just come from lecturing to my class in Precepts. A real hell! It was a wonderful lecture: "Concept and Definition of Harmony." But the children weren't interested at all—and what children! For me, since they see I am disabled, they have a little respect. Now and then some pin or other in the chair, or a little paper doll on my back; but to my companions they do horrible things. They are the children of the rich and, since they pay, we can't punish them. This the Director is always telling us. Yesterday they insisted that poor Mr. Canito, the new geography teacher, wore a corset, because his figure is a little bit drawn in; and when he was alone in the patio the big bullies and the boarders undressed him from the waist up, tied him to one of the columns of the corridor and threw a jar of water on him from the balcony.

AUNT: Poor creature!

Doña Rosita

DON MARTÍN: Every day I enter the school trembling, waiting to see what they are going to do to me. Although, as I say, they respect my misfortune somewhat. A while ago they made a great uproar because Mr. Consuegra, who explains Latin admirably, had found a cat excrement on his class roll.

AUNT: They are the enemy!

DON MARTÍN: They are the ones who pay and we have to live with them. And, believe me, the fathers laugh afterwards at their infamies because—since we are the ones that always pass them, and we're not going to give examinations to their sons—they consider us men without feeling—like persons on the lowest level of the class that still wear a tie and an ironed collar.

AUNT: Oh, Don Martín! What a world this is!

DON MARTÍN: What a world! I dreamt always of being a poet. I was born with a talent, a natural flower, and I wrote a play that was never produced.

AUNT: "The Chieftain's Daughter"?

DON MARTÍN: That's it.

AUNT: Rosita and I read it. You lent it to us. We read it four or five times.

DON MARTÍN (*Eagerly*): And what . . . ?

AUNT: I liked it very much. I've always told you that. Especially when she is going to die and she remembers her mother and calls her.

DON MARTÍN: It is strong, isn't it? A real drama. A drama of contour and concept. It was never possible to produce it. (*Beginning to recite*):

> O mother unexcelled! Now turn your gaze
> to her who lies in abject trance undone;
> receive you these refulgent jewels of mine
> and the horrid death rattle of my combat!

And is this bad? And doesn't this verse sound well as to

accent and cesura? "And the horrid death rattle of my combat!"

AUNT: Charming! Charming!

DON MARTÍN: And when Glucinio goes to challenge Isaias and raises the tent's tapestry . . .

HOUSEKEEPER (*Interrupting him*): Through here.

(*Two Workmen dressed in denim suits enter.*)

FIRST WORKMAN: Good afternoon.

DON MARTÍN AND AUNT (*Together*): Good afternoon.

HOUSEKEEPER: This is it!

(*She points to a large divan at the back of the room. The Men take it out slowly as if they were carrying a coffin. The Housekeeper follows them. Silence. Two strokes of a bell are heard while the Two Men go out with the divan.*)

DON MARTÍN: Is it the novena of St. Gertrude the Great?

AUNT: Yes, at St. Anthony's.

DON MARTÍN: It's very difficult to be a poet.

(*The Men go out.*)

Afterward, I wanted to be a pharmacist. It's a peaceful life.

AUNT: My brother, may he be in glory, was a pharmacist.

DON MARTÍN: But I couldn't. I had to help my mother and I became a teacher. That's why I envied your husband so much. He was what he wanted to be.

AUNT: And it brought him to ruin.

DON MARTÍN: Yes, but this of mine is worse.

AUNT: But you go on writing.

DON MARTÍN: I don't know why I write since I have no more hope. But, it's the only thing I like. Did you read my story yesterday? In the second issue of *The Granada Mentality*?

AUNT: "The Birthday of Matilda"? Yes, we read it. A charming thing.

DON MARTÍN: Yes, isn't it? There I tried to renew myself by writing something with a present-day atmosphere. I even mention an airplane. The truth is, that one has to be modern. But naturally, what I like best are my sonnets.

AUNT: To the nine muses of Parnassus!

DON MARTÍN: To the ten, to the ten! Don't you remember that I named Rosita the tenth muse?

HOUSEKEEPER (*Entering*): Mistress, you help me fold this sheet. (*The two of them begin folding it.*) Don Martín with his little red hair! Why didn't you marry, man of God? You wouldn't be so alone in this life!

DON MARTÍN: No one ever loved me!

HOUSEKEEPER: It's just that there's no more taste. With such a precious manner of speaking as you have!

AUNT: Watch out you don't make love to him!

DON MARTÍN: Let her try!

HOUSEKEEPER: When he lectures in the lower room of the school I go to the coal bin to listen to him: "What is idea?" "The Intellectual representation of a thing or an object." Isn't that it?

DON MARTÍN: Look at her! Look at her!

HOUSEKEEPER: Yesterday he was shouting: "No; there is hyperbole there!" and then . . . "the Epinicio" . . . I'd like to be able to understand, but since I don't understand, it makes me laugh. And the coal man who is always reading a book called "The Ruins of Palmyra" throws glances at me like two fighting-mad cats, but even though I laugh, ignorant as I am, I realize that Don Martín has much merit.

DON MARTÍN: Today no merit is assigned to rhetoric and poetry, nor to universitarian culture.

(*The Housekeeper goes out quickly with the folded sheet.*)

AUNT: What can we do! We have very little time left on this stage.

DON MARTÍN: And we must devote that to kindness and sacrifice.

(*Shouts are heard.*)

AUNT: What's happening?

HOUSEKEEPER (*Appearing*): Don Martín, they want you to go to the school because the children have stuck a nail in the piping and all the classrooms are flooded.

DON MARTÍN: Let's go then. I dreamt of Parnassus and I have to be a mason and a plumber. Just so they don't push me or I slip . . .

(*The Housekeeper helps Don Martín to rise.*)

HOUSEKEEPER: He's coming! Calm down! Watch out the water doesn't rise until not a single child is left alive!

DON MARTÍN (*Leaving*): Blessed be to God!

AUNT: Poor thing. What a fate!

HOUSEKEEPER: Just look at him! He irons his own collars and darns his own socks. And the time he was sick, when I took him some custard, his bed had some sheets on it that were black as coal, and his walls and his washbasin . . . Oh my!

AUNT: And others have so much.

HOUSEKEEPER: That's why I'll always say: "Damned, damned be the rich!" May not even their fingernails be left!

AUNT: Let them be!

HOUSEKEEPER: But I'm sure that they are going to hell headfirst. Where do you think Don Rafael Sale, exploiter of the poor, who was buried yesterday, can be, God preserve him!—with so many priests and nuns and so much mumbo-jumbo? In hell! And he will say: "I have twenty million pesetas, don't pinch me with the tongs! I will give you forty thousand dollars if you take these coals from my feet!" But the devils, prodding here, prodding there, kicking him for all they're worth, hitting him in the face, until his blood is turned to little pieces of charcoal . . .

Doña Rosita

AUNT: All we Christians know that no rich man is going to enter the kingdom of heaven, but be careful that you too don't land head-first in hell for speaking that way.

HOUSEKEEPER: Me, in hell? The first push I give the furnace of Old Nick will make the hot water reach to the edges of the earth. No, madam, no. I'll get into heaven by force. (*Sweetly.*) With you. Each one in a chair of celestial blue silk, rocking herself and with fans of scarlet satin. Between the two of us, on a swing of jasmin and rosemary plants, Rosita swinging herself, and behind her your husband covered with roses, the way he left this house in his coffin; with the same smile, with the same forehead white as crystal. And you rock like this, and I like this, and Rosita like this, and behind us God throwing roses at us as if the three of us were a mother-of-pearl float in a Holy Week procession full of wax candles and flounces.

AUNT: And let the handkerchiefs for tears stay here below.

HOUSEKEEPER: That's it! Confusion to them! For us, a celestial blow out!

AUNT: Because we don't have a single tear left within our hearts!

FIRST WORKMAN (*Entering*): At your service.

HOUSEKEEPER: Come! (*As they are leaving, from the door.*) Courage!

AUNT: God bless you!

(*The Aunt sits down slowly. Rosita appears with a package of letters in her hand. Silence.*)

Have they taken the bureau?

ROSITA: Just now. Your cousin Hope sent a child for a screwdriver.

AUNT: They are probably putting together the beds for tonight. We should have gone early and done things as we wanted them. My cousin has probably placed the furniture just anywhere.

ROSITA: But I'd rather leave here when the street is dark. If I could I'd put out the street lamp. The neighbors will be watching for us anyway. With the moving the door has been full of children all day as if there were a dead person in the house.

AUNT: If I had known, I would by no means have permitted your uncle to mortgage the house with furniture and everything. What we have left are the barest necessities. A chair to sit on and a bed to sleep in.

ROSITA: To die in.

AUNT: That was a fine thing he did for us! Tomorrow the new owners come. I would like your uncle to see us. Foolish old man! Weak in business matters. Rose specialist! A man with no idea of the value of money! He bankrupted me day by day. "There is so and so." And he would say: "Show him in." And he would come in with empty pockets and leave with them overflowing with silver. And always: "Don't let my wife find out." The extravagant thing! The weakling! And there was no calamity he didn't remedy, nor children he did not take in because . . . because . . . he had the greatest heart a man ever had . . . the purest Christian soul. . . . No, no. Be quiet, old lady! Be quiet, babbler, and respect God's will! Penniless! Very well. So, silence! But I see you . . .

ROSITA: Don't worry about me, Aunt. I know that the mortgage was to pay for my furniture and my trousseau, and that's what hurts me.

AUNT: He did right. You deserved everything and everything he bought is worthy of you and will be beautiful the day you use it.

ROSITA: The day I use it?

AUNT: Of course, your wedding day.

ROSITA: Don't make me speak of it.

AUNT: That's a failing of the decent women of these lands,

not speaking. We don't speak, but we have to speak. (*Shouting.*) Ama! Has the postman come?

ROSITA: What do you propose to do?

AUNT: Live—and let you take a lesson from me.

ROSITA: (*Embracing her*): Hush!

AUNT: I have to talk out loud sometime. Leave your four walls, my child. Don't give yourself over to misfortune.

ROSITA (*Kneeling before her*): I've grown accustomed to living for many years outside of myself, thinking of things that were far away, and now that these things no longer exist, I continue going around and around in a cold place, looking for a way out that I shall never find. I knew everything. I knew he had married; some kind soul took care to tell me that. And full of tears I have been receiving his letters with an illusion that surprised even me. If people had not talked; if you had not learned it: if no one but I had known of it: his letters and his lie would have fed my illusion like the first year of his absence. But every one knew it, and I found myself pointed out with a finger that made my engaged girl's modesty ridiculous, and gave a grotesque air to my maidenly fan. Every year that passed was like an intimate garment torn from my body. And today one friend gets married, and another and another, and tomorrow she has a son and he grows up and comes to show me his examination marks, and they have their new houses and new songs and I the same, with the same trembling, the same; I, just as before, cutting the same carnations, looking at the same clouds; and one day out walking I realize I don't know anybody. Girls and boys leave me behind because I get tired, and one of them says, "There's the old maid," and another, beautiful, with a curly head, comments: "No one would sink his teeth in her any more." And I hear him, and I can't even shout, but go on, with a mouth full of poison and an overpowering desire to flee, to take off my shoes, to rest, and never, never move out of my corner again.

AUNT: Child! Rosita!

ROSITA: I'm old. Yesterday I heard the housekeeper say that I could still marry. By no means! Don't think it. I lost all hope of marrying the one I loved with all my blood, the one I loved and still do. Everything is finished, and yet, with all illusion lost, I go to bed and get up again with the most terrible of all feelings—the feeling of having hope dead. I want to flee. I don't want to see. I want to be left serene, empty. Doesn't a poor woman have the right to breathe freely? And yet, hope pursues me, encircles me, bites me; like a dying wolf tightening his grip for the last time.

AUNT: Why didn't you listen to me? Why didn't you marry another?

ROSITA: I was tied. And besides, what man came to this house sincerely and overflowing to gain my affection? Not one.

AUNT: You wouldn't pay attention to any of them. You were blinded by a deceiver.

ROSITA: I've always been serious.

AUNT: You clung to your idea without regard to reality and without thinking of your future.

ROSITA: I am as I am. And I can't make myself change. Now the only thing left for me is my dignity. What is inside of me, I keep to myself.

AUNT: That's what I don't want.

HOUSEKEEPER (*Coming in suddenly*): Nor I either! Speak, unburden yourself, we'll cry until the three of us are tired and we will share our feelings.

ROSITA: And what am I going to tell you? There are things that cannot be told because there are no words to tell them; and even if there were, no one would understand their meaning. You understand me if I ask for bread or water, or even for a kiss, but you would never be able to understand, nor remove, this dark hand that freezes or embraces my heart—I don't know which—every time I'm left alone.

HOUSEKEEPER: You're saying something now.

AUNT: There's consolation for everything.

ROSITA: It would be a never-ending story. I know that my eyes will always be young, but I also know that my back will bend more each day. After all, what has happened to me has happened to a thousand women. (*Pause.*) But why am I saying all this? (*To the Housekeeper.*) You go straighten things up because in a few minutes we're going to leave this house with its garden, and you, Aunt, please don't worry about me. (*Pause. To the Housekeeper.*) Go on! I don't like you to look at me like that. Those glances like a faithful dog bother me.

(*The Housekeeper leaves.*)

Those pitying looks that perturb and anger me.

AUNT: Child, what do you want me to do?

ROSITA: Leave me as a lost thing. (*Pause. She walks up and down.*) I know you are remembering your sister, the old maid . . . the old maid like me. She was bitter and hated children and every one who put on a new dress . . . but I won't be like that. (*Pause.*) I ask your forgiveness.

AUNT: What nonsense.

(*At the back, an eighteen-year-old Boy appears.*)

ROSITA: Come in.

BOY: But . . . are you moving?

ROSITA: In a few minutes. When it grows dark.

AUNT: Who is it?

ROSITA: It's Mary's son.

AUNT: Which Mary?

ROSITA: The oldest of the three Manolas.

AUNT: Oh, those who go up to the Alhambra "The three and the four alone." Forgive my bad memory, son.

BOY: You've seen me very few times.

AUNT: Yes, but I was very fond of your mother. How charming she was! She died about the same time as my husband.

ROSITA: Before.

BOY: Eight years ago.

ROSITA: He has the same face.

BOY (*Happy*): A little bit worse. Mine was hammered out.

AUNT: And the same features; the same character!

BOY: Why, of course I resemble her. At carnival time, I put on one of mother's dresses . . . a dress she had a long time ago, green . . .

ROSITA (*Melancholy*): With black laces . . . and nile-green silk flounces.

BOY: Yes.

ROSITA: And a great belt of velvet at the waist.

BOY: The same.

ROSITA: Falling on one side and the other of the bustle.

BOY: Exactly. What an absurd style! (*He smiles.*)

ROSITA (*Sad*): It was a pretty style!

BOY: Don't tell me that! Well, I was coming down the stairs almost dying of laughter with that old thing on, filling all the corridor with the smell of mothballs, and suddenly my aunt began to cry bitterly because she said it was exactly like seeing my mother. It made an impression on me, naturally, and I left the dress and the mask on my bed.

ROSITA: Since there is nothing more alive than a memory. It comes to the point of making our lives impossible. That's why I well understand those drunken little old ladies who go through the streets trying to blot out the world, and sit singing on the benches in the park.

AUNT: And your aunt, the married one?

BOY: She writes from Barcelona. Each time less.

ROSITA: Had she any children?

BOY: Four of them. (*Pause.*)

HOUSEKEEPER (*Entering*): Give me the keys to the wardrobe. (*The Aunt gives them to her. Then, for the Boy.*) Here, this young man was walking yesterday with his sweetheart. I saw them at the new plaza. She wanted to go one side and he wouldn't let her. (*Laughs.*)

AUNT: Come now, leave the boy alone!

BOY (*Confused*): We were just joking.

HOUSEKEEPER: Don't blush! (*She leaves.*)

ROSITA: Now be quiet.

BOY: What a beautiful garden you have!

ROSITA: We used to have!

AUNT: Come and cut some flowers.

BOY: I hope everything goes well with you, Doña Rosita.

ROSITA: God go with you, child!

(*They leave. Afternoon is falling.*)

Doña Rosita! Doña Rosita!

> When it opens in the morning
> red as blood it is.
> The evening turns her white
> with a whiteness of spume and salt
> and when night comes
> her petals begin to fall.

(*Pause.*)

HOUSEKEEPER (*Comes in with a shawl*): Let us be going.

ROSITA: Yes. I am going to throw on a coat.

HOUSEKEEPER: Since I have taken down the hanger, you will find it hooked on the window handle.

(*The Third Spinster comes in wearing a dark dress with a mourning veil on her head and still with the leg-o'-mutton sleeves that were used in 1912. They speak low.*)

THIRD SPINSTER: Ama!

HOUSEKEEPER: You find us here for a few minutes.

THIRD SPINSTER: I came to give a piano lesson near by and dropped in to see if you needed something.

HOUSEKEEPER: May God repay you!

THIRD SPINSTER: What a catastrophe!

HOUSEKEEPER: Yes, yes. But don't touch my heart. Don't lift this veil of sorrow because I am the one who has to give encouragement in this wake without a corpse, that you are witnessing.

THIRD SPINSTER: I'd like to see them.

HOUSEKEEPER: But it's better for you not to see them. Go to the other house.

THIRD SPINSTER: That's better. But if you need something, you know that I'm here to do anything I can.

HOUSEKEEPER: This misfortune will surely pass!

(*The wind is heard.*)

THIRD SPINSTER: A wind has come up.

HOUSEKEEPER: Yes, it looks like rain.

(*The Third Spinster leaves.*)

AUNT (*Entering*): If this wind keeps up there won't be a rose left alive. The cypresses at the center almost touch the walls of my room. It's almost as if the garden wanted to become ugly so that we should feel no pain at leaving it.

HOUSEKEEPER: If you are talking about beauty, beautiful it has never been. Have you put on your coat? And this scarf. That's it. Well covered. (*Helps her.*) Now when we get there, dinner will be ready. For dessert, custard. You like it. A custard as golden as a mignonette.

(*The Housekeeper speaks with a voice shrouded by deep emotion. A thud is heard.*)

AUNT: That's the greenhouse door. Why don't you close it?

HOUSEKEEPER: It can't be closed because of the dampness.

AUNT: It will be banging all night.

HOUSEKEEPER: Well, since we won't hear it . . . !

(*The stage is in a sweet half-light of evening.*)

AUNT: I will. I'll hear it.

(*Rosita appears. She is pale, dressed in white, with a coat down to the hem of her dress.*)

HOUSEKEEPER (*Courageously*): Come!

ROSITA (*In a weak voice*): It's begun to rain. Like this there will be no one in the balconies to see us leave.

AUNT: That's preferable.

ROSITA (*She wavers a little, leans against a chair, and falls supported by the Housekeeper and the Aunt who prevent her from fainting completely*):
        And when the night arrives
        its petals begin to fall.

(*They leave and at their exit the stage is left empty. The door is heard banging. Suddenly a balcony window at the back opens and the white curtains flutter in the wind.*)

CURTAIN